TRAEGER GRILL & SMOKER COOKBOOK

*Complete Guide for Beginner to Master Traeger
Wood Pellet Grill With Delicious, Affordable, &
Easy Pitmaster Recipes | Smoker Cooking Bible
For All Types Of Meat*

Daniel Truman

Table of Contents

Introduction

This book includes many grilling recipes for you to use and enjoy, from typical fares like burgers and steaks to more exotic dishes like curry pulled pork or ginger grilled pineapple.

Apart from the recipes themselves, the Traeger Grill & Smoker cookbook also includes some helpful pointers on how best to grill different meats and vegetables-everything from what heat level is appropriate for which type of food to how long it should be cooked at that level before being removed. There are also some pointers on how to prepare your meal ahead of time and how to polish it up before serving.

This book offers many ways to have fun with your Traeger grill, even if you're grilling for a crowd and need something different than the usual fare. You can try making some simple dishes outside while using your Traeger grill as a smoker or even preparing drinks for yourself or your guests inside using Traeger's side burner. You also won't be stuck with a menu that you always make; there are many options in this book that will allow you to mix things up so that you never get bored with grilling.

The Traeger Grill & Smoker cookbook also includes useful hints on using Traeger's different features to make your food taste better. For example, a "how-to" on cleaning out the drip tray will ensure that you never have to do it yourself again and makes finding and replacing filters much simpler.

This handbook is not only devoid of language obstacles, but it will appeal to newcomers to grilling, seasoned grillers, and meat lovers.

The Traeger Grill & Smoker cookbook is a fantastic place to develop your grilling abilities if you're just starting.

The recipes in this book will also appeal to those who have been grilling for a long time. It is because many recipes featured in the Traeger Grill & Smoker cookbook offer new and exciting ways of approaching standard grilling fare. For example, instead of having burgers or hot dogs on the grill, you could make a bacon cheeseburger using ground meat mixed with bacon pieces or put cheese and pineapple slices on top of hamburgers before grilling them for an added flavor boost.

The Traeger Grill & Smoker cookbook also features some tips for hostesses on ensuring that their pots and pans and serving dishes are kept in great condition when used with the Traeger.

The Traeger Grill & Smoker cookbook is a very helpful guide for anyone who wants the flexibility to create many different grilling dishes. It also makes getting more out of your Traeger grill easier and ensures you will never burn food again

What Is the Traeger Grill?

The Traeger Grill is a hybrid of a charcoal grill and an oven, which allows you to sear over an open flame while infusing smoky flavors for that signature wood-fired grill taste.

When it's too cold to cook outside in the winter, you can turn your Traeger Grill into a genuine wood-burning oven with our smooth cooking process. It's the perfect way to enjoy your favorite grilled foods like bacon-wrapped asparagus in the middle of winter.

The Traeger Grill was designed with versatility from its inception and through every detail, from lid size and handle position to grease management and temperature control. In addition to the advanced Traeger digital control system, Traeger grills feature a large cooking area.

The Traeger Grill has superior pellet distribution providing precise temperature control from one end of the grill to the other. The Traeger grills have generous racks measuring 14 ½" (L) x 15" (W) x 6" (H) while still being able to accommodate most barbecuing accessories with enough room for two additional racks for side dishes. For extra convenience, there are two grease management systems and a small storage drawer inside the grill, which is only accessible when the lid is in place. With its heavy-duty cast-iron base, this unit is designed for durability.

The Traeger line of grills offers a variety of useful features:

- Charcoal grills for the purist are the original, classic charcoal grill. These grills allow you to control the temperature precisely. They are great for quick searing and cooking at high temperatures or slow smoking. If you prefer the true smoke-filled flavor, this grill is for you. It's also great when experimenting with new recipes and flavors.

- Searing grills with an innovative ceramic-brazed lid allows you to cook multiple foods simultaneously through a unique 18000 BTU hood. These grills are perfect for the outdoor chef traveling by car or boat.

- Digital control units are available that let you monitor grill temperature, set precise cooking times and cycles, and turn your Traeger Grill into a custom smoker with numerous features available in digital control. For example, you can preheat your second cook zone for smoking while you keep the first side in the desired temperature range.

Pellet grills have become very popular recently, and the Traeger Pellet Grill is one of the top-selling models. It's easy to see why once you learn about the versatility of these machines.

They are like traditional charcoal grills, except they use wood pellets instead of charcoal or gas for fuel. In addition, pellet grills don't need vents or gas lines to function correctly, so they are easier to maintain.

Components of Traeger Wood Pellet Grill

Traeger makes a few additions to most of their models, including the firebox, heat exchanger, side shelf, and cabinet. Each model has a specific focus that allows customers to decide which grill will fit their needs. Below is a brief description of what makes each model different. Some components are shared among the models. Traeger's entire line of grills shares the firebox and heat exchanger.

The firebox is the heart of every Traeger grill. The wood pellets are loaded into the firebox from the front of the grill. The firebox is a rectangular box with the fires for the grill in it. After the wood pellets are loaded in, the lid is closed, igniting the pellets. First, as the wood pellets ignite, they begin to release smoke. As the fire burns, smoke carries the heat to the heating element inside the grill, turning it into heat used for cooking the meat and then convection that distributes the heat evenly throughout the grill.

The heating element is what does most of the work. It is made of aluminum blocks stacked to create a column and is covered in Therma-cast insulation that prevents heat from exiting the grill too much. When a customer grills on the Traeger Pellet grill, they are grilling on the heating element, which slowly cooks the meat evenly.

The side shelf is where most tools and wood pellets are kept on the Traeger Pellet grill. It has a coated surface that prevents the tool and pellets from damaging the grill's finish. Tools are kept on the side shelf while the grill is in use and don't need quick access. If a tool does need to be used in mid-grilling, it can be placed in the warming drawer with the wood pellets.

The warming drawer is found on all but one Traeger grill; the RecTec, its warming drawer, can be found on the side table at the front of the grill. The warming drawer is more of a compartment than a drawer. It provides a place where the tools that need to be kept hot can stay warm while their job is finished. It also provides a place where novices can keep wood pellets until they are ready to be put into the firebox.

The secondary cooking chamber is used on the 4-burner grill and the 4-burner grill with the side burner. The extra space on the firebox is left open for maximum heat exposure. The customer can place their meat on the exposed grates in the secondary cooking chamber to give them more options for cooking their food.

The cabinet holds accessories for Traeger Pellet grills. Every Traeger pellet grill has specific accessories purchased from the Traeger website and applied to the grill. Accessories range from the backup cable to protect and isolate electronic components to the cabinet, allowing more accessories and attachments to be added. The Traeger pellet grill cabinet is offered for extra smoke when cooks desire more smoke or if the grill is in an outdoor environment where the temperature fluctuates a lot; waterproofing the firebox can add protection to the grill.

The rear-mounted fill tray is unique to Traeger Pellet grills. It can be folded and used as a table or set up at the back of the grill. The rear-mounted fill tray is equipped with a Velcro latch that can hold the tray in an upright position. The rear-mounted fill tray allows for easier and more accessible adding of wood pellets.

Traeger's general purpose was to cook food with wood pellets. Almost all Traeger models have the capability of smoking and grilling. However, all Traeger grills can grill and smoke except for the smaller Traeger Junior Elite.

How to Maintain the Traeger Grill and Cleaning?

A barbecue grill can be quite a significant investment. It can cost $1000 or more. You need to learn how to take care of your investment when you spend that much. Regarding barbecue, taking care of it needs to become a habit. After every use, you should ensure that your grill is thoroughly cleaned. It doesn't matter if you're using an indoor electric grill like the Breville Smart Grill, a barbecue model like a Weber grill, or even a gas grill; most maintenance tips will follow, not change.

Phase 1-Using the Right Equipment

You don't have to go to the hardware store and spend hundreds of dollars to find the right tools to clean your barbecue. All you need are steel wool sheets, a mild dish cleaner, baking soda, spray cooking oil, a grill brush, aluminum foil, and a cloth. Take a few moments to pick and keep these things close to your barbecue, but note that you should store them inside so that the weather does not harm them.

Phase 2- Give a Good Brushing to Your Grill

You should provide your grill with a regular brushing after every single use. One thing you were supposed to get when you gathered materials earlier was a grill brush. They are commonly made of brass wires that can be used to brush the grilling surface to remove all of the unpleasant accumulation to become permanent. The longer that all grease and stuck-on food is left on the grilling board, the more difficult it will be to clean.

Phase 3-The Other Products Are Used.

Mix just a bit of baking soda with water to make the nasty bits nice and clean, and put it on your wire brush. Using this baking soda mixture, you can clean every portion of your grill. Next, to make it clean, crumple up some aluminum foil and wipe down the grill surfaces with a light circular motion. Once your grill is cold and washed off, spray it with the cooking oil. That is important because it will avoid the rusting of the grilling surface.

Phase 4-Do Not Think About the Soap.

Get the soap out and wash your shelves. You can combine a bit of soap and water in a bucket and use a tissue to clean your racks. That may seem like there's a lot of work, but if you spent a lot of money on your grill, you would certainly want it to be always perfect. It can make them last longer. On top of that, the soap's anti-bacterial properties will help kill off any bacteria left on your food. The steel wool pads can also be used to remove some of the residual grime.

If you have started having chronic problems with your barbecue, consider getting a cover. Some of the bad things you can expose your grill to are weather conditions, like rain and snow, so it is best to cover it up. Make this maintenance routine a habit, and your grill will support you for years and years.

You cannot use your grill very much, or maybe you choose to cook in your kitchen because you're not a jockey on the grill or don't have enough time for a barbecue. Well, whatever the reason is, there is no excuse not to take care of it, be it gas or charcoal.

Much like the other appliances you have in your home, you also shelled money on your gas or charcoal grill, so it only fits that you find time to clean and maintain it. How? Here you can find four simple tips for taking care of your grill. Don't worry; it's so much easier to clean it than to clean the charcoal.

Powder the Grill Grates Before Cooking

Don't put meat and vegetables (also called grids) directly on the grill grates. Instead, before cooking, make it a habit to coat the grill grates with some oil. That prevents excessive food and particles from sticking onto your grates. It may be hard to extract food trapped in the grates. Also, a well-oiled grill grate gives the food better grill marks.

To oil the grill grates, you can use any of these three options: an oiled paper towel or rag, some bacon or beef fat, or cooking spray. If you use the first option, it is best if the grill grates are very hot. Some recommend using bacon or beef fat because it gives the food an extra taste. The third choice is the most convenient; however, ensure you apply the spray before turning the grill on; as the spray appears to catch fire, never spray the grates over the flame.

Clean the Whole Grill

The most important part of the grill is the grate since this is where you put your food. That's why it has a priority when it comes to cleaning the grill. Clean the grill grates only after grilling so it is easy to remove any food particles that may have stuck on them. To clean the grates, use a wire brush. Long-handled rigid wire brushes are the favorite of serious grillers. Scrub the grates twice; then, you can wash them with soapy water if you are still not pleased.

Next, the whole grill is washed. Wait for the grill and let it cool down fully. Then, clean off the surfaces' grease with a wet paper towel or a damp rag. Grease can cause corrosion if not removed immediately.

You are also advised to schedule a daily to clean your grill thoroughly. Create a combination of half water and half white vinegar. Clean the grill by spraying it inside the grill with the mixture. Leave it for about an hour to 30 minutes. Wipe the whole thing with a wet rag or paper towel afterward.

Drain the drip pan and clear the ash catcher; grilling usually helps produce many food drippings, such as beef and poultry. Expect that the drip pan (which you ideally set up correctly) is guaranteed to be full of fat and oil after your grilling session. Don't throw the fat instantly. Let the drip pan cool off first.

Don't dump the drippings directly into the field once it has cooled down. Use something close to an empty milk carton and pour the fat into it. You may use this fat again. You'll never know. Just ensure that when you decide to use it again, the drippings are free of ash.

Besides the drip pan, many charcoal grills come with an ash catcher. Usually, it is shaped like a saucepan and placed at the grill's bottom. Their name suggests their primary purpose is to catch the ashes produced during your grilling session. Remove the ash catcher from the base and toss the ashes after using the grill; however, ensure the ashes are still cold before dumping them in the garbage. If you throw them when still hot, it can cause flame among your other flammable garbage. Wait one day to be sure and secure.

Tips and Tricks

It's been two years since we bought our Traeger grill, and I have a few suggestions to help new users with pellet smokers avoid any issues—usually due to inexperience or negligence. Let's start on the right foot.

Pellet Storage

You must be vigilant in storing your pellets, especially if you live in a humid climate. Damp pellets will not lead to the best grilling experience—you won't be able to get a fire going. What's worse, damp pellets will damage the drill since it won't be able to rotate and will burn out the motor.

I bought some 5-gallon pails, and my husband went hunting for sealing lids since storing your pellets in an open container is counterproductive. We found that screw-on covers work best to keep moisture out and are convenient—you won't have to break your fingers trying to pry them open.

Temperature Readings

After using your grill a few times, you may notice that the temperature fluctuates quite a bit. It is because grease and soot build-up on the temperature probe used to regulate the temperature. An effortless way to stop this is to clean the probe and cover it with foil. Consequently, cooking temperature readings will be more accurate.

Cover Your Grill

You may think a grill cover isn't necessary, but believe me, it's crucial. Your Traeger grill is an appliance and one with electronics inside to boot! If you want to ensure your pellet smoker's durability, protect it from the elements. Move your grill under a rooftop after having a barbeque, and use a grill cover. You don't want your pellet smoker to stop working suddenly due to water damage.

Clean Your Grill

A lot of people fail at keeping their grill clean. This step is crucial to guard against overfilling the firepot and protect against flare-ups. Not to mention that your grill will look brand-new for longer if you care for it in this simple way. I recommend cleaning your Traeger grill after cooking something for an extended period or after you're done using it for the weekend. You'll have to clean your grill more often if you love cooking greasier foods. Here are the steps you should follow:
1. Use an all-natural degreaser/cleaner to spray the grill grate and the inside of the chimney.
2. Remove and clean the sides of the grill grates.
3. Throw away the old foil and drip tray liners.
4. Remove the drip tray and heat baffle.
5. Use a vacuum inside the grill and firepot to remove any food particles.
6. Clean the inside of the chimney.
7. Again, use an all-natural degreaser/cleaner to spray the inside and outside of the grill. Wait a few minutes before wiping clean.
8. Put all components back in their place, including the heat baffle, drip tray, and foil liners. You're all set for your next barbeque!
Tip: Avoid using wire brushes as they will scratch your Traeger grill. Heavy-duty paper towels or a cleaning cloth will work nicely.

Be Adventurous

It is vital to your grilling success—you won't enjoy your Traeger grill for long if you have to make the same recipes repeatedly. Moreover, you own a 6-in-1 appliance and can't let that versatility go unused. As you get used to a pellet grill, you may cook simple meals, but once you feel confident in your grilling abilities, try new things! Don't limit yourself to cooking only traditional barbeque foods—what about making a smoky bean stew in your Traeger grill? Don't worry; later in this cookbook, you'll see recipes that spark your adventurous side.

These aren't the only elements that will contribute to your grilling success, but they cover some rookie mistakes many, myself included, make. It put a real downer on my grilling plans!

Choosing Pellets

It is sometimes stated that modern society is evolving at such a breakneck speed that it is impossible to stay up. Learning to choose a pellet grill is just one of many skills we have had to learn. Some individuals are afraid of choosing a grill because they feel they will never be able to make a final decision and that it will always be too complicated and time-consuming. However, buying a pellet grill requires just as much dedication as any other purchase you might make; you need to be knowledgeable about this product and get one that suits your needs perfectly. Choosing the right pellet grill is a delicate process, and this book will help you do that.

What to look for in a pellet grill?
Buying a new pellet grill might be daunting, but it's critical to understand what to look for. When shopping around for your new cooking surface, there are several points to consider: its size and shape and the type of pellet fuel you will use.

The size of the grill
One of the most important aspects to consider when choosing a pellet grill is its size and shape. The first step is to measure the available space in your home to estimate how much space you have to work with. If you plan to use your new grill regularly, you will need about 25 square feet for every 100 square inches of grilling space.

The type of grilling you want to do
The other important aspect to consider will be the kind of grilling you want to do on your new pellet grill. First off, we recommend getting one that is propane-powered and charcoal-powered. It will ensure that you have a safe, efficient fire in the grill, which requires no maintenance or refills on your wood pellets. Propane and charcoal are relatively easy to light up, but neither is as easy as an electric ignition-type of gas or wood pellet. They are both very effective ways of cooking and allow for great versatility regarding the flavor and nutrition of your food.

On the other hand, if you are a diehard fan of electric ignition-type grills, you can still find many great options. Make sure your electric pellet grill includes a built-in meat probe that will let you know when your food is done.

I have made a careful selection of recipes because my intent is to offer the reader the opportunity to prepare meals with ever changing flavors. Since a diet or eating pattern might be boring in the long run, I want to reassure the reader that thanks to the recipes collected in this book he/she will have delicious and ever changing dishes for a very long time....at least 1500 days!

Chapter 4. Appetizer and Snacks

1. Grilled Corn

Preparation time: 15 minutes
Cooking time: 25 minutes
Servings: 6
Ingredients:
- 6 fresh corn ears
- Salt
- Black pepper
- Olive oil
- Vegetable seasoning
- Butter for serving

Directions:
9. Preheat the grill to high with a closed lid.
10. Peel the husks. Remove the corn's silk. Rub with black pepper, salt, vegetable seasoning, and oil.
11. Close the husks and grill for 25 minutes. Turn them occasionally.
12. Serve topped with butter, and enjoy.
Nutrition: Calories: 70 │ Protein: 3 g. │ Carbs: 18 g. │ Fat: 2 g.

2. Easy Eggs

Preparation time: 10 minutes
Cooking time: 30 minutes
Servings: 12
Ingredients:
- 12 hardboiled eggs, peeled and rinsed

Directions:
1. Provide wood pellets to your smoker and follow the manufacturer's particular start-up procedure—Preheat the grill to 120°F (49°C) with the lid closed.
2. Smoke the eggs directly on the grill grate for 30 minutes.
3. They'll start to get a little brown gloss.
4. Refrigerate the eggs for at least 30 minutes before serving.
5. Keep any leftovers in an airtight jar/container in the refrigerator for 1 to 2 weeks.
Nutrition: Calories: 57 │ Total Fat: 3 g. │ Saturated Fat: 1 g. │ Total Carbs: 6 g. │ Net Carbs: 4 g. │ Protein: 4 g. │ Sugar: 2 g. │ Fiber: 2 g. │ Sodium: 484 mg.

3. Thyme-Rosemary Mash Potatoes

Preparation time: 20 minutes
Cooking time: 1 hour
Servings: 6
Ingredients:
- 4 ½ lbs. potatoes, russet
- Salt
- 1-pint heavy cream
- 3 thyme sprigs + 2 tbsp. for garnish
- 2 rosemary sprigs
- 6–7 sage leaves
- 6–7 black peppercorns
- Black pepper to taste
- 2 stick butter softened.
- 2 garlic cloves, chopped.

Directions:
1. Preheat the grill to 350°F with a closed lid.
2. Peel the russet potatoes.
3. Cut into small pieces and place them in a baking dish; fill it with water (1 ½ cup), place on the grill and cook with a closed lid for about 1 hour.
4. In the meantime, in a saucepan, combine the garlic, peppercorns, herbs, and cream. Place on the grate and cook covered for about 15 minutes. Once done, strain to remove the garlic and herbs. Keep warm.
5. Take out the water from the potatoes and place them in a stockpot. Mash them with a fork and pour 2/3 of the mixture. Add one stick of softened butter and salt.
6. Serve right away.
Nutrition: Calories: 180 │ Protein: 4 g. │ Carbs: 28 g. │ Fat: 10 g.

4. Brisket Baked Beans

Preparation time: 20 minutes
Cooking time: 2 hours
Servings: 10
Ingredients:
- 2 tbsp. extra-virgin olive oil
- 1 large diced onion
- 1 diced green pepper
- 1 red pepper diced
- 2–6 Jalapeño peppers diced
- 3 pieces Texas-style brisket flat chopped
- 1 baked bean, like Bush's country-style baked beans
- 1 pork and beans
- 1 red kidney beans, rinse, drain
- 1 cup barbecue sauce like Sweet Baby Ray's barbecue sauce
- ½ cup stuffed brown sugar
- 3 garlic, chopped
- 2 tsp. mustard
- ½ tsp. Kosher salt
- ½ tsp. black pepper

Directions:
1. Heat the skillet with olive oil over medium heat and add the diced onion, peppers, and Jalapeño. Sauté the food for about 8–10 minutes until the onion is translucent.
2. In a 4-quart casserole dish, mix chopped brisket, baked beans, pork beans, kidney beans, cooked onions, peppers, barbecue sauce, brown sugar, garlic, mustard, salt, and black pepper.
3. Using the selected pellets, configure a wood pellet-smoking grill for indirect cooking and preheat to 325°F. Cook the beans baked in the brisket for 1.5–2 hours until they become raw beans. Rest for 15 minutes before eating.

Nutrition: Calories: 199 | Carbs: 35 g. | Fat: 2 g. | Protein: 9 g.

5.   Grilled Broccoli

Preparation time: 15 minutes
Cooking time: 10 minutes
Servings: 4–6
Ingredients:
• 4 broccoli bunches
• 4 tbsp. olive oil
• Black pepper and salt to taste
• ½ lemon, the juice
• ½ lemon cut into wedges
Directions:
1. Preheat the grill to high with a closed lid.
2. In a bowl, add the broccoli and drizzle with oil. Coat well—season with salt.
3. Grill for 5 minutes and then flip. Cook for 3 minutes more.
4. Once done, transfer to a plate. Squeeze lemon on top and serve with lemon wedges. Enjoy!
Nutrition: Calories: 35 g. | Protein: 2.5 g. | Carbs: 5 g. | Fat: 1 g.

6.   Smoked Coleslaw

Preparation time: 15 minutes
Cooking time: 25 minutes
Servings: 8
Ingredients:
• 1 purple cabbage, shredded
• 1 green cabbage, shredded
• 2 scallions, sliced.
• 1 cup carrots, shredded
• Dressing:
• 1 tbsp. celery seed
• 1/8 cup white vinegar
• 1 ½ cups mayo
• Black pepper and salt to taste
Directions:
1. Preheat the grill to 180°F with a closed lid.
2. On a tray, spread the carrots and cabbage. Place the tray on the grate and smoke for about 25 minutes.
3. Transfer to the fridge to cool.
4. In the meantime, make the dressing. In a bowl, combine the ingredients. Mix well.
5. Transfer the veggies to a bowl. Drizzle with the sauce and toss
6. Serve sprinkled with scallions.
Nutrition: Calories: 35 g. | Protein: 1 g. | Carbs: 5 g. | Fat: 5 g.

7.   The Best Potato Roast

Preparation time: 15 minutes
Cooking time: 35 minutes
Servings: 6
Ingredients:

• 4 potatoes, large, scrubbed
• 1 ½ cups gravy (beef or chicken)
• Rib seasoning to taste
• 1 ½ cup Cheddar cheese
• Black pepper and salt to taste
• 2 tbsp. scallions, sliced
Directions:
1. Preheat the grill to high with a closed lid.
7. Slice each potato into wedges or fries. Transfer into a bowl and drizzle with oil—season with Rib seasoning.
8. Spread the wedges/fries on a baking sheet (rimmed)—roast for about 20 minutes. Turn the wedges/fries and cook for 15 minutes more.
9. In the meantime, warm the chicken/beef gravy in a saucepan.
10. Cut the cheese into small cubes.
11. Once cooking is complete, place the potatoes on a plate or bowl. Distribute the cut cheese and pour the hot sauce on top.
12. Serve garnished with scallion—season with pepper.
13. Enjoy!
Nutrition: Calories: 220 | Protein: 3 g. | Carbs: 38 g. | Fat: 15 g.

8.   Traeger Smoked Vegetables

Preparation time: 5 minutes
Cooking time: 20 minutes
Servings: 4
Ingredients:
• 1 broccoli head
• 4 carrots
• 16 oz. snow peas
• 1 tbsp. olive oil
• 1 ½ tbsp. pepper
• 1 tbsp. garlic powder
Directions:
1. Cut broccoli and carrots into bite-size pieces. Add snow peas and combine.
2. Toss the veggies with oil and seasoning.
3. Now cover a pan with parchment paper. Place veggies on top.
4. Meanwhile, set your wood pellet smoker to 180°F.
5. Place the pan into the smoker—smoke for about 5 minutes.
6. Adjust smoker temperature to 400°F and cook for another 10–15 minutes until slightly brown broccoli tips.
7. Remove, serve, and enjoy.
Nutrition: Calories 111 | Total Fat: 4 g. | Saturated Fat: 1 g. | Total Carbs: 15 g. | Net Carbs: 9 g. | Protein: 5 g. | Sugars: 7 g. | Fiber: 6 g. | Sodium: 0 mg. | Potassium: 109 mg.

9.   Grilled Carrots

Preparation time: 5 minutes
Cooking time: 20 minutes
Servings: 6
Ingredients:
• 1 lb. carrots, large
• ½ tbsp. salt
• 6 oz. butter
• ½ tbsp. black pepper
• Fresh thyme
Directions:
1. Thoroughly wash the carrots and do not peel them. Pat them dry and coat them with olive oil.
2. Add salt to your carrots.
3. Meanwhile, preheat a Traeger grill to 350°F.
4. Now place your carrots directly on the grill or on a raised rack.
5. Close and cook for about 20 minutes.
6. While carrots cook, cook butter in a small saucepan over medium heat until browned. Stir constantly to avoid it from burning. Remove from heat.
7. Remove carrots from the grill onto a plate, and drizzle with browned butter.
8. Add pepper and splash with thyme.
9. Serve and enjoy.
Nutrition: Calories: 250 | Fat: 25 g. | Saturated Fat: 15 g. | Carbs: 6 g. | Net Carbs: 4 g. | Protein: 1 g. | Sugars: 3 g. | Fiber: 2 g. | Sodium: 402 mg. | Potassium: 369 mg.

10.   Grilled Brussels Sprouts

Preparation time: 15 minutes
Cooking time: 20 minutes
Servings: 8
Ingredients:
• ½ lb. bacon, grease reserved
• 1 lb. Brussels sprouts
• ½ tbsp. pepper
• ½ tbsp. salt
Directions:
1. Cook bacon until crispy on a stovetop, reserve its grease, then chop it into small pieces.
2. Meanwhile, wash the Brussels sprouts, trim off the dry end, and remove dried leaves, if any. Half them and set aside.
3. Place ¼ cup reserved grease in a pan, cast-iron, over medium-high heat.
4. Season the Brussels sprouts with pepper and salt.
5. Brown the sprouts on the pan with the cut side down for about 3–4 minutes.
6. In the meantime, preheat your Traeger grill to 350–375°F.
7. Place bacon pieces and browned sprouts into your grill-safe pan.
8. Cook for about 20 minutes.
9. Serve immediately.

Nutrition: Calories: 153 | Fat: 10 g. | Saturated Fat: 3 g. | Carbs: 5 g. | Net Carbs: 3 g. | Protein: 11 g. | Sugars: 1 g. | Fiber: 2 g. | Sodium: 622 mg. | Potassium: 497 mg.

11.   Traeger Spicy Brisket

Preparation time: 20 minutes
Cooking time: 9 hours
Servings: 10
Ingredients:
• 2 tbsp. garlic powder
• 2 tbsp. onion powder
• 2 tbsp. paprika
• 2 tbsp. chili powder
• 1/3 cup salt
• 1/3 cup black pepper
• 12 lb. whole packer brisket, trimmed
• 1-½ cup beef broth
Directions:
1. Set your Traeger temperature to 225°F. Let preheat for 15 minutes with the lid closed.
2. Meanwhile, mix garlic, onion, paprika, chili, salt, and pepper in a mixing bowl.
3. Put on the brisket generously on all sides.
4. Place the meat on the grill with the fat side down and let it cool until the internal temperature reaches 160°F.
5. Remove the meat from the grill and double-wrap it with foil. Return it to the grill and cook until the internal temperature reaches 204°F.
6. Remove from grill, unwrap the brisket and let rest for 15 minutes.
7. Slice and serve.
Nutrition: Calories: 270 | Fat: 20 g. | Saturated Fat: 8 g. | Carbs: 3 g. | Net Carbs: 3 g. | Protein: 20 g. | Sugar: 1 g. | Fiber: 0 g. | Sodium: 1220 mg.

12.   Smoked Cashews

Preparation time: 5 minutes
Cooking time: 1 hour
Servings: 4–6
Ingredients:
• 1 lb. (454 g.) roasted, salted cashews
Directions:
1. Supply your smoker with pellets and follow the manufacturer's specific start-up procedure. Preheat the grill, with the lid closed, to 120°F (49°C).
2. Pour the cashews onto a rimmed baking sheet and smoke for 1 hour, stirring once about halfway through the smoking time.
3. Remove the cashews from the grill, let cool, and store them in an airtight container for as long as you can resist.
Nutrition: Calories: 57 | Total Fat: 3 g. | Saturated Fat: 1 g. | Total Carbs: 6 g. | Net Carbs: 4 g. | Protein: 4 g. | Sugar: 2 g. | Fiber: 2 g. | Sodium: 484 mg.

13.   Traeger Grill Funeral Potatoes

Preparation time: 10 minutes
Cooking time: 60 minutes
Servings: 8
Ingredients:
• 1, 32 oz., package frozen hash browns
• ½ cup Cheddar cheese, grated
• 1 can cream chicken soup
• 1 cup sour cream
• 1 cup mayonnaise
• 3 cups corn flakes, whole or crushed
• ¼ cup melted butter

Directions:
1. Preheat your Traeger grill to 350°F.
2. Spray a 13 x 9 baking pan, aluminum, using a cooking spray, non-stick.
3. Mix hash browns, cheddar cheese, chicken soup cream, sour cream, and mayonnaise in a bowl, large.
4. Spoon the mixture into a baking pan gently.
5. Mix cornflakes and melted butter, then sprinkle over the casserole.
6. Grill for about 1–½ hour until potatoes become tender. Cover with a foil until the potatoes are done if the top browns too much.
7. Remove from the grill and serve hot.

Nutrition: Calories: 403 | Fat: 37 g. | Saturated Fat: 12 g. | Carbs: 14 g. | Net Carbs: 14 g. | Protein: 4 g. | Sugars: 2 g. | Fiber: 0 g. | Sodium: 620 mg. | Potassium: 501 mg.

14.   Smoky Caramelized Onions on the Traeger Grill

Preparation time: 5 minutes
Cooking time: 60 minutes
Servings: 4
Ingredients:
8. 5 large, sliced onions
9. ½ cup fat your choice
10. Pinch sea salt

Directions:
1. Place all the ingredients into a pan. For a deep rich brown caramelized onion, cook them off for about 1 hour on a stovetop.
2. Keep the grill temperatures not higher than 250–275°F.
3. Now transfer the pan to the grill.
4. Cook for about 1–1½ hours until brown. Check and stir with a wooden spoon after every 15 minutes. Make sure not to run out of Traeger's.
5. Now remove from the grill and season with more salt if necessary.
6. Serve immediately or place in a refrigerator for up to 1 week.

Nutrition: Calories: 286 | Fat: 25.8 g. | Saturated Fat: 10.3 g. | Carbs: 12.8 g. | Net Carbs: 9.8 g. | Protein: 1.5 g. | Sugars: 5.8 g. | Fiber: 3 g. | Sodium: 6 mg. | Potassium: 201 mg.

15.   Hickory Smoked Green Beans

Preparation time: 15 minutes
Cooking time: 3 hours
Servings: 10
Ingredients:
• 6 cups fresh green beans, halved and ends cut off
• 2 cups chicken broth
• 1 tbsp. pepper, ground
• ¼ tbsp. salt
• 2 tbsp. apple cider vinegar
• 6–8 bite-size bacon slices
• Optional: sliced almonds

Directions:
1. Add green beans to a colander, then rinse well. Set aside.
2. Place large chicken broth, pepper, salt, and apple cider in a large pan. Add green beans.
3. Blanch over medium heat for about 3–4 minutes, then remove from heat.
4. Transfer the mixture into an aluminum pan, disposable. Ensure all mixture goes into the pan, so do not drain them.
5. Place bacon slices over the beans and place the pan into the Traeger smoker.
6. Smoke for about 3 hours uncovered.
7. Remove from the smoker and top with almond slices.
8. Serve immediately.

Nutrition: Calories: 57 | Fat: 3 g. | Saturated Fat: 1 g. | Carbs: 6 g. | Net Carbs: 4 g. | Protein: 4 g. | Sugars: 2 g. | Fiber: 2 g. | Sodium: 484 mg. | Potassium: 216 mg.

16.   Smoked Corn on the Cob

Preparation time: 5 minutes
Cooking time: 60 minutes
Servings: 4
Ingredients:
• 4 corn ears, husk removed
• 4 tbsp. olive oil
• Pepper and salt to taste

Directions:
9. Preheat your smoker to 225°F.
10. Meanwhile, brush your corn with olive oil. Season with pepper and salt.
11. Place the corn on a smoker and smoke for about 1 hour and 15 minutes.
12. Remove from the smoker and serve.
13. Enjoy!

Nutrition: Calories: 180°Fat: 7 g. | Saturated Fat: 4 g. | Carbs: 31 g. | Net Carbs: 27 g. | Protein: 5 g. | Sugars: 5 g. | Fiber: 4 g. | Sodium: 23 mg. | Potassium: 416 mg.

17. Easy Grilled Corn

Preparation time: 5 minutes
Cooking time: 40 minutes
Servings: 6
Ingredients:
• 6 fresh corn ears, still in the husk
• Pepper, salt, and butter
Directions:
14. Preheat your Traeger grill to 375–400°F.
15. Cut off the large silk ball and any hanging or loose husk pieces from the corn top.
16. Place the corn on your grill grate directly, and do not peel off the husk.
17. Grill for about 30–40 minutes. Flip a few times to grill evenly all around.
18. Transfer the corn to a platter, serve, and let guests peel their own.
19. Now top with pepper, salt, and butter.
20. Enjoy!
Nutrition: Calories: 77 | Fat: 1 g. | Saturated Fat: 1 g. | Carbs: 17 g. | Net Carbs: 15 g. | Protein: 3 g. | Sugars: 6 g. | Fiber: 2 g. | Sodium: 14 mg. | Potassium: 243 mg.

18. Seasoned Potatoes on Smoker

Preparation time: 10 minutes
Cooking time: 45 minutes
Servings: 6
Ingredients:
• 1–½ lb. creamer potatoes
• 2 tbsp. olive oil
• 1 tbsp. garlic powder
• ¼ tbsp. oregano
• ½ tbsp. thyme, dried
• ½ tbsp. parsley, dried
Directions:
1. Preheat your Traeger grill to 350°F.
2. Spray an 8x8 inch foil pan using non-stick spray.
3. Mix all ingredients in the pan and place it on the grill.
4. Cook for about 45 minutes until the potatoes are done. Stir after every 15 minutes.
5. Serve and enjoy!
Nutrition: Calories: 130 | Fat: 4 g. | Saturated Fat: 2 g. | Carbs: 20 g. | Net Carbs: 18 g. | Protein: 2 g. | Sugars: 2 g. | Fiber: 2 g. | Sodium: 7 mg. | Potassium: 483 mg.

19. Atomic Buffalo Turds

Preparation time: 30–45 minutes
Cooking time: 1.5 hours to 2 hours
Servings: 6–10
Ingredients:
• 10 medium Jalapeño pepper
• 8 oz. regular cream cheese at room temperature
• ¾ cup Monterey Jack and Cheddar Cheese Blend Shred (optional)
• 1 tsp. smoked paprika
• 1 tsp. garlic powder
• ½ tsp. cayenne pepper
• ½ tsp. red pepper flakes (optional)
• 20 smoky sausages
• 10 slices bacon, cut in half
Directions:
1. Wear food service gloves when using. Jalapeño peppers are washed vertically and sliced. Carefully remove seeds and veins using a spoon or paring knife and discard. Place jalapeno on a grilled vegetable tray and set aside.
2. In a small bowl, mix cream cheese, shredded cheese, paprika, garlic powder, cayenne pepper, and red pepper flakes, if used, until thoroughly mixed.
3. Mix cream cheese with half of the jalapeno pepper.
4. Place the Little Smokies sausage on half of the filled jalapeno pepper.
5. Wrap half of the thin bacon around half of each jalapeno pepper.
6. Fix the bacon to the sausage with a toothpick, so the pepper does not pierce. Place the ABT on the grill tray or pan.
7. Set the Traeger smoker grill for indirect cooking and preheat to 250°F using hickory Traeger's or blends.
8. Suck jalapeno peppers at 250°F for about 1.5–2 hours until the bacon is cooked and crisp.
9. Remove the ABT from the grill and let it rest for 5 minutes before hors d'oeuvres
Nutrition: Calories: 334 | Carbs: 14 g. | Protein: 22 g. | Fat: 28 g.

20. Smashed Potato Casserole

Preparation time: 30–45 minutes
Cooking time: 45–60 minutes
Servings: 8
Ingredients:
• 8–10 bacon slices
• ¼ cup (½ stick) salt butter or bacon grease
• 1 sliced red onion
• 1 small pepper, sliced
• 1 small red pepper, sliced
• 1 small pepper, sliced
• 3 cups mashed potatoes
• ¾ cup sour cream
• 1.5 tsp. Texas BBQ Love
• 3 cups sharp Cheddar cheese
• 4 cups hashed brown potato
Directions:
1. Cook the bacon in a large skillet over medium heat until both sides are crispy for about 5 minutes. Set the bacon aside.
2. Transfer the rendered bacon grease to a glass container.
3. In the same large frying pan, heat the butter or bacon grease over medium heat and fry the red onions and peppers until they become al dente. Set aside.

4. Spray a 9x11-inch casserole dish with a non-stick cooking spray and spread the mashed potatoes to the bottom of the dish.

5. Layer sour cream on mashed potatoes and season with Texas BBQ Love.

6. Layer the stir-fried vegetables on the potatoes and pour butter or bacon grease into a pan.

7. Sprinkle 1.5 cups of sharp cheddar cheese followed by frozen hash brown potatoes.

8. Spoon the butter or bacon grease from the stir-fried vegetables over the hash browns and place the crushed bacon.

9. Place the remaining 1.5 cups of sharp cheddar cheese and cover the casserole dish with a lid or aluminum foil.

10. Set up a Traeger smoking grill for indirect cooking and preheat to 350°F.

11. Bake the crushed potato casserole for 45–60 minutes until the cheese foams.

12. Rest for 10 minutes before eating.

Nutrition: Calories: 330 | Carbs: 13 g. | Protein: 11 g. | Fat: 20 g.

21.   Deviled Eggs

Preparation time: 15 minutes
Cooking time: 30 minutes
Servings: 4–6
Ingredients:
• 3 tsp. diced chives
• 3 tbsp. mayonnaise
• 7 eggs, hard-boiled, peeled
• 1 tsp. cider vinegar
• 1 tsp. mustard, brown
• 1/8 tsp. hot sauce
• 2 tbsp. crumbled bacon
• Black pepper and salt to taste
• For dusting: paprika
Directions:
1. Preheat the grill to 180°F with a closed lid.
2. Place the cooked eggs on the grate. Smoke for 30 minutes. Set aside and let them cool.
3. Slice the eggs in half lengthwise. Scoop the yolks and transfer them into a zip lock bag; now, add the black pepper, salt, hot sauce, vinegar, mustard, chives, and mayo. Close the bag and knead the ingredients until smooth.
4. Cut one corner and squeeze the mixture into the egg whites.
5. Top with bacon and dust with paprika.
6. Serve and enjoy! On the other hand, chill in the fridge until serving.
Nutrition: Calories: 140 | Protein: 6 g. | Carbs: 2 g. | Fat: 6 g.

22.   Cranberry-Almond Broccoli Salad

Preparation time: 10 minutes
Cooking time: 60 minutes
Servings: 8
Ingredients:
• ¼ cup finely chopped red onion
• ⅓ cup canola mayonnaise
• 3 tbsp. 2% reduced-fat Greek yogurt
• 1 tbsp. cider vinegar
• 1 tbsp. honey
• ¼ tsp. salt
• ¼ tsp. freshly ground black pepper
• 4 cups coarsely chopped broccoli florets
• ⅓ cup slivered almonds, toasted
• ⅓ cup reduced-sugar dried cranberries
• 4 center-cut bacon slices, cooked and crumbled
Directions:
1. Put the red onion in cold water for 5 minutes.
2. Put together the mayonnaise with the next 5 ingredients (through pepper), blending well with a whisk.
3. Mix in red onion, broccoli, and the remaining ingredients. Cover and chill 1 hour before serving.
Nutrition: Calories 104 | Fat: 5.9 g. Carb 11 g. | Sugars: 5 g.

23.   Onion Bacon Ring

Preparation time: 10 minutes
Cooking time: 1 hour and 30 minutes
Servings: 6–8
Ingredients:
• 2 large onions, cut into ½-inch slices
• 1 bacon package
• 1 tsp. honey
• 1 tbsp. mustard, yellow
• 1 tbsp. garlic chili sauce
Directions:
1. Wrap Bacon around onion rings. Wrap until you are out of bacon. Place on skewers.
2. Preheat the grill to 400°F with a closed lid.
3. In the meantime, in a bowl, combine the mustard and garlic chili sauce. Add honey and stir well.
4. Grill the onion bacon rings for 1 hour and 30 minutes. Flip once.
5. Serve with the sauce, and enjoy!
Nutrition: Calories: 90 | Protein: 2 g. | Carbs: 9 g. | Fat: 7 g.

24.   Grilled Watermelon Juice

Preparation time: 10 minutes
Cooking time: 15 minutes
Servings: 4
Ingredients:
• 2 limes
• 2 tbsp. oil
• ½ watermelon, sliced into wedges
• ¼ tsp. pepper flakes
• 2 tbsp. salt
Directions:
1. Preheat the grill to high with a closed lid.
2. Brush the watermelon with oil. Grill for 15 minutes. Flip once.
3. In a blender, mix the salt and pepper flakes until combined.
4. Transfer the watermelon to a plate.
5. Serve and enjoy!
Nutrition: Calories: 40 | Protein: 1 g. | Carbs: 10 g. | Fat: 0

25.   Smoked Popcorn With Parmesan Herb

Preparation time: 10 minutes
Cooking time: 10 minutes
Servings: 2–4
Ingredients:
• ¼ cup popcorn kernels
• 1 tsp. salt
• 1 tsp. garlic powder
• ½ cup grated parmesan
• 2 tsp. Italian seasoning
• 2 tbsp. oil
• 4 tbsp. butter
Directions:
1. Preheat the grill to 250°F with a closed lid.
2. In a saucepan, add the butter and oil. Melt and add the salt, garlic powder, and Italian seasoning.
3. Add the kernels to a paper bag. Fold it twice to close.
4. Place in the microwave. Turn on high heat and sit for 2 minutes.
5. Open and transfer to a bowl.
6. Pour the butter. Toss. Transfer to a baking tray and grill for about 10 minutes. Toss with parmesan cheese to serve.
7. Serve and enjoy!
Nutrition: Calories: 60 | Protein: 1 g. | Carbs: 5 g. | Fat: 3 g.

26.   Smoked Mushrooms 1

Preparation time: 5 minutes
Cooking time: 45 minutes
Servings: 4–6
Ingredients:
• 4 cups mushrooms (whole) baby Portobello, cleaned
• 1 tsp. onion powder
• 1 tbsp. canola oil
• 1 tsp. garlic, granulated
• 1 tsp. pepper
• 1 tsp. salt
Directions:
1. Add the ingredients to a bowl.
2. Preheat the grill to smoke with a closed lid.
3. Smoke the mushrooms for about 30 minutes.
4. Serve and enjoy!
Nutrition: Calories: 55 | Protein: 2.5 g. | Carbs: 3 g. | Fat: 3.5 g.

27.   Smoked Summer Sausage

Pellet: Apple
Preparation time: 15 minutes
Cooking time: 4 hours and 15 minutes
Servings: 4–6
Ingredients:
• 1½ tsp. Morton salt
• ½ lb. ground venison
• ½ lb. ground boar
• 1 tbsp. salt
• ½ tsp. mustard seeds
• ½ tsp. garlic powder
• ½ tsp. black pepper
Directions:
1. Add all ingredients into a bowl and mix until combined. Cover the bowl with a plastic bag and let it rest in the fridge overnight
2. Form a log from the mixture and wrap it with plastic wrap. Twist the log's end tightly. Now unwrap carefully.
3. Preheat the grill to 225°F with closed lit.
4. Grill the meat for 4 hours. Set aside and let it cool for 1 hour.
5. Once cooled, wrap and store in the fridge.
1.   Serve and enjoy!
Nutrition: Calories: 170 | Protein: 8 g. | Carbs: 0 g. | Fat: 14 g.

28.   Roasted Tomatoes

Preparation time: 10 minutes
Cooking time: 3 hours
Servings: 2–4
Ingredients:
• 3 ripe tomatoes, large
• 1 tbsp. black pepper
• 2 tbsp. salt
• 2 tsp. basil
• 2 tsp. sugar
• Oil
Directions:
1. Place parchment paper on a baking sheet. Preheat the grill to 225°F with a closed lid.
2. Remove the stems from the tomatoes. Cut them into slices (½ inch).
3. Mix the basil, sugar, pepper, and salt in a bowl. Mix well.
4. Pour oil on a plate. Dip the tomatoes (just one side) in the oil—transfer to the prepared baking sheet.
5. Dust each slice with the mixture.
6. Grill the tomatoes for 3 hours.
7. Serve and enjoy! (You can serve it with mozzarella pieces).
Nutrition: Calories: 40 | Protein: 1 g. | Carbs: 2 g. | Fat: 3 g.

29.   Turkey Jerky

Preparation time: 30 minutes
Cooking time: 2 hrs. 30 minutes
Servings: 8
Ingredients:
• 1 tbsp. Asian chili-garlic paste
• 1 tbsp. curing salt
• ½ cup soy sauce
• ¼ cup water
• 2 tbsp. honey
• 2 tbsp. lime juice
• 2 pounds boneless, skinless turkey breast
Directions:
1. Mix the salt, water, lime juice, chili-garlic paste, honey, and soy sauce.
2. Slice the turkey into thin strips. Lay the slices into a large zip-top baggie. If there is more meat than you can, fit it into one bag, and use as much as you need. Pour marinade over the turkey.
3. Seal the bag and shake it around, so each slice gets coated with the marinade. Place the bag into the refrigerator overnight.
4. Add wood pellets to your smoker and follow your cooker's startup procedure. Preheat your smoker with your lid closed until it reaches 350°F.
5. Take the sliced turkey out of the bags. Use paper towels to pat them dry. Place them evenly over the grill into one layer. Smoke the turkey for 2 hours. The jerky should feel dry but still chewable when done.
6. Place into the zip-top bag to keep fresh until ready to eat.

Nutrition: Calories: 80 | Protein: 13 g. | Carbs: 5.1 g. | Fat: 0.8 g.

30.   Smoked Veggie Medley

Preparation time: 30 minutes
Cooking time: 1 hour
Servings: 4
Ingredients:
• 1 Spanish red onion, peeled and cut into quarters
• 1 red pepper, seeded and sliced
• 2 zucchinis, sliced
• 1 yellow summer squash, sliced
• 2 tbsp. olive oil
• 2 tbsp. balsamic vinegar
• 6 garlic cloves, peeled, minced
• 1 tsp. sea salt
• ½ tsp. black pepper
Directions:
1. Preheat the pellet grill to 350°F.
2. In a large bowl, combine the red onion, red pepper, zucchinis, summer squash, olive oil, balsamic vinegar, garlic, sea salt, and black pepper. Toss to combine.
3. Transfer the veggies to the smoker and, with the lid closed, cook for between 30–45 minutes until cooked through and caramelized.
4. Serve and enjoy.
Nutrition: Calories: 63 | Protein: 3 g. | Carbs: 9 g. | Fat: 3 g.

Chapter 5. Beef Recipes

31.   Mustard Beef Short Ribs

Preparation time: 15 minutes
Cooking time: 3 hours
Servings: 6
Ingredients:
For mustard sauce:
- 1 cup prepared yellow mustard
- ¼ cup red wine vinegar
- ¼ cup dill pickle juice
- 2 tbsp. soy sauce
- 2 tbsp. Worcestershire sauce
- 1 tsp. ground ginger
- 1 tsp. granulated garlic
For the spice rub:
- 2 tbsp. salt
- 2 tbsp. freshly ground black pepper
- 1 tbsp. white cane sugar
- 1 tbsp. granulated garlic
For ribs:
- 6 (14 oz.) (4–5-inch long) beef short ribs
Directions:
1. Preheat the Z Grills Traeger Grill & Smoker on smoke setting to 230–250°F, using charcoal.
2. For the sauce:
3. In a bowl, mix all ingredients.
4. For the rub:
5. In a small bowl, mix all ingredients.
6. Coat the ribs with sauce generously and then sprinkle with spice rub evenly.
7. Place the ribs onto the grill over indirect heat, bone side down.
8. Cook for about 1–1½ hours.
9. Flip the side and cook for about 45 minutes.
10. Flip the side and cook for about 45 minutes more.
11. Remove the ribs from the grill and place them onto a cutting board for about 10 minutes before serving.
12. Cut the ribs into equal-sized individual pieces with a sharp knife and serve.
Nutrition: Calories: 867 | Fat: 37.5 g. | Saturated Fat: 13.7 g. | Cholesterol: 361 mg. | Sodium: 3462 mg. | Carbs: 7.7 g. | Fiber: 2.1 g. | Sugar: 3.6 g. | Protein: 117.1 g.

32.   Sweet & Spicy Beef Brisket

Preparation time: 10 minutes
Cooking time: 7 hours
Servings: 10
Ingredients:
- 1 cup paprika
- ¾ cup sugar
- 3 tbsp. garlic salt
- 3 tbsp. onion powder
- 1 tbsp. celery salt
- 1 tbsp. lemon pepper
- 1 tbsp. ground black pepper
- 1 tsp. cayenne pepper
- 1 tsp. mustard powder
- ½ tsp. dried thyme, crushed
- 1 (5–6 lb.) beef brisket, trimmed
Directions:
1. Place all ingredients except beef brisket in a bowl and mix well.
2. Rub the brisket with spice mixture generously.
3. With plastic wrap, cover the brisket and refrigerate overnight.
4. Preheat the Z Grills Traeger Grill & Smoker on the grill setting to 250°F.
5. Place the brisket onto the grill over indirect heat and cook for about 3–3½ hours.
6. Flip and cook for about 3–3½ hours more.
7. Remove the brisket from the grill and place it on a cutting board for 10–15 minutes before slicing.
8. With a sharp knife, cut the brisket into desired-sized slices and serve.
Nutrition: Calories: 536 | Fat: 15.6 g. | Saturated Fat: 5.6 g. | Cholesterol: 203 mg. | Sodium: 158 mg. | Carbs: 24.8 g. | Fiber: 4.5 g. | Sugar: 17.4 g. | Protein: 71.1 g.

33.   Brandy Beef Tenderloin

Preparation time: 15 minutes
Cooking time: 2 hours 2 minutes
Servings: 6
Ingredients:
For brandy butter:
- ½ cup butter
- 1 oz. brandy
For brandy sauce:
- 2 oz. brandy
- 8 garlic cloves, minced
- ¼ cup mixed fresh herbs (parsley, rosemary, and thyme), chopped
- 2 tsp. honey
- 2 tsp. hot English mustard
For tenderloin:
- 1 (2 lb.) center-cut beef tenderloin
- Salt and cracked black peppercorns, as required
Directions:
1. Preheat the Z Grills Traeger Grill & Smoker on grill setting to 230°F.
2. For brandy butter:
3. In a pan, melt butter over medium-low heat.
4. Stir in brandy and remove from heat.
5. Set aside, covered to keep warm.
6. For brandy sauce:
7. In a bowl, add all ingredients and mix until well combined.
8. Season the tenderloin with salt and black peppercorns generously.

9. Coat tenderloin with brandy sauce evenly.

10. With a baster injector, inject tenderloin with brandy butter.

11. Place the tenderloin onto the grill and cook for about ½–2 hours, injecting with brandy butter occasionally.

12. Remove the tenderloin from the grill and place it on a cutting board for 10–15 minutes before serving.

13. With a sharp knife, cut the tenderloin into desired-sized slices and serve.

Nutrition: Calories: 496 | Fat: 29.3 g. | Saturated Fat: 15 g. | Cholesterol: 180 mg. | Sodium: 240 mg. | Carbs: 4.4 g. | Fiber: 0.7 g. | Sugar: 2 g. | Protein: 44.4 g.

34.　Beef Rump Roast

Preparation time: 10 minutes
Cooking time: 6 hours
Servings: 8
Ingredients:
14. 1 tsp. smoked paprika
15. 1 tsp. cayenne pepper
16. 1 tsp. onion powder
17. 1 tsp. garlic powder
18. Salt and ground black pepper, as required
19. 3 lbs. beef rump roast
20. ¼ cup Worcestershire sauce
Directions:
1. Preheat the Z Grills Traeger Grill & Smoker on the smoke setting to 200°F, using charcoal.
2. In a bowl, mix all spices.
3. Coat the rump roast with Worcestershire sauce evenly and then rub with spice mixture generously.
4. Place the rump roast onto the grill and cook for about 5–6 hours.
5. Remove the roast from the grill and place it on a cutting board for about 10–15 minutes before serving.
6. With a sharp knife, cut the roast into desired-sized slices and serve.

Nutrition: Calories: 252 | Fat: 9.1 g. | Saturated Fat: 3 g. | Cholesterol: 113 mg. | Sodium: 200 mg. | Carbs: 2.3 g. | Fiber: 0.2 g. | Sugar: 1.8 g. | Protein: 37.8 g.

35.　Herbed Prime Rib Roast

Preparation time: 10 minutes
Cooking time: 3 hours 50 minutes
Servings: 10
Ingredients:
• 1 (5 lb.) prime rib roast
• Salt, as required
• 5 tbsp. olive oil
• 2 tsp. dried thyme, crushed
• 2 tsp. dried rosemary, crushed
• 2 tsp. garlic powder
• 1 tsp. onion powder
• 1 tsp. paprika
• ½ tsp. cayenne pepper
• Ground black pepper, as required

Directions:
1. Season the roast with salt generously.
2. With plastic wrap, cover the roast and refrigerate for about 24 hours.
3. Mix the remaining ingredients in a bowl and set aside for about 1 hour.
4. Rub the roast with oil mixture from both sides evenly.
5. Arrange the roast on a large baking sheet and refrigerate for about 6–12 hours.
6. Preheat the Z Grills Traeger Grill & Smoker on smoke setting to 225–230°F, using pecan wood chips.
7. Place the roast onto the grill and cook for about 3–3½ hours.
8. Meanwhile, preheat the oven to 500°F.
9. Remove the roast from the grill and place it on a large baking sheet.
10. Place the baking sheet in the oven and roast for about 15–20 minutes.
11. Remove the roast from the oven and place it on a cutting board for about 10–15 minutes before serving.
12. With a sharp knife, cut the roast into desired-sized slices and serve.

Nutrition: Calories: 605 | Fat: 47.6 g. | Saturated Fat: 17.2 g. | Cholesterol: 135 mg. | Sodium: 1285 mg. | Carbs: 3.8 g. | Fiber: 0.3 g. | Sugar: 0.3 g. | Protein: 38 g.

36.　Spicy Chuck Roast

Preparation time: 10 minutes
Cooking time: 4½ hours
Servings: 8
Ingredients:
• 2 tbsp. onion powder
• 2 tbsp. garlic powder
• 1 tbsp. red chili powder
• 1 tbsp. cayenne pepper
• Salt and ground black pepper, as required
• 1 (3 lb.) beef chuck roast
• 16 fluid ounces warm beef broth
Directions:
1. Preheat the Z Grills Traeger Grill & Smoker on the grill setting to 250°F.
2. In a bowl, mix spices, salt, and black pepper.
3. Rub the chuck roast with spice mixture evenly.
4. Place the rump roast onto the grill and cook for about 1½ hours per side.
5. Now, arrange chuck roast in a steaming pan with beef broth.
6. Cover the pan with foil and cook for about 2–3 hours.
7. Remove the chuck roast from the grill and place it on a cutting board for about 20 minutes before slicing.
8. With a sharp knife, cut the chuck roast into desired-sized slices and serve.

Nutrition: Calories: 645 | Fat: 48 g. | Saturated Fat: 19 g. | Cholesterol: 175 mg. | Sodium: 329 mg. | Carbs: 4.2 g. | Fiber: 1 g. | Sugar: 1.4 g. | Protein: 46.4 g.

37.   BBQ Spiced Flank Steak

Preparation time: 15 minutes
Cooking time: 30 minutes
Servings: 6
Ingredients:
- 1 (2 lb.) beef flank steak
- 2 tbsp. olive oil
- ¼ cup BBQ rub
- 3 tbsp. blue cheese, crumbled
- 2 tbsp. butter, softened
- 1 tsp. fresh chives, minced

Directions:
1. Preheat the Z Grills Traeger Grill & Smoker on the grill setting to 225°F.
2. Coat the steak with oil evenly and season with BBQ rub.
3. Place the steak onto the grill and cook for about 10–15 minutes per side.
4. Remove the steak from the grill and place it on a cutting board for about 10 minutes before slicing.
5. Meanwhile, in a bowl, add blue cheese, butter, and chives and mix well.
6. Cut the steak into thin strips across the grain with a sharp knife.
7. Top with cheese mixture and serve.

Nutrition: Calories: 370 | Fat: 19.1 g. | Saturated Fat: 7.5 g. | Cholesterol: 148 mg. | Sodium: 1666 mg. | Carbs: 0.1 g. | Fiber: 0 g. | Sugar: 0 g. | Protein: 46.8 g.

38.   Beef Stuffed Bell Peppers

Preparation time: 20 minutes
Cooking time: 1 hour
Servings: 6
Ingredients:
- 6 large bell peppers
- 1 lb. ground beef
- 1 small onion, chopped
- 2 garlic cloves, minced
- 2 cups cooked rice
- 1 cup frozen corn, thawed
- 1 cup cooked black beans
- ⅔ cup salsa
- 2 tbsp. Cajun rub
- 1½ cups Monterey Jack cheese, grated

Directions:
1. Cut each bell pepper in half lengthwise through the stem.
2. Carefully remove the seeds and ribs.
3. For stuffing:
4. Heat a large frying pan and cook the beef for about 6–7 minutes or until browned completely.
5. Add onion and garlic and cook for about 2–3 minutes.
6. Stir in the remaining ingredients except for cheese and cook for about 5 minutes.
7. Remove from the heat and set aside to cool slightly.
8. Preheat the Z Grills Traeger Grill & Smoker on the grill setting to 350°F.

9. Stuff each bell pepper half with the stuffing mixture evenly.
10. Arrange the peppers onto the grill, stuffing side up, and cook for about 40 minutes.
11. Sprinkle each bell pepper half with cheese and cook for about 5 minutes.
12. Remove the bell peppers from the grill and serve hot.

Nutrition: Calories: 675 | Fat: 14.8 g. | Saturated Fat: 7.5 g. | Cholesterol: 93 mg. | Sodium: 1167 mg. | Carbs: 90.7 g. | Fiber: 8.7 g. | Sugar: 9.1 g. | Protein: 43.9 g.

39.   BBQ Meatloaf

Preparation time: 20 minutes
Cooking time: 2 ½ hours
Servings: 8
Ingredients:
For the meatloaf:
- 3 lb. ground beef
- 3 eggs
- ½ cup panko breadcrumbs
- 1 (10 oz.) can diced tomatoes with green chili peppers
- 1 large white onion, chopped
- 2 hot banana peppers, chopped
- 2 tbsp. seasoned salt
- 2 tsp. liquid smoke flavoring
- 2 tsp. smoked paprika
- 1 tsp. onion salt
- 1 tsp. garlic salt
- Salt and ground black pepper, as required
- For the sauce:
- ½ cup ketchup
- ¼ cup tomato-based chili sauce
- ¼ cup white sugar
- 2 tsp. Worcestershire sauce
- 2 tsp. hot pepper sauce
- 1 tsp. red pepper flakes, crushed
- 1 tsp. red chili pepper
- Salt and ground black pepper, as required

Directions:
1. Preheat the Z Grills Traeger Grill & Smoker on the smoke setting to 225°F, using charcoal.
2. Grease a loaf pan.
3. For the meatloaf: in a bowl, add all ingredients, and with your hands, mix until well combined.
4. Place the mixture into the prepared loaf pan evenly.
5. Place the pan onto the grill and cook for about 2 hours.
6. Add all ingredients to a bowl for the sauce and beat until well combined.
7. Remove the pan from the grill and drain excess grease from the meatloaf.
8. Place sauce over meatloaf evenly and place the pan onto the grill.
9. Cook for about 30 minutes.
10. Remove the meatloaf from the grill and set it aside for about 10 minutes before serving.

11. Carefully invert the meatloaf onto a platter.

12. Cut the meatloaf into desired-sized slices and serve.

Nutrition: Calories: 423 | Fat: 13 g. | Saturated Fat: 4.7 g. | Cholesterol: 213 mg. | Sodium: 1879 mg. | Carbs: 15.7 g. | Fiber: 1.5 g. | Sugar: 12.3 g. | Protein: 54.9 g.

40. Smoked Beef Brisket in Sweet and Spicy Rub

Preparation time: 15 minutes

Cooking time: 1 hour

Servings: 10

Ingredients:
• Beef Brisket (6 lbs., 2.7-kgs)
• 1 cup paprika
• ½ cup salt
• 1 cup brown sugar
• ½ cup cumin
• ½ cup pepper
• ½ cup chili powder
• ¼ cup cayenne pepper

Directions:

1. Combine paprika, salt, brown sugar, cumin, pepper, chili powder, and cayenne pepper in a bowl, then stir until incorporated.

2. Rub the beef brisket with the spice mixture, then marinate overnight. Store in the refrigerator to keep it fresh.

3. Remove the beef brisket from the refrigerator, then thaw until it reaches room temperature.

4. Preheat the smoker to 250°F (121°C) with charcoal and hickory chips—using indirect heat. Don't forget to soak the wood chips before using them.

5. When the smoker has reached the desired temperature, wrap the beef brisket with aluminum foil, then place it in the smoker.

6. Smoke the wrapped beef brisket for 8 hours. Check the temperature every hour, then add more charcoal and hickory chips if necessary.

7. Once the smoked beef brisket is ready, remove it from the smoker, then let it sit for a few minutes until warm.

8. Unwrap the smoked beef brisket, then place it on a flat surface.

9. Cut the smoked beef brisket into thick slices, then place on a serving dish.

10. Serve and enjoy.

Nutrition: Calories: 180 | Carbs: 3 g. | Fat: 3 g. | Protein: 35 g.

41. Simple Smoked Beef Brisket With Mocha Sauce

Preparation time: 15 minutes

Cooking time: 1 hour

Servings: 10

Ingredients:
• 5 lbs. beef brisket
• 1 ½ tbsp. garlic powder
• 1 ½ tbsp. onion powder
• 4 tbsp. salt
• 4 tbsp. pepper
• 2 ½ tbsp. olive oil
• 1 cup chopped onion
• 2 tsp. salt
• ¼ cup chopped chocolate dark
• ¼ cup sugar
• ½ cup beer
• 2 shots expresso

Directions:

1. Rub the beef brisket with garlic powder, onion powder, salt, and black pepper.

2. Wrap the seasoned beef brisket with a sheet of plastic wrap, then store it in the refrigerator overnight.

3. In the morning, remove the beef brisket from the refrigerator and thaw for about an hour.

4. Preheat the smoker to 250°F (121°C) with charcoal and hickory chips—using indirect heat. Place the beef brisket in the smoker and smoke for 8 hours.

5. Keep the temperature at 250°F (121°C) and add more charcoal and hickory chips if necessary.

6. Meanwhile, preheat a saucepan over medium heat, then pour olive oil into the saucepan.

7. Once the oil is hot, stir in chopped onion, then sauté until wilted and aromatic.

8. Reduce the heat to low, then add the remaining sauce ingredients to the saucepan. Mix well, then bring to a simmer.

9. Remove the sauce from heat, then set aside.

10. When the smoked beef brisket is ready, or the internal temperature has reached 190°F (88°C), remove it from the smoker, then transfer it to a serving dish.

11. Drizzle the mocha sauce over the smoked beef brisket, then serve.

12. Enjoy warm.

Nutrition: Calories: 210 | Carbs: 1 g. | Fat: 13 g. | Protein: 19 g.

42. Lemon Ginger Smoked Beef Ribs

Preparation time: 10 minutes
Cooking time: 10 hours
Servings: 10
Ingredients:
• 6 lb. beef ribs
• 3 tbsp. paprika
• ¼ cup brown sugar
• 1 ½ tbsp. dry mustard
• 1 ½ tbsp. ginger
• 1 tbsp. onion powder
• 1 ½ tbsp. salt
• 1 tbsp. pepper
• 3 tbsp. lemon juice
Directions:
1. Combine the paprika with brown sugar, dry mustard, onion powder, salt, and pepper, then mix well.
2. Rub the beef ribs with the spice mixture, then place them on a sheet of aluminum foil.
3. Splash lemon juice over the beef ribs, then sprinkles ginger on top.
4. Wrap the seasoned beef ribs with aluminum foil, then set them aside.
5. Preheat the smoker to 250°F (121°C) with charcoal and hickory chips—don't forget to soak the wood chips before using them.
6. Place the wrapped beef ribs in the smoker and smoke for 10 hours.
7. If necessary, check the temperature at 250°F (121°C) and add more charcoal and hickory chips.
8. Once the smoked beef ribs are done, remove them from the smoker.
9. Unwrap the smoked beef ribs, then place them on a serving dish.
10. Serve and enjoy.
Nutrition: Calories: 415 | Fat: 35 g. | Protein: 25 g.

43. Chocolate Smoked Beef Ribs

Preparation time: 15 minutes
Cooking time: 19 hours
Servings: 10
Ingredients:
• 6 lb. beef ribs
• 1 ¼ cups cocoa powder
• ¾ cup chili powder
• ¾ cup sugar
• ¾ cup salt
• ¼ cup black pepper
• ¼ cup cumin
Directions:
1. Place the cocoa powder in a bowl, then add chili powder, sugar, salt, black pepper, and cumin. Mix well.
2. Rub the beef ribs with the cocoa powder mixture, then cover with plastic wrap.

3. Marinate the beef ribs overnight and store them in the refrigerator to keep them fresh.
4. In the morning, remove the beef ribs from the refrigerator and thaw for about an hour.
5. Preheat the smoker to 250°F (121°C) with charcoal and hickory chips—using indirect heat. Place the beef ribs in the smoker and smoke for 10 hours.
6. Keep the temperature at 250°F (121°C) and add more charcoal and hickory chips if necessary.
7. Once it is done or the internal temperature has reached 170°F (77°C), take the smoked beef ribs from the smoker and transfer them to a serving dish.
8. Serve and enjoy warm.
Nutrition: Calories: 415 | Carbs: 0 g. | Fat: 35 g. | Protein: 25 g.

44. Smoked Beef With Smoked Garlic Mayo Dip

Preparation time: 15 minutes
Cooking time: 8 hours
Servings: 10
Ingredients:
• 5 lb. beef tenderloin
• ¼ cup minced garlic
• 2 tsp. black pepper
• 2 tsp. salt
• 1 ½ tsp. olive oil
• 5 garlic cloves
• ½ cup mayonnaise
• ¼ cup water
• 2 tbsp. red wine vinegar
• 2 tbsp. chives
Directions:
1. Preheat, the smoker to 250°F (121°C). Soak the hickory wood chips for about an hour before using them.
2. Combine minced garlic, black pepper, salt, and olive oil and stir until mixed.
3. Rub the beef tenderloin with the spice mixture, then place it in the smoker.
4. Wrap the garlic cloves with aluminum foil, then place them next to the beef tenderloin.
5. Smoke the beef tenderloin and garlic for about 8 hours or until the internal temperature of the beef tenderloin reaches 145°F (63°C).
6. Remove the smoked beef tenderloin and garlic from the smoker, then cut the smoked beef tenderloin into slices. Set aside.
7. Place mayonnaise and chives in a blender and pour water and red wine vinegar over the mayonnaise.
8. Add the smoked garlic to the blender and blend until smooth.
9. Transfer the garlic and mayonnaise dip to a small bowl and place next to the smoked beef tenderloin.
10. Serve and enjoy.

Nutrition: Calories: 205 | Carbs: 4 g. | Fat: 12 g. | Protein: 19 g.

45.   Simple Smoked Pulled Beef

Preparation time: 15 minutes
Cooking time: 9 hours
Servings: 10
Ingredients:
• 1 6 lb. chuck roast
• 2 ½ tbsp. salt
• 2 ½ tbsp. black pepper
• 2 ½ tbsp. garlic powder
• ½ cup chopped onion
• 3 cups beef broth
Directions:
1. Preheat, the smoker to 225°F (107°C). Let the lid close and wait for 15 minutes.
2. Mix garlic powder with black pepper and salt until combined.
3. Rub the chuck roast with the spice mixture and massage the roast using your hand until it is thoroughly seasoned.
4. Place the seasoned roast on the grill and cook the roast for 3 hours. Spray the roast with beef broth once every hour.
5. After 3 hours, sprinkle chopped onion on the bottom of a pan, then pour the remaining beef broth over the onion— about 2 cups.
6. Transfer the cooked roast to the pan, then place the pan on the grill.
7. Increase the smoker's temperature to 250°F (121°C) and cook for 3 hours.
8. After 3 hours, cover the pan with aluminum foil, then lower the temperature to 165°F (74°C).
9. Cook the roast for another 3 hours until done.
10. Once done, transfer the smoked beef to a flat surface and let it cool.
11. Once it is cold, using a fork, shred the beef, then place it on a serving dish.
12. Serve and enjoy!
Nutrition: Calories: 104 | Carbs: 6 g. | Fat: 2 g. | Protein: 16 g.

46.   Smoked Beef Churl Barbecue

Preparation time: 20 minutes
Cooking time: 4 hours
Servings: 10
Ingredients:
• 1 (5-lb.) beef chuck rolls
• 5 tbsp. ground black peppercorns
• ¼ cup Kosher salt
Directions:
1. Combine salt and black peppercorns in a bowl. Mix until combined.
2. Rub the beef chuck with the spice mixture, then set aside.
3. Preheat a grill over medium heat for about 10 minutes.
4. Place the charcoal on the grill, then waits until the grill reaches 275°F (135°C).

5. Wrap the beef with aluminum foil, then place it on the grill. Keep the grill's temperature to 275°F (135°C)
6. Cook the beef chuck for 5 hours.
7. When the smoked beef is done, please remove it from the grill and let it cool for a few minutes.
8. Cut the smoked beef into thin slices, then serve with any roasted vegetables you desire.
Nutrition: Calories: 230 | Carbs: 22 g. | Fat: 9 g. | Protein: 15 g.

47.   Honey Glazed Smoked Beef

Preparation time: 10 minutes
Cooking time: 8 hours
Servings: 10
Ingredients:
• 1 (6 lb.) beef brisket
• 2 ½ tbsp. salt
• 2 ½ tbsp. pepper
• ¾ cup barbecue sauce
• 3 tbsp. red wine
• 3 tbsp. raw honey
Directions:
1. Preheat, the smoker to 225°F (107°C). Spread the charcoal on one side.
2. Meanwhile, rub the beef brisket with salt, pepper, and barbecue sauce.
3. When the smoker has reached the desired temperature, place the brisket on the grill with the fat side up. Splash red wine over beef brisket.
4. Smoke the beef brisket for 8 hours. Check the smoker every 2 hours and add more charcoal if necessary.
5. Once it is done, take the smoked beef brisket from the smoker and transfer it to a serving dish.
6. Drizzle raw honey over the beef and let it sit for about an hour before slicing.
7. Serve with roasted or sautéed vegetables according to your desire.
Nutrition: Calories: 90 | Carbs: 8 g. | Fat: 1 g. | Protein: 11 g.

48.   Spiced Smoked Beef With Oregano

Preparation time: 10 minutes
Cooking time: 8 hours
Servings: 10
Ingredients:
• 1 (8 lb.) untrimmed brisket
• 6 tbsp. paprika
• ¼ cup salt
• 3 tbsp. garlic powder
• 2 tbsp. onion powder
• 1 ½ tbsp. black pepper
• 1 ½ tbsp. dried parsley
• 2 ½ tsp. cayenne pepper
• 2 ½ tsp. cumin
• 1 ½ tsp. coriander
• 2 tsp. oregano

- ½ tsp. hot chili powder

Directions:

8. Preheat the smoker before smoking.

9. Woodchips during the smoking time.

10. Cook the brisket for 6 hours.

11. After 6 hours, the smoker's temperature usually decreases to 170°F (77°C).

12. Take the brisket out from the smoker and wrap it with aluminum foil.

13. Return the brisket to the smoker, then cooks again for 2 hours—this will increase the tenderness of the smoked beef.

14. Once it is done, remove the smoked beef from the smoker, then place it in a serving dish.

15. Cut the smoked beef into slices and enjoy!

Nutrition: Calories: 267 | Carbs: 0 g. | Fat: 21 g. | Protein: 20 g.

49.   BBQ Sweet Pepper Meatloaf

Preparation time: 20 minutes
Cooking time: 3 hours and 15 minutes
Servings: 8
Ingredients:
- 1 cup red sweet peppers, chopped
- 5 lb. ground beef
- 1 cup green onion, chopped
- 1 tbsp. salt
- 1 tbsp. black pepper, grounded
- 1 cup panko breadcrumbs
- 2 tbsp. BBQ rub and more as needed
- 1 cup ketchup
- 2 eggs

Directions:

1. Switch on the Traeger grill, fill the grill hopper with Texas beef blend flavored Traeger's, power the grill on by using the control panel, select 'smoke' on the temperature dial, or set the temperature to 225°F and let it preheat for a minimum of 5 minutes.

2. Meanwhile, take a large bowl, place all the ingredients except ketchup, and then stir until well combined.

3. Shape the mixture into meatloaf and then sprinkle with some BBQ rub.

4. When the grill has preheated, open the lid, place meatloaf on the grill grate, shut the grill, and smoke for 2 hours and 15 minutes.

5. Then change the smoking temperature to 375°F, insert a food thermometer into the meatloaf, and cook for 45 minutes or more until the internal temperature of the meatloaf reaches 155°F.

6. Brush the top of the meatloaf with ketchup and then continue cooking for 15 minutes until glazed.

7. Transfer food to a dish, let it rest for 10 minutes, cut it into slices and serve.

Nutrition: Calories: 160.5 | Fat: 2.8 g. | Carbs: 13.2 g. | Protein: 17.2 g. | Fiber: 1 g.

50.   Blackened Steak

Preparation time: 10 minutes
Cooking time: 60 minutes
Servings: 4
Ingredients:
- 2 steaks, about 40 ounces each
- 4 tbsp. blackened rub
- 4 tbsp. butter, unsalted

Directions:

1. Switch on the Traeger grill, fill the grill hopper with hickory-flavored Traeger's, power the grill on the control panel, select 'smoke' on the temperature dial, or set the temperature to 225°F and let it preheat for a minimum of 15 minutes.

2. Transfer steaks to a dish and then repeat with the remaining steak.

3. Let seared steaks rest for 10 minutes, then slice each steak across the grain and serve.

Nutrition: Calories: 184.4 | Fat: 8.8 g. | Carbs: 0 g. | Protein: 23.5 g.

51.   BBQ Brisket

Preparation time: 12 hours
Cooking time: 10 hours
Servings: 8
Ingredients:
- 1 beef brisket, about 12 lb.
- Beef rub as needed

Directions:

1. Season beef brisket with beef rub until well coated, place it in a large plastic bag, seal it and let it marinate for a minimum of 12 hours in the refrigerator.

2. When ready to cook, switch on the Traeger grill, fill the grill hopper with hickory-flavored Traeger's, power the grill on by using the control panel, select 'smoke' on the temperature dial, or set the temperature to 225°F and let it preheat for a minimum of 15 minutes.

3. When the grill has preheated, open the lid, place marinated brisket on the grill, grate fat-side down, shut the grill, and smoke for 6 hours until the internal temperature reaches 160°F.

4. Then wrap the brisket in foil, return it to the grill grate and cook for 4 hours until the internal temperature reaches 204°F.

5. Transfer brisket to a cutting board, let it rest for 30 minutes, then cut it into slices and serve.

Nutrition: Calories: 328 | Fat: 21 g. | Protein: 32 g.

52.   Perfect Beef Tenderloin

Preparation time: 10 minutes
Cooking time: 1 hour 19 minutes
Servings: 12
Ingredients:
• 1 (5 lb.) beef tenderloin, trimmed
• Kosher salt, to taste
• ¼ cup olive oil
• Ground black pepper to taste
Directions:
1. Tie the tenderloin with kitchen strings at 7–8 places.
2. Season tenderloin with salt generously.
3. Cover the tenderloin with plastic wrap and set it aside at room temperature for 1 hour.
4. Preheat the Traeger Grill at 250°F with a closed lid for 15 minutes.
5. Now, coat the tenderloin with oil and season with black pepper.
6. Arrange tenderloin onto the grill and cook for 55–65 minutes.
7. Now, place the cooking grate directly over hot coals and sear tenderloin for 2 minutes per side.
8. Remove the tenderloin and rest for 10 minutes.
9. Slice and serve.
Nutrition: Calories: 425 | Fat: 21.5 g. | Carbs: 0 g. | Protein: 54.7 g.

53.   Versatile Beef Tenderloin

Preparation time: 15 minutes
Cooking time: 2 hours 5 minutes
Servings: 6
Ingredients:
For brandy butter:
• ½ cup butter
• 1 oz. brandy
For brandy sauce:
• 2 oz. brandy
• 8 garlic cloves, minced
• ¼ cup mixed fresh herbs (parsley, rosemary, and thyme), chopped
• 2 tsp. honey
• 2 tsp. hot English mustard
For tenderloin:
• 1 (2 lb.) center-cut beef tenderloin
• Salt and cracked black peppercorns to taste
Directions:
1. Set the temperature of Traeger Grill to 230°F and preheat with a closed lid for 15 minutes.
2. For brandy butter: in a pan, melt butter, then stir in brandy and remove from heat. Cover and set aside. Keep warm.
3. For brandy sauce, add all the ingredients in a bowl and mix well.
4. Season tenderloin with salt and black peppercorns generously.
5. Coat tenderloin with brandy sauce evenly.

6. With a baster injector, inject tenderloin with brandy butter.
7. Place the tenderloin onto the grill and cook for 1 ½–2 hours. Injecting with brandy butter occasionally.
8. Remove the tenderloin from the grill and rest for 10 minutes.
9. Slice and serve.
Nutrition: Calories: 496 | Fat: 29.3 g. | Carbs: 4.4 g. | Protein: 44.4 g.

54.   Buttered Tenderloin

Preparation time: 10 minutes
Cooking time: 45 minutes
Servings: 8
Ingredients:
• 1 (4 lb.) beef tenderloin, trimmed
• Cracked black pepper and smoked salt to taste
• 3 tbsp. butter, melted
Directions:
1. Set the temperature of Traeger Grill to 300°F and preheat with a closed lid for 15 minutes.
2. Season the tenderloin with salt and pepper, and then rub with butter.
3. Place the tenderloin onto the grill and cook for 45 minutes.
4. Remove the tenderloin from the grill and rest for 10 minutes.
5. Slice and serve.
Nutrition: Calories: 505 | Fat: 25.1 g. | Carbs: 0 g. | Protein: 65.7 g.

55.   Delicious Beef Brisket

Preparation time: 10 minutes
Cooking time: 7 hours
Servings: 10
Ingredients:
• 1 cup paprika
• ¾ cup sugar
• 3 tbsp. garlic salt
• 3 tbsp. onion powder
• 1 tbsp. celery salt
• 1 tbsp. lemon pepper
• 1 tbsp. black pepper, grounded
• 1 tsp. cayenne pepper
• 1 tsp. mustard powder
• ½ tsp. dried thyme, crushed
• 1 (5–6 lb.) beef brisket, trimmed
Directions:
1. Place all ingredients in a bowl, except for beef brisket, and mix well.
2. Rub the brisket with the spice mixture.
3. Cover the brisket with plastic wrap and refrigerate overnight.
4. Set the temperature of Traeger Grill to 250°F and preheat with a closed lid for 15 minutes.

5. Place the brisket onto the grill over indirect heat and cook for 3–3 ½ hours.

6. Flip and cook for 3–3 ½ hours more.

7. Remove the brisket from the grill and rest for 10 minutes.

8. Slice and serve.

Nutrition: Calories: 536 | Fat: 15.6 g. | Carbs: 24.8 g. | Protein: 71.1 g.

56.   St. Patrick Day's Corned Beef

Preparation time: 15 minutes

Cooking time: 7 hours

Servings: 14

Ingredients:

• 6 lb. corned beef brisket, drained, rinsed, and pat dried

• Ground black pepper to taste

• 8 oz. light beer

Directions:

1. Set the temperature of Traeger Grill to 275°F and preheat with a closed lid for 15 minutes.

2. Sprinkle the beef brisket with the spice packet evenly.

3. Place the brisket onto the grill and cook for 3–4 hours.

4. Remove from grill and transfer briskets into an aluminum pan.

5. Add enough beer just to cover the bottom of the pan.

6. Cover the pan with a piece of foil, leaving one corner open to let out steam.

7. Cook for 2–3 hours.

8. Remove the brisket from the grill and rest for 10 minutes.

9. Slice and serve.

Nutrition: Calories: 337 | Fat: 24.3 g. | Carbs: 0.6 g. | Protein: 26.1 g.

57.   Spiced Rump Roast

Preparation time: 10 minutes

Cooking time: 6 hours

Servings: 8

Ingredients:

• 1 tsp. smoked paprika

• 1 tsp. cayenne pepper

• 1 tsp. onion powder

• 1 tsp. garlic powder

• Salt and ground black pepper to taste

• 3 lb. beef rump roast

• ¼ cup Worcestershire sauce

Directions:

1. Set the temperature of Traeger Grill to 200°F and preheat with a closed lid for 15 minutes, using charcoal.

2. Mix all the spices in a bowl.

3. Coat the rump roast with Worcestershire sauce evenly and then rub with spice mixture generously.

4. Place the rump roast onto the grill and cook for 5–6 hours.

5. Remove the roast from the grill and rest for 10 minutes.

6. Slice and serve.

Nutrition: Calories: 252 | Fat: 9.1 g. | Carbs: 2.3 g. | Protein: 37.8 g.

58.   Prime Rib Roast

Preparation time: 10 minutes

Cooking time: 3 hours 50 minutes

Servings: 10

Ingredients:

• 1 (5 lb.) prime rib roast

• Salt, to taste

• 5 tbsp. olive oil

• 4 tsp. dried rosemary, crushed

• 2 tsp. garlic powder

• 1 tsp. onion powder

• 1 tsp. paprika

• ½ tsp. cayenne pepper

• Ground black pepper to taste

Directions:

1. Season the roast with salt.

2. Cover the roast with plastic wrap and refrigerate for 24 hours.

3. Mix the remaining ingredients in a bowl and set aside for 1 hour.

4. Rub the roast with the oil mixture.

5. Arrange the roast on a baking sheet and refrigerate for 6–12 hours.

6. Set the temperature of Traeger Grill to 225–230°F and preheat with a closed lid for 15 minutes.

7. Place the roast onto the grill and cook for 3–3 ½ hours.

8. Meanwhile, preheat the oven to 500°F.

9. Remove the roast from the grill and place it on a baking sheet.

10. Bake the roast in the oven for 15–20 minutes.

11. Remove the roast and rest for 10 minutes.

12. Slice and serve.

Nutrition: Calories: 605 | Fat: 47.6 g. | Carbs: 3.8 g. | Protein: 38 g.

59.   Real Treat Chuck Roast

Preparation time: 10 minutes

Cooking time: 4 ½ hours

Servings: 8

Ingredients:

• 2 tbsp. onion powder

• 2 tbsp. garlic powder

• 1 tbsp. red chili powder

• 1 tbsp. cayenne pepper

• Salt and ground black pepper to taste

• 1 (3 lb.) beef chuck roast

• 16 fluid oz. warm beef broth

Directions:

1. Set the temperature of Traeger Grill to 250°F and preheat with a closed lid for 15 minutes.

2. In a bowl, mix spices, salt, and black pepper.

3. Rub the chuck roast with a spice mixture.

4. Place the rump roast onto the grill and cook for 1 ½ hour per side.

5. Now, arrange the chuck roast in a steaming pan with beef broth.

6. Cover the pan with a piece of foil and cook for 2–3 hours.

7. Remove the chuck roast from the grill and rest for 20 minutes.

8. Slice and serve.

Nutrition: Calories: 645 | Fat: 48 g. | Carbs: 4.2 g. | Protein: 46.4 g.

60. Tri-Tip Roast

Preparation time: 10 minutes
Cooking time: 35 minutes
Servings: 8
Ingredients:
• 1 tbsp. onion, granulated
• 1 tbsp. garlic, granulated
• Salt and ground black pepper to taste
• 1 (3-lb.) tri-tip roast, trimmed
Directions:

1. Add all ingredients except the roast to a bowl and mix well.

2. Coat the roast with the spice mixture. Set aside until grill heats.

3. Set the temperature of Traeger Grill to 250°F and preheat with a closed lid for 15 minutes.

4. Place the roast onto the grill and cook for 25 minutes.

5. Now, set the grill to 350–400°F and preheat with a closed lid for 15 minutes. Sear roast for 3–5 minutes per side.

6. Remove the roast and rest for 20 minutes.

7. Slice and serve.

Nutrition: Calories: 313 | Fat: 14.2 g. | Carbs: 0.8 g. | Protein: 45.7 g.

61. Flank Steak

Preparation time: 15 minutes
Cooking time: 30 minutes
Servings: 6
Ingredients:
• 1 (2-lb.) beef flank steak
• 2 tbsp. olive oil
• ¼ cup BBQ rub
• 2 tbsp. butter, melted
Directions:

1. Set the temperature of Traeger Grill to 225°F and preheat with a closed lid for 15 minutes.

2. Coat the steak with oil and season with BBQ rub.

3. Place the steak onto the grill and cook for 10–15 minutes per side.

4. Remove the steak from the grill and rest for 10 minutes.

5. Slice and drizzle with melted butter. Serve.

Nutrition: Calories: 355 | Fat: 17.9 g. | Carbs: 0 g. | Protein: 45.9 g.

62. Tender Flank Steak

Preparation time: 15 minutes
Cooking time: 10 minutes
Servings: 6
Ingredients:
• ½ cup olive oil
• ⅓ cup fresh lemon juice
• ⅓ cup soy sauce
• ¼ cup brown sugar
• 2 tbsp. Worcestershire sauce
• 5 garlic cloves, minced
• 1 tsp. red chili powder
• 1 tsp. red pepper flakes, crushed
• 2 lb. flank steak
Directions:

1. Add all ingredients except steak to a resealable plastic bag and mix well.

2. Add the steak and seal the bag. Shake well to coat.

3. Refrigerate to marinate overnight.

4. Set the temperature of Traeger Grill to 450°F and preheat with a closed lid for 15 minutes.

5. Place the steak onto the grill and cook for 5 minutes per side.

6. Remove the steak from the grill and rest for 10 minutes.

7. Slice and serve.

Nutrition: Calories: 482 | Fat: 29.6 g. | Carbs: 9.5 g. | Protein: 43.3 g.

63. Restaurant-Style Rib-Eye Steak

Preparation time: 10 minutes
Cooking time: 20 minutes
Servings: 2
Ingredients:
• 2 rib-eye steaks (1 3/8-inch thick), trimmed
• 1 tbsp. olive oil
• 1 tbsp. steak seasoning
Directions:

1. Season each steak with steak seasoning and coat both sides with oil.

2. Let steaks sit at room temperature for 15 minutes.

3. Set the Traeger Grill to 325°F and warm for 15 minutes with the lid covered.

4. Grill the steaks for 15–20 minutes on each side.

5. Every 6 minutes, flip the container.

6. Serve immediately after removing from the grill.

Nutrition: Calories: 527 | Fat: 44.6 g. | Carbs: 0 g. | Protein: 30.1 g.

64. 3-Ingredient Mignon Fillet

Preparation time: 10 minutes
Cooking time: 10 minutes
Servings: 2
Ingredients:
• 2 Mignon fillets
• Salt and ground black pepper to taste
Directions:
1. Set the Traeger Grill to 450°F and preheat for 15 minutes with the lid covered.
2. Season the steaks with salt and pepper.
3. Place the filet mignons onto the grill and cook for 5 minutes per side.
4. Remove from grill and serve.
Nutrition: Calories: 254 │ Fat: 9.3 g. │ Carbs: 0 g. │ Protein: 39.8 g.

65. Fall-Of-The-Bones Short Ribs

Preparation time: 15 minutes
Cooking time: 5 ½ hours
Servings: 4
Ingredients:
• 2½ lb. beef short ribs, trimmed
• 4 tbsp. extra-virgin olive oil
• 4 tbsp. beef rub
• 1 cup apple juice
• 1 cup apple cider vinegar
• 1 cup red wine
• 1 cup beef broth
• 2 tbsp. butter
• 2 tbsp. Worcestershire sauce
• Salt and ground black pepper to taste
Directions:
1. Preheat the Traeger Grill to 225°F for 15 minutes with the lid closed.
2. Coat the ribs with olive oil and season with rub evenly.
3. Arrange the ribs on the grill and cook for 1 hour.
4. In a spray bottle, mix apple juice and vinegar.
5. After 1 hour, spray the ribs with vinegar mixture evenly.
6. Cook for 2 hours, spraying with vinegar mixture after every 15 minutes.
7. In a mixing bowl, combine the remaining ingredients.
8. Transfer the ribs to a baking dish with the wine mixture.
9. Cover the baking dish tightly with a piece of foil. Cook for 2–2 ½ hours.
10. Remove the ribs from the grill and rest for 15 minutes.
11. Slice and serve.
Nutrition: Calories: 859 │ Fat: 45.7 │ Carbs: 10.9 g. │ Protein: 83.2 g.

66. Favorite American Short Ribs

Preparation time: 15 minutes
Cooking time: 3 hours
Servings: 6
Ingredients:
For the mustard sauce:
• 1 cup prepared yellow mustard
• ¼ cup red wine vinegar
• ¼ cup dill pickle juice
• 2 tbsp. soy sauce
• 2 tbsp. Worcestershire sauce
• 1 tsp. ginger, grounded
• 1 tsp. garlic, granulated
For the spice rub:
• 2 tbsp. salt
• 2 tbsp. ground black pepper
• 1 tbsp. white cane sugar
• 1 tbsp. granulated garlic
For ribs:
• 6 (14-oz.) (4–5-inch long) beef short ribs
Directions:
1. Set the temperature of Traeger Grill to 230–250°F and preheat with a closed lid for 15 minutes.
2. For the sauce: in a bowl, add all the ingredients and whisk to mix.
3. For the rub, in a bowl, mix everything.
4. Coat the ribs with sauce and then sprinkle with spice rub evenly.
5. Place the ribs onto the grill over indirect heat, bone side down, and cook for 1–1 ½ hours.
6. Flip the side and cook for 45 minutes. Flip the side and cook for 45 minutes more.
7. Remove the ribs from the grill and rest for 10 minutes. Slice and serve.
Nutrition: Calories: 867 │ Fat: 37.5 g. │ Carbs: 7.7 g. │ Protein: 117.1 g.

67. Super-Easy Short Ribs

Preparation time: 15 minutes
Cooking time: 10 hours
Servings: 8
Ingredients:
• 2 tsp. smoked paprika
• 2 tsp. garlic powder
• Salt and ground black pepper to taste
• 1 (4-lb.) rack of beef short ribs, trimmed and silver skin removed
• 2 tbsp. olive oil
• 1 cup apple cider vinegar
Directions:
1. Set the temperature of Traeger Grill to 250°F and preheat with a closed lid for 15 minutes.
2. In a bowl, mix spices, salt, and black pepper.
3. Coat ribs with oil and then rub with spice mixture.

4. Place the ribs onto the grill (over indirect heat), bone side down, and cook for 6–10 hours.

5. Add the apple cider vinegar to a food-safe spray bottle.

6. After 5 hours, spray the ribs with vinegar.

7. Remove the ribs from the grill and rest for 10 minutes.

8. Slice and serve.

Nutrition: Calories: 461 | Fat: 17.7 g. | Carbs: 1.1 g. | Protein: 69 g.

68.   Texas-Style Beef Ribs

Preparation time: 15 minutes

Cooking time: 6 hours and 3 minutes

Servings: 4

Ingredients:
- 2 tbsp. butter
- 1 cup white vinegar
- 1 cup yellow mustard
- 2 tbsp. brown sugar
- 2 tbsp. Tabasco sauce
- 1 tsp. Worcestershire sauce
- 2 beef rib racks
- Salt and ground black pepper to taste

Directions:

9. For the BBQ sauce: melt the butter in a pan. Stir in the vinegar, mustard, brown sugar, Tabasco, and Worcestershire sauce and remove from the heat. Set aside to cool completely.

10. Set the temperature of Traeger Grill to 225°F and preheat with a closed lid for 15 minutes.

11. Season the rib racks with salt and black pepper.

12. Coat rib rack with cooled sauce.

13. Arrange the rib racks onto the grill and cook for 5–6 hours. Coating with sauce after every 2 hours.

14. Remove the rib racks from the grill and rest for 15 minutes.

15. Slice and serve.

Nutrition: Calories: 504 | Fat: 19.7 g. | Carbs: 5.7 g. | Protein: 70.7 g.

Chapter 6. Pork Recipes

69.   Bacon-Wrapped Sausages in Brown Sugar

Preparation time: 20 minutes
Cooking time: 30 minutes
Servings: 8
Ingredients:
• 1 lb. bacon strips, halved
• 14 oz. cocktail sausages
• ½ cup brown sugar
Directions:
1. Place bacon strips on a clean working space, roll them using a rolling pin, and then wrap a sausage with a bacon strip, securing with a toothpick.
2. Repeat with the remaining sausages, placing them in a single layer in the casserole dish, covering them with sugar, and refrigerating for 30 minutes.
3. When ready to cook, switch on the Traeger grill, fill the grill hopper with apple-flavored wood pellets, power the grill on by using the control panel, select 'smoke' on the temperature dial, or set the temperature to 350°F and let it preheat for a minimum of 15 minutes.
4. Meanwhile, take the casserole dish out of the fridge and put the sausage on a baking sheet coated with parchment paper.
5. After preheating the grill, open the lid, set a cookie sheet on the grill grate, close the grill, and smoke for 30 minutes.
6. When finished, move the sausages to a serving dish and serve.
Nutrition: Calories: 270 Kcal │ Fat: 27 g. │ Carbs: 18 g. │ Protein: 9 g. │ Fiber: 2 g.

70.   Sweet and Hot BBQ Ribs

Preparation time: 10 minutes
Cooking time: 5 hours and 10 minutes
Servings: 4
Ingredients:
• 2 pork rib racks, bone-in, membrane removed
• 6 oz. pork and poultry rub
• 8 oz. apple juice
• 16 oz. sweet and heat BBQ sauce
Directions:
1. Sprinkle pork and poultry rub evenly over all sides of pork ribs, rub well, and marinate for at least 30 minutes.
2. When you're ready to cook, turn on the Traeger grill, fill the grill hopper with pecan-flavored wood pellets, turn on the grill with the control panel, select 'smoke' on the temperature dial, or set the temperature to 225°F, and let it warm for at least 15 minutes.
3. When the grill is hot, open the lid, set the pork ribs bone-side down on the grill grate, close the top, and smoke for 1 hour, spraying with 10 ounces of apple juice regularly.

4. Wrap the ribs in aluminum foil, pour the remaining 6 ounces of apple juice, and securely wrapped.
5. Return the wrapped ribs to the grill grate, meat-side down, and smoke for 3–4 hours, or until the internal temperature reaches 203°F.
6. Remove the wrapped ribs from the grill, uncover them, and coat them liberally with the sauce.
7. Return the pork ribs to the grill grate and cook for 10 minutes, or until glazed.
8. Place the ribs on a cutting board for 10 minutes before slicing and serving.
Nutrition: Calories: 250.8 Kcal │ Fat: 16.3 g. │ Carbs: 6.5 g. │ Protein: 18.2 g. │ Fiber: 0.2 g.

71.   Lemon Pepper Pork Tenderloin

Preparation time: 20 minutes
Cooking time: 20 minutes
Servings: 6
Ingredients:
• 2 oz. pork tenderloin, fat trimmed
For the marinade:
• ½ tsp. garlic, minced
• 2 lemons, zested
• 1 tsp. parsley, minced
• ½ tsp. salt
• ¼ tsp. ground black pepper
• 1 tsp. lemon juice
• 2 tbsp. olive oil
Directions:
1. To make the marinade, whisk together all ingredients in a small basin.
2. Take a large plastic bag, pour marinade in it, add pork tenderloin, seal the bag, turn it upside down to coat the pork, and let it marinate for a minimum of 2 hours in the refrigerator.
3. When ready to cook, switch on the Traeger grill, fill the grill hopper with apple-flavored wood pellets, power the grill on by using the control panel, select 'smoke' on the temperature dial, or set the temperature to 375°F and let it preheat for a minimum of 15 minutes.
4. When the grill has preheated, open the lid, place pork tenderloin on the grill grate, shut the grill, and smoke for 20 minutes until the internal temperature reaches 145°F, turning the pork halfway.
5. Place the pork on a cutting board for 10 minutes to rest before slicing and serving.
Nutrition: Calories: 288.5 Kcal │ Fat: 16.6 g. │ Carbs: 6.2 g. │ Protein: 26.4 g. │ Fiber: 1.2 g

72.   Chinese BBQ Pork

Preparation time: 10 minutes
Cooking time: 2 hours
Servings: 8
Ingredients:
• 2 pork tenderloins, silver skin removed
For the marinade:
• ½ tsp. minced garlic
• 1 ½ tbsp. brown sugar
• 1 tsp. Chinese five-spice
• ¼ cup honey
• 1 tbsp. Asian sesame oil
• ¼ cup Hoisin sauce
• 2 tsp. red food coloring
• 1 tbsp. oyster sauce, optional
• 3 tbsp. soy sauce
For the Five-spice sauce:
• ¼ tsp. Chinese five-spice
• 3 tbsp. brown sugar
• 1 tsp. yellow mustard
• ¼ cup ketchup
Directions:
1. Prepare the marinade and for this, take a small bowl, place all its ingredients in it and whisk until combined.
2. Take a large plastic bag, pour marinade in it, add pork tenderloin, seal the bag, turn it upside down to coat the pork, and let it marinate for a minimum of 8 hours in the refrigerator.
3. Switch on the Traeger grill, fill the grill hopper with maple-flavored wood pellets, power the grill on by using the control panel, select 'smoke' on the temperature dial, or set the temperature to 225°F and let it preheat for a minimum of 5 minutes.
4. Meanwhile, remove pork from the marinade, transfer marinade into a small saucepan, place it over medium-high heat and cook for 3 minutes, and then set aside until cooled.
5. When the grill has preheated, open the lid, place pork on the grill grate, shut the grill, and smoke for 2 hours, basting with the marinade halfway.
6. Meanwhile, prepare the five-spice sauce and for this, take a small saucepan, place it over low heat, add all of its ingredients, stir until well combined and sugar has dissolved, and cook for 5 minutes until hot and thickened, set aside until required.
7. When done, transfer pork to a dish, let rest for 15 minutes, and meanwhile, change the smoking temperature of the grill to 450°F and let it preheat for a minimum of 10 minutes.
8. Then return pork to the grill grate and cook for 3 minutes per side until slightly charred.
9. Transfer pork to a dish, let rest for 5 minutes and then serve with prepared five-spice sauce.
Nutrition: Calories: 280 Kcal | Fat: 8 g. | Carbs: 12 g. | Protein: 40 g. | Fiber: 0 g.

73.   Smoked Sausages

Preparation time: 15 minutes
Cooking time: 3 hours
Servings: 4
Ingredients:
• 3 lb. pork, grounded
• 1 tbsp. onion powder
• 1 tbsp. garlic powder
• 1 tsp. curing salt
• 4 tsp. black pepper
• ½ tbsp. salt
• ½ tbsp. mustard, grounded
• Hog casings, soaked
• ½ cup ice water
Directions:
1. Switch on the Traeger grill, fill the grill hopper with flavored wood pellets, power the grill on by using the control panel, select 'smoke' on the temperature dial, or set the temperature to 225°F and let it preheat for a minimum of 15 minutes.
2. Meanwhile, take a medium bowl, place all the ingredients except water and hog casings, and stir until well mixed.
3. Pour in water, stir until incorporated, place the mixture in a sausage stuffer, then stuff the hog casings and tie the link to the desired length.
4. When the grill has preheated, open the lid, place the sausage links on the grill grate, shut the grill, and smoke for 2–3 hours until the internal temperature reaches 155°F.
5. When done, transfer sausages to a dish, let them rest for 5 minutes, then slice and serve.
Nutrition: Calories: 230 Kcal | Fat: 22 g. | Carbs: 2 g. | Protein: 14 g. | Fiber: 0 g.

74.   BBQ Baby Back Ribs

Preparation time: 15 minutes
Cooking time: 6 hours
Servings: 8
Ingredients:
• 2 baby back pork rib racks, membrane removed
• Pork and poultry rub as needed
• ½ cup brown sugar
• ⅓ cup honey, warmed
• ⅓ cup yellow mustard
• 1 tbsp. Worcestershire sauce
• 1 cup BBQ sauce
• ½ cup apple juice, divided
Directions:
1. Switch on the Traeger grill, fill the grill hopper with hickory-flavored wood pellets, power the grill on by using the control panel, select 'smoke' on the temperature dial, or set the temperature to 180°F and let it preheat for a minimum of 15 minutes.
2. Meanwhile, take a small bowl, place mustard and Worcestershire sauce in it, pour in ¼ cup apple juice, and whisk until combined and smooth paste comes together.

3. Brush this paste on all sides of ribs and then season with pork and poultry rub until coated.

4. When the grill has preheated, open the lid, place ribs on the grill meat-side up, shut the grill, and smoke for 3 hours.

5. After 3 hours, transfer ribs to a rimmed baking dish, let rest for 15 minutes, and meanwhile, change the smoking temperature of the grill to 225°F and let it preheat for a minimum of 10 minutes.

6. Then return the pork to the rimmed baking sheet to the grill grate and cook for 3 minutes per side until slightly charred.

7. When done, remove the baking sheet from the grill and work on one rib at a time; sprinkle half of the sugar over the rib, drizzle with half of the honey and half of the remaining apple juice, and cover with aluminum foil to seal completely.

8. Repeat with the remaining ribs, return foiled ribs to the grill grate, shut with lid, and then smoke for 2 hours.

9. After 2 hours, uncover the grill, brush them with BBQ sauce generously, arrange them on the grill grate, and grill for 1 hour until glazed.

10. When done, transfer ribs to a cutting board, let it rest for 15 minutes, slice into pieces and then serve.

Nutrition: Calories: 334 Kcal │ Fat: 22.5 g. │ Carbs: 6.5 g. │ Protein: 24 g. │ Fiber: 0.1 g.

75. Roasted Whole Ham in Apricot Sauce

Preparation time: 15 minutes
Cooking time: 2 hours
Servings: 12
Ingredients:
• 8 lb. whole ham, bone-in
• 16 oz. apricot BBQ sauce
• 2 tbsp. Dijon mustard
• ¼ cup horseradish
Directions:
1. Switch on the Traeger grill and fill the grill hopper with apple-flavored wood pellets. Then, power the grill on the control panel, select 'smoke' on the temperature dial, or set the temperature to 325°F and let it preheat for a minimum of 15 minutes.

2. In the meantime, take a large roasting pan, line it with foil, and place ham on it.

3. When the grill has preheated, open the lid, place the roasting pan containing ham on the grill grate, shut the grill, and smoke for 1 hour and 30 minutes.

4. While ham is smoking, prepare the glaze by taking a medium saucepan. Place it over medium heat, add BBQ sauce, mustard, and horseradish, stir until mixed and cook for 5 minutes. Then, set aside until required.

5. After 1 hour and 30 minutes of smoking, brush ham generously with the prepared glaze and continue smoking for 30 minutes until the internal temperature reaches 135°F.

6. When done, remove the roasting pan from the grill. Let ham rest for 20 minutes and then cut into slices.

7. Serve ham with remaining glaze.

Nutrition: Calories: 157.7 Kcal │ Fat: 5.6 g. │ Carbs: 4.1 g. │ Protein: 22.1 g. │ Fiber: 0.1 g.

76. Pork Belly

Preparation time: 10 minutes
Cooking time: 3 hours and 30 minutes
Servings: 8
Ingredients:
• 3 lb. pork belly, skin removed
• Pork and poultry rub as needed
• 4 tbsp. salt
• ½ tsp. ground black pepper
Directions:
1. Switch on the Traeger grill, fill the grill hopper with apple-flavored wood pellets, then power the grill on by using the control panel, select 'smoke' on the temperature dial, or set the temperature to 275°F. Let it preheat for a minimum of 15 minutes.

2. In the meantime, prepare the pork belly by sprinkling pork and poultry rub, salt, and black pepper on all sides of the pork belly until well coated.

3. When the grill has preheated, open the lid, and place the pork belly on the grill grate. Then, shut the grill and smoke the pork belly for 3 and 30 minutes until the internal temperature reaches 200°F.

4. When done, put the pork belly on a cutting board and let it rest for 15 minutes. Then cut it into slices and serve.

Nutrition: Calories: 430 Kcal │ Fat: 44 g. │ Carbs: 1 g. │ Protein: 8 g. │ Fiber: 0 g.

77. Pulled Pork

Preparation time: 10 minutes
Cooking time: 9 hours
Servings: 12
Ingredients:
• 9 lb. pork shoulder, bone-in, fat trimmed
• Game rub as needed and more as required
• 2 cups apple cider
Directions:
1. Switch on the Traeger grill, fill the grill hopper with apple-flavored wood pellets, power the grill on by using the control panel, select 'smoke' on the temperature dial, or set the temperature to 250°F and let it preheat for a minimum of 15 minutes.

2. Meanwhile, prepare the pork shoulder, and season it generously with game rub until well coated.

3. When the grill has preheated, open the lid, place pork on the grill grate fat-side up, shut the grill and smoke for 5 hours, and then remove pork from the grill.

4. Take a large baking sheet, line it with 4 large aluminum foil pieces to wrap pork, place pork in the center, bring up the sides of the foil, pour in apple cider, and then wrap tightly.

5. Transfer the baking sheet containing wrapped pork to the grill grate and cook for 4 hours until the internal temperature reaches 204°F.

6. When done, remove the baking sheet from the grill, let it rest for 45 minutes, then uncover it, place the pork into a large dish and drain excess liquid into a bowl.

7. Shred pork using 2 forks, remove and discard excess fat and bone, drizzle with reserved liquid, and season with some game rub.

8. Serve straight away.

Nutrition: Calories: 220.1 Kcal | Fat: 15 g. | Carbs: 1 g. | Protein: 20 g. | Fiber: 0 g.

78.   Pork Steak

Preparation time: 10 minutes
Cooking time: 20 minutes
Servings: 4
Ingredients:
For the brine:
• 2-inch piece of orange peel
• 2 sprigs of thyme
• 4 tbsp. salt
• 4 black peppercorns
• 1 sprig of rosemary
• 2 tbsp. brown sugar
• 2 bay leaves
• 10 cups water
For pork steaks:
• 4 pork steaks, fat trimmed
• Game rub as needed
Directions:
1. Prepare the brine by placing all ingredients in a large container and stirring until the sugar has dissolved.

2. Place the steaks in it, add some weights to submerge them in the brine, and refrigerate for 24 hours.

3. When you're ready to cook, turn on the Traeger grill, load the grill hopper with hickory-flavored wood pellets, turn on the grill using the control panel, select 'smoke' on the temperature dial, or set the temperature to 225°F, and let it preheat for at least 15 minutes.

4. Meanwhile, remove steaks from the brine, rinse well, pat dry with paper towels and then season well with game rub until coated.

5. When the grill has preheated, open the lid, place steaks on the grill grate, shut the grill, and smoke for 10 minutes per side until the internal temperature reaches 140°F.

6. When done, transfer steaks to a cutting board

7. Let them rest for 10 minutes

8. Cut into slices

9. Serve.

Nutrition: Calories: 260 Kcal | Fat: 21 g. | Carbs: 1 g. | Protein: 17 g. | Fiber: 0 g.

79.   Smoked Baby Back Ribs

Preparation time: 10 minutes
Cooking time: 2 hours
Servings: 6
Ingredients:
10. 3 baby back rib racks
11. Salt and pepper to taste
Directions:
1. Clean the ribs by removing the extra membrane that covers them. Pat dries the ribs with a clean paper towel. Season the baby rack ribs with salt and pepper to taste. Allow resting in the fridge for at least 4 hours before cooking.

2. Once ready to cook, fire the Traeger Grill to 2250°F. Use hickory wood pellets when cooking the ribs. Close the lid and preheat for 15 minutes.

3. Place the ribs on the grill grate and cook for 2 hours. Carefully flip the ribs halfway through the cooking time for even cooking.

Nutrition: Calories per servings: 1037 | Protein: 92.5 g. | Carbs: 1.4 g. | Fat: 73.7 g. | Sugar: 0.2 g.

80.   Smoked Apple Pork Tenderloin

Preparation time: 10 minutes
Cooking time: 3 hours
Servings: 6
Ingredients:
• ½ cup apple juice
• 3 tbsp. honey
• 3 tbsp. Traeger pork and poultry rub
• ¼ cup brown sugar
• 2 tbsp. thyme leaves
• ½ tbsp. black pepper
• 2 pork tenderloin roasts, skin removed
Directions:
1. Mix the apple juice, honey, pork and poultry rub, brown sugar, thyme, and black pepper in a bowl. Whisk to mix everything.

2. Add the pork loins into the marinade and allow them to soak for 3 hours in the fridge.

3. Once ready to cook, fire the Traeger Grill to 2250°F. Use hickory wood pellets when cooking the ribs. Close the lid and preheat for 15 minutes.

4. Place the marinated pork loin on the grill grate and cook until the temperature registers to 145°F. Cook for 2–3 hours on low heat.

5. Meanwhile, place the marinade in a saucepan. Place the saucepan on the grill and allow it to simmer until the sauce has reduced.

6. Before taking the meat out, baste the pork with the reduced marinade.

7. Allow resting for 10 minutes before slicing.

Nutrition: Calories per serving: 203 | Protein: 26.4 g. | Carbs: 15.4 g. | Fat: 3.6 g. | Sugar: 14.6 g.

81.   Competition Style BBQ Pork Ribs

Preparation time: 10 minutes
Cooking time: 2 hours
Servings: 6
Ingredients:
• 2 St. Louis-style rib racks
• 1 cup Traeger pork and poultry rub
• ⅛ cup brown sugar
• 4 tbsp. butter
• 4 tbsp. agave
• 1 bottle Traeger Sweet and Heat BBQ sauce
Directions:
1. Place the ribs on the working surface and remove the thin film of connective tissues covering it. In a smaller bowl, combine the Traeger pork and Poultry rub, brown sugar, butter, and agave. Mix until well combined.
2. Massage the rub onto the ribs and allow them to rest in the fridge for at least 2 hours.
3. When ready to cook, fire the Traeger Grill to 2250°F. Use desired wood pellets when cooking the ribs. Close the lid and preheat for 15 minutes.
4. Place the ribs on the grill grate and close the lid. Smoke for 1 hour and 30 minutes. Make sure to flip the ribs halfway through the cooking time.
5. 10 minutes before the cooking time ends, brush the ribs with BBQ sauce.
6. Remove from the grill and allow to rest before slicing.
Nutrition: Calories per serving: 399 | Protein: 47.2 g. | Carbs: 3.5 g. | Fat: 20.5 g. | Sugar: 2.3 g. Smoked

82.   Apple BBQ Ribs

Preparation time: 10 minutes
Cooking time: 2 hours
Servings: 6
Ingredients:
• 2 St. Louis-style rib racks
• ¼ cup Traeger Big Game rub
• 1 cup apple juice
• A bottle of Traeger BBQ sauce
Directions:
1. Place the ribs on a working surface and remove the film of connective tissues covering it.
2. Mix the Game rub and apple juice in another bowl until well combined.
3. Massage the rub onto the ribs and allow them to rest in the fridge for at least 2 hours.
4. When ready to cook, fire the Traeger Grill to 2250°F. Use apple wood pellets when cooking the ribs. Close the lid and preheat for 15 minutes.
5. Place the ribs on the grill grate and close the lid. Smoke for 1 hour and 30 minutes. Make sure to flip the ribs halfway through the cooking time.
6. 10 minutes before the cooking time ends, brush the ribs with BBQ sauce.
7. Remove from the grill and allow to rest before slicing.

Nutrition: Calories per serving: 337 | Protein: 47.1 g. | Carbs: 4.7 g. | Fat: 12.9 g. | Sugar: 4 g.

83.   Citrus-Brined Pork Roast

Preparation time: 10 minutes
Cooking time: 45 minutes
Servings: 6
Ingredients:
• ½ cup salt
• ¼ cup brown sugar
• 3 garlic cloves, minced
• 2 dried bay leaves
• 6 peppercorns
• 1 lemon, juiced
• ½ tsp. dried fennel seeds
• ½ tsp. red pepper flakes
• ½ cup apple juice
• ½ cup orange juice
• 5 lb. pork loin
• 2 tbsp. extra-virgin olive oil
Directions:
1. In a bowl, combine the salt, brown sugar, garlic, bay leaves, peppercorns, lemon juice, fennel seeds, pepper flakes, apple juice, and orange juice. Mix to form a paste rub.
2. Rub the mixture onto the pork loin and marinate in the fridge for at least 2 hours.
3. Add in the oil.
4. When ready to cook, fire the Traeger Grill to 300°F.
5. Use apple wood pellets when cooking.
6. Close the lid and preheat for 15 minutes.
7. Place the seasoned pork loin on the grill grate and close the lid. Cook for 45 minutes.
8. Make sure to flip the pork halfway through the cooking time.
Nutrition: Calories per serving: 869 | Protein: 97.2 g. | Carbs: 15.2 g. | Fat: 43.9 g. | Sugar: 13 g.

84.   Pork Collar and Rosemary Marinade

Preparation time: 15 minutes
Cooking time: 30 minutes
Servings: 6
Ingredients:
• 1 pork collar, 3–4 lb.
• 3 tbsp. rosemary, fresh
• 3 shallots, minced
• 2 tbsp. garlic, chopped
• ½ cup bourbon
• 2 tsp. coriander, ground
• 1 apple ale bottle
• 1 tsp. ground black pepper
• 2 tsp. salt
• 3 tbsp. oil
Directions:
1. Take a zip bag and add pepper, salt, canola oil, apple ale, bourbon, coriander, garlic, shallots, and rosemary, and mix well.

2. Cut meat into slabs, add them to the marinade and let it refrigerate overnight.

3. Preheat your smoker to 450°F.

4. Transfer meat to smoker and smoke for 5 minutes, lower temperature to 325°F.

5. Pour marinade and cook for 25 minutes until the internal temperature reaches 160°F.

6. Serve and enjoy!

Nutrition: Calories: 420 | Fat: 26 g. | Carbs: 4 g. | Fiber: 2 g.

85.   Roasted Ham

Preparation time: 15 minutes
Cooking time: 2 hours 15 minutes
Servings: 6
Ingredients:
• 8–10 lb. ham, bone-in
• 2 tbsp. Dijon mustard
• ¼ cup horseradish
• 1 bottle BBQ Apricot sauce

Directions:
1. Preheat your smoker to 325°F.

2. Cover a roasting pan with foil, place the ham, transfer to the smoker, and smoke for 1 hour and 30 minutes.

3. Take a small pan and add sauce, mustard and horseradish, place it over medium heat and cook for a few minutes.

4. Keep it on the side.

5. After 1 hour and 30 minutes of smoking, glaze ham and smoke for 30 minutes more until the internal temperature reaches 135°F.

6. Let it rest for 20 minutes, slice, and enjoy!

Nutrition: Calories: 460 | Fat: 43 g. | Carbs: 10 g. | Fiber: 1 g.

86.   Smoked Pork Loin

Preparation time: 15 minutes
Cooking time: 3 hours
Servings: 6
Ingredients:
• ½ quart apple juice
• ½ quart apple cider vinegar
• ½ cup sugar
• ¼ cup salt
• 2 tbsp. fresh ground pepper
• 1 pork loin roast
• ½ cup Greek seasoning

Directions:
1. Take a large container and mix the brine by adding apple juice, vinegar, salt, pepper, sugar, and liquid smoke, and stir.

2. Keep stirring until the sugar and salt dissolve, and add the loin.

3. Add more water if needed to submerge the meat.

4. Cover and chill overnight.

5. Preheat your smoker to 250°F with hickory wood.

6. Coat the meat with Greek seasoning and transfer to your smoker.

7. Smoker for 3 hours until the internal temperature of the thickest part registers 160°F.

8. Serve and enjoy!

Nutrition: Calories: 169 | Fat: 5 g. | Carbs: 3 g. | Fiber: 3 g.

87.   Smoke Pulled Pork

Preparation time: 15 minutes
Cooking time: 3 hours
Servings: 4
Ingredients:
• 6–9 lb. whole pork shoulder
• 2 cups apple cider
• Big game rub

Directions:
1. Set the temperature to 250°F and put it on preheat by keeping the lid closed for 15 minutes.

2. Now take off the excess fat from the butt of the pork and season it with a big game rub on all sides.

3. Put the pork butt on the grill grate, keeping the fat side up.

4. Smoke it until the internal temperature reaches 160°F. It should take approx. 3–5 hours.

5. Remove it from the grill and keep it aside.

6. Now take a large baking sheet and keep 4 large pieces of aluminum foil, one on top of the other. It should be wide enough to wrap the pork butt entirely.

7. Keep the pork butt in the very center of the foil and bring up the sides a little.

8. Pour apple cider on the pork and wrap the foil tightly around it.

9. Keep it back on the grill with the fat side up and cook till the internal temperature reaches 200°F. It should take 3–4 hours approx.

10. Remove it from the grill and let it rest for 45 minutes inside the foil packet.

11. Take off the foil and pour off the extra liquid.

12. Keep the pork in a dish and remove the bones and excess fat.

13. Add the separated liquid to the pork and season it with a big game rub.

14. Serve and enjoy!

Nutrition: Calories: 169 | Fat: 5 g. | Carbs: 3 g. | Fiber: 3 g.

88. Easy Pork Chuck Roast

Preparation time: 15 minutes
Cooking time: 4 hours
Servings: 6
Ingredients:
- 1 whole (4–5 lb.) chuck roast
- ¼ cup olive oil
- ¼ cup firm packed brown sugar
- 2 tbsp. Cajun seasoning
- 2 tbsp. paprika
- 2 tbsp. cayenne pepper

Directions:
1. Preheat your smoker to 225°F using oak wood
2. Rub chuck roast all over with olive oil
3. Take a small bowl and add brown sugar, paprika, Cajun seasoning, cayenne
4. Coat the roast well with the spice mix
5. Transfer the chuck roast to the smoker rack and smoke for 4–5 hours
6. Once the internal temperature reaches 165°Fahrenheit, take the meat out and slice
7. Enjoy!

Nutrition: Calories: 219 | Fat: 16 g. | Carbs: 0 g. | Fiber: 3 g.

89. Pineapple Pork BBQ

Preparation time: 10 minutes
Cooking time: 60 minutes
Servings: 4
Ingredients:
- 1 lb. pork sirloin
- 4 cups pineapple juice
- 3 garlic cloves, minced
- 1 cup Carne Asada marinade
- 2 tbsp. salt
- 1 tsp. ground black pepper

Directions:
1. Place all ingredients in a bowl. Massage the pork sirloin to coat with all ingredients. Place inside the fridge to marinate for at least 2 hours.
2. When ready to cook, fire the Traeger Grill to 300°F. Use desired wood pellets when cooking the ribs. Close the lid and preheat for 15 minutes.
3. Place the pork sirloin on the grill grate and cook for 45–60 minutes. Make sure to flip the pork halfway through the cooking time.
4. At the same time, when you put the pork on the grill grate, place the marinade in a pan and place it inside the smoker. Allow the marinade to cook and reduce.
5. Baste the pork sirloin with the reduced marinade before the cooking time ends.
6. Allow resting before slicing.

Nutrition: Calories per serving: 347 | Protein: 33.4 g. | Carbs: 45.8 g. | Fat: 4.2 g. | Sugar: 36 g.

90. BBQ Spareribs With Mandarin Glaze

Preparation time: 10 minutes
Cooking time: 60 minutes
Servings: 6
Ingredients:
- 3 large spareribs, membrane removed
- 3 tbsp. yellow mustard
- 1 tbsp. Worcestershire sauce
- 1 cup honey
- 1 ½ cup brown sugar
- 13 oz. Traeger Mandarin Glaze
- 1 tsp. sesame oil
- 1 tsp. soy sauce
- 1 tsp. garlic powder

Directions:
1. Place the spare ribs on a working surface and carefully remove the connective tissue membrane that covers the ribs.
2. In another bowl, mix the rest of the ingredients until well combined.
3. Massage the spice mixture onto the spareribs. Allow resting in the fridge for at least 3 hours.
4. When ready to cook, fire the Traeger Grill to 300°F.
5. Use hickory wood pellets when cooking the ribs.
6. Close the lid and preheat for 15 minutes.
7. Place the seasoned ribs on the grill grate and cover the lid.
8. Cook for 60 minutes.
9. Once cooked, allow resting before slicing.

Nutrition: Calories per serving: 1263 | Protein: 36.9 g. | Carbs: 110.3 g. | Fat: 76.8 g. | Sugar: 107 g.

91. Braised Pork Chile Verde

Preparation time: 10 minutes
Cooking time: 40 minutes
Servings: 6
Ingredients:
- 3 lb. pork shoulder, bone removed and cut into ½-inch cubes
- 1 tbsp. all-purpose flour
- Salt and pepper to taste
- 1 lb. tomatillos, husked and washed
- 2 Jalapeños, chopped
- 1 medium yellow onion, peeled and sliced
- 4 garlic cloves
- 4 tbsp. extra-virgin olive oil
- 2 cup chicken stock
- 2 cans green chilies
- 1 tbsp. cumin
- 1 tbsp. oregano
- ½ lime, juiced
- ¼ cup cilantro

Directions:
1. Put the pork shoulder chunks in a bowl and toss using flour. Season with salt and pepper to taste.

2. Use desired wood pellets when cooking. Place a large cast-iron pan on the lower rack of the grill. Hen, close the cover and preheat for 15 minutes.

3. Put the tomatillos, Jalapeño, onion, and garlic on a sheet tray lined with foil and drizzle with 2 tbsp. olive oil. Season using salt and pepper to taste.

4. Place the remaining olive oil in the heated cast iron skillet and cook the pork shoulder. Spread the meat evenly, then close.

5. Before closing the grill's lid, put the vegetables on the rack tray. Now, you can close the lid.

6. Cook for 20 minutes without opening the lid or stirring the pork. Remove the vegetables from the grill after 20 minutes and place them in a blender. Pulse until smooth and put it into the pan with the pork. Stir in the chicken stock, green chilies, cumin, oregano, and lime juice. Season using salt and pepper to taste. Close the grill lid and cook for another 20 minutes. Once cooked, stir in the cilantro.

Nutrition: Calories per serving: 389 | Protein: 28.5 g. | Carbs: 4.5 g. | Fat: 24.3 g. | Sugar: 2.1 g.

92.   BBQ Pulled Pork Sandwiches

Preparation time: 10 minutes
Cooking time: 1 hour 30 minutes
Servings: 6
Ingredients:
• 8–10 lb. bone-in pork butt roast
• 12 Kaiser rolls
• 1 cup yellow mustard
• Coleslaw
• 1 bottle BBQ sauce
• 5 oz. sugar
Directions:
7. Push the temperature to 225°F and set your smoker to preheat.

8. Take the pork roast from the packaging and keep it on a cookie sheet.

9. Rub it thoroughly with yellow mustard.

10. Now take a bowl and mix the BBQ sauce and sugar.

11. Use this mix to rub the roast thoroughly and give time for the rub to seep inside and melt in the meat.

12. Now place this roast in the smoker and allow it to cook for 6 hours.

13. When done, remove it from the smoker and then wrap it in tin foil.

14. Push the temperature to 250°F and cook it for a couple of hours. The internal temperature should reach 200°F.

15. Let the pork butt rest in the foil for an hour before pulling it out.

16. Now take the Kaiser roll and cut it in half.

17. Mix the pulled pork with BBQ sauce and pile it on the top of each halved roll.

18. Top it with coleslaw and serve.

Nutrition: Calories per serving: 426 | Protein: 65.3 g. | Carbs: 20.4 g. | Fat: 8.4 g. | Sugar: 17.8 g.

93.   Roasted   Pork   With   Balsamic Strawberry Sauce

Preparation time: 15 minutes
Cooking time: 35 minutes
Servings: 3
Ingredients:
• 2 lb. pork tenderloin
• Salt and pepper to taste
• 2 tbsp. rosemary, dried
• 2 tbsp. olive oil
• 12 strawberries, fresh
• 1 cup balsamic vinegar
• 4 tbsp. sugar
Directions:
1. Set the wood pellet grill to 350°F and preheat for 15 minutes with a closed lid.

2. Meanwhile, rinse the pork and pat it dry—season with salt, pepper, and rosemary.

3. In an oven skillet, heat oil until smoking. Add the pork and sear on all sides until golden brown.

4. Set the skillet on the grill and cook for 20 minutes or until the meat is no longer pink and the internal temperature is 150°F.

5. Remove the pork from the grill and let rest for 10 minutes.

6. Add berries to the skillet and sear over the stovetop for a minute. Remove the strawberries from the skillet.

7. Add vinegar to the same skillet and scrape any browned bits from the skillet bottom. Bring it to a boil, then reduce heat to low. Stir in sugar and cook until it has been reduced by half.

8. Slice the meat, place the strawberries on top, and drizzle vinegar sauce. Enjoy.

Nutrition: Calories 244 | Total Fat: 9 g. | Saturated Fat: 3 g. | Total Carbs: 15 g. | Net Carbs: 13 g. | Protein: 25 g. | Sugar: 12 g. | Fiber: 2 g. | Sodium: 159 mg.

94.   Wet-Rubbed St. Louis Ribs

Preparation time: 15 minutes
Cooking time: 4 hours
Servings: 3
Ingredients:
• ½ cup brown sugar
• 1 tbsp. cumin, ground
• 1 tbsp. Ancho chili powder
• 1 tbsp. smoked paprika
• 1 tbsp. garlic salt
• 3 tbsp. balsamic vinegar
• 1 St. Louis style rib rack
• 2 cups apple juice
Directions:
1. Add all the ingredients except ribs to a mixing bowl and mix until well mixed. Place the rub on both ribs and sit for 10 minutes.

2. Set the wood pellet temperature to 180°F and preheat for 15 minutes. Smoke the ribs for 2 hours.

3. Increase the temperature to 250°F and wrap the ribs and apple juice with foil or tinfoil.

4. Place back the pork and cook for an additional 2 hours.

5. Remove from the grill and let rest for 5 minutes before serving. Enjoy.

Nutrition: Calories: 210 | Total Fat: 13 g. | Saturated Fat: 4 g. | Total Carbs: 0 g. | Net Carbs: 0 g. | Protein: 24 g. | Sodium: 85 mg.

95.   Cocoa Crusted Pork Tenderloin

Preparation time: 30 minutes

Cooking time: 25 minutes

Servings: 5

Ingredients:

• 1 pork tenderloin

• ½ tbsp. fennel, ground

• 2 tbsp. cocoa powder, unsweetened

• 1 tbsp. smoked paprika

• ½ tbsp. Kosher salt

• ½ tbsp. black pepper

• 1 tbsp. extra-virgin olive oil

• 3 green onions

Directions:

1. Remove the silver skin and the connective tissues from the pork loin.

2. Combine the rest of the ingredients in a mixing bowl, then rub the mixture on the pork. Refrigerate for 30 minutes.

3. Preheat the wood pellet grill for 15 minutes with the lid closed.

4. Sear all sides of the loin at the front of the grill, then reduce the temperature to 350°F and move the pork to the center grill.

5. Cook for 15 more minutes or until the internal temperature is 145°F.

6. Remove from grill and let rest for 10 minutes before slicing. Enjoy.

Nutrition: Calories: 264 | Total Fat: 13.1 g. | Saturated Fat: 6 g. | Total Carbs: 4.6 g. | Net Carbs: 1.2 g. Protein: 33 g. | Sugar: 0 g. | Fiber: 3.4 g. | Sodium: 66 mg.

96.   Wood Pellet Grilled Bacon

Preparation time: 30 Minutes

Cooking time: 25 Minutes

Servings: 6

Ingredients:

• 1 lb. bacon, thickly cut

Directions:

1. Preheat your wood pellet grill to 375 degrees Fahrenheit.

2. Line a baking sheet with parchment paper and arrange the bacon in a single layer.

3. Bake for 20 minutes with the cover closed. Close the lid and bake for a further 5 minutes.

4. Enjoy with your favorite side dish.

Nutrition: Calories: 315 | Total Fat: 14 g. | Saturated Fat: 10 g. | Protein: 9 g. | Sodium: 500 mg.

97.   Wood Pellet Blackened Pork Chops

Preparation time: 5 minutes

Cooking time: 20 minutes

Servings: 6

Ingredients:

• 6 pork chops

• ¼ cup blackening seasoning

• Salt and pepper to taste

Directions:

1. Preheat your grill to 375 degrees Fahrenheit.

2. Meanwhile, season the pork chops well with the blackening seasoning, salt, and pepper.

3. Close the lid of the grill and place the pork chops on it.

4. Allow the chops to cook for 8 minutes before flipping. Cook until the internal temperature of the chicken reaches 142°F.

5. Remove the chops from the grill and set aside for 10 minutes to rest before slicing.

6. Serve immediately and enjoy.

Nutrition: Calories 333 | Total Fat: 18 g. | Saturated Fat: 6 g. | Total Carbs: 1 g. | Protein: 40 g. | Fiber: 1 g. | Sodium: 3175 mg.

98.   Teriyaki Pineapple Pork Tenderloin Sliders

Preparation time: 20 minutes

Cooking time: 20 minutes

Servings: 6

Ingredients:

• 1-½ lb. pork tenderloin

• 1 can pineapple rings

• 1 package king's Hawaiian rolls

• 8 oz. teriyaki sauce

• 1-½ tbsp. salt

• 1 tbsp. onion powder

• 1 tbsp. paprika

• ½ tbsp. garlic powder

• ½ tbsp. cayenne pepper

Directions:

1. Add all the ingredients for the rub to a mixing bowl and mix until well mixed. Generously rub the pork loin with the mixture.

2. Heat the pellet to 325°F. Place the meat on a grill and cook while you turn it every 4 minutes.

3. Cook until the internal temperature reaches 145°F.remove from the grill and let it rest for 5 minutes.

4. Meanwhile, open the pineapple can and place the pineapple rings on the grill. Flip the crews when they have a dark brown color.

5. At the same time, half the rolls and place them on the grill and grill them until toasty browned.

6. Assemble the slider by putting the bottom roll first, followed by the pork tenderloin, pineapple ring, a drizzle of sauce, and top with the other roll half. Serve and enjoy.

Nutrition: Calories 243 | Total Fat: 5 g. | Saturated Fat: 2 g. | Total Carbs: 4 g. | Net Carbs: 15 g. | Protein: 33 g. | Sugar: 10 g. | Fiber: 1 g. | Sodium: 2447 mg.

99. Lovable Pork Belly

Preparation time: 15 minutes
Cooking time: 4 hours and 30 minutes
Servings: 4
Ingredients:
• 5 lb. pork belly
• 1 cup dry rub
• 3 tbsp. olive oil
For sauce:
• 2 tbsp. honey
• 3 tbsp. butter
• 1 cup BBQ sauce
Directions:
1. Take your drip pan and add water. Cover with aluminum foil.
2. Pre-heat your smoker to 250°F
3. Add pork cubes, dry rub, and olive oil into a bowl and mix well
4. Use water to fill the water pan halfway through and place it over the drip pan.
5. Add wood chips to the side tray
6. Transfer pork cubes to your smoker and smoke for 3 hours (covered)
7. Remove pork cubes from the smoker and transfer to foil pan; add honey, butter, BBQ sauce, and stir
8. Cover the pan with foil and move back to a smoker, smoke for 90 minutes more
9. Remove foil and smoke for 15 minutes more until the sauce thickens
10. Serve and enjoy!
Nutrition: Calories: 1164 | Fat: 68 g. | Carbohydrates: 12 g. | Protein: 104 g.

100. County Ribs

Preparation time: 15 minutes
Cooking time: 3 hours
Servings: 4
Ingredients:
• 4 lb. country-style ribs
• Pork rub to taste
• 2 cups apple juice
• ½ stick butter, melted
• 18 oz. BBQ sauce
Directions:
1. Take your drip pan and add water. Cover with aluminum foil.
2. Pre-heat your smoker to 275°F.
3. Season country-style ribs from all sides

4. Use water to fill the water pan halfway through and place it over the drip pan.
5. Add wood chips to the side tray.
6. Transfer the ribs to your smoker and smoke for 1 hour and 15 minutes until the internal temperature reaches 160°F.
7. Take a foil pan and mix melted butter, apple juice, and 15 ounces BBQ sauce, and put ribs back in the pan; cover with foil.
8. Transfer back to the smoker and smoke for 1 hour 15 minutes more until the internal temperature reaches 195°F.
9. Take ribs out from the liquid, place them on racks, glaze with more BBQ sauce, and smoke for 10 minutes more.
10. Take them out and let them rest for 10 minutes, serve and enjoy!
Nutrition: Calories: 251 | Fat: 25 g. | Carbohydrates: 35 g. | Protein: 76 g.

101. Wow-Pork Tenderloin

Preparation time: 15 minutes
Cooking time: 3 hours
Servings: 4
Ingredients:
• 1 pork tenderloin
• ¼ cup BBQ sauce
• 3 tbsp. dry rub
Directions:
1. Take your drip pan and add water. Cover with aluminum foil.
2. Pre-heat your smoker to 225°F
3. Rub the spice mix all over the pork tenderloin
4. Use water to fill the water pan halfway through and place it over the drip pan.
5. Add wood chips to the side tray
6. Transfer pork meat to your smoker and smoke for 3 hours until the internal temperature reaches 145°F
7. Brush the BBQ sauce over the pork and let it rest
8. Serve and enjoy!
Nutrition: Calories: 405 | Fat: 9 g. | Carbohydrates: 15 g. | Protein: 59 g.

102. Awesome Pork Shoulder

Preparation time: 15 minutes + 24 hours
Cooking time: 12 hours
Servings: 4
Ingredients:
• 8 lb. pork shoulder
For rub:
• 1 tsp. dry mustard
• 1 tsp. black pepper
• 1 tsp. cumin
• 1 tsp. oregano
• 1 tsp. cayenne pepper
• ⅓ cup salt
• ¼ cup garlic powder
• ½ cup paprika
• ⅓ cup brown sugar
• ⅔ cup sugar
Directions:
1. Bring your pork under salted water for 18 hours.
2. Pull the pork out from the brine and let it sit for 1 hour
3. Rub mustard all over the pork.
4. Take a bowl and mix all the rub ingredients. Rub mixture all over the meat
5. Wrap meat and leave it overnight.
6. Take your drip pan and add water. Cover with aluminum foil. Pre-heat your smoker to 250°F.
7. Use water to fill the water pan halfway through and place it over the drip pan. Add wood chips to the side tray.
8. Transfer meat to smoker and smoke for 6 hours
9. Take the pork out, wrap it in foil, and smoke for 6 hours more at 195°F.
10. Shred and serve.
Nutrition: Calories: 965 │ Fat: 65 g. │ Carbohydrates: 19 g. │ Protein: 71 g.

103. Herbed Prime Rib

Preparation time: 15 minutes
Cooking time: 4 hours
Servings: 4
Ingredients:
• 5 lb. prime rib
• 2 tbsp. black pepper
• ¼ cup olive oil
• 2 tbsp. salt
Herb paste:
• ¼ cup olive oil
• 1 tbsp. fresh sage
• 1 tbsp. fresh thyme
• 1 tbsp. fresh rosemary
• 3 garlic cloves
Directions:
1. Take a blender and add herbs; blend until thoroughly combined.
2. Take your drip pan and add water. Cover with aluminum foil.

3. Pre-heat your smoker to 225°F.
4. Use water to fill the water pan halfway through and place it over the drip pan.
5. Add wood chips to the side tray.
6. Coat rib with olive oil and season it well with salt and pepper.
7. Transfer seasoned rib to your smoker and smoke for 4 hours.
8. Remove rib from the smoker and keep it on the side. Let it cool for 30 minutes
9. Cut into slices and serve.
10. Enjoy!
Nutrition: Calories: 936 │ Fat: 81 g. │ Carbohydrates: 2 g. │ Protein: 46 g.

104. Carolina Smoked Ribs

Preparation time: 30 minutes
Cooking time: 4 hours and 30 minutes
Servings: 10
Ingredients:
• ½ a cup brown sugar
• ⅓ cup fresh lemon juice
• ¼ cup white vinegar
• ¼ cup apple cider vinegar
• 1 tbsp. Worcestershire sauce
• ¼ cup molasses
• 2 cups prepared mustard
• 2 tsp. garlic, minced
• 2 tsp. salt
• 1 tsp. ground black pepper
• 1 tsp. crushed red pepper flakes
• ½ a tsp. white pepper
• ¼ tsp. cayenne pepper
• 2 racks pork spare ribs
• ½ cup barbeque seasoning
Directions:
1. Take a medium-sized bowl and whisk in brown sugar, white vinegar, lemon juice, mustard, Worcestershire sauce, mustard, and molasses
2. Mix well and season the mixture with granulated garlic, pepper, salt, red pepper flakes, white pepper flakes, and cayenne pepper
3. Take your drip pan and add water; cover with aluminum foil.
4. Pre-heat your smoker to 225°F
5. Use water to fill the water pan halfway through and place it over the drip pan.
6. Add wood chips to the side tray
7. Rub the ribs with your prepared seasoning and transfer to your smoker
8. Cover the meat with aluminum foil and smoke for 4 hours, making sure to add chips after every 60 minutes
9. After the first 3 and a ½ hours, make sure to uncover the meat and baste it generously with the prepared mustard sauce

10. Take the heart out and serve with the remaining sauce

11. Enjoy!

Nutrition: Calories: 750 | Fat: 50 g. | Carbohydrates: 24 g. | Fiber: 2.2 g.

105. Explosive Smoky Bacon

Preparation time: 20 minutes
Cooking time: 2 hours and 10 minutes
Servings: 10
Ingredients:
- 1 lb. thick-cut bacon
- 1 tbsp. BBQ spice rub
- 2 lb. bulk pork sausage
- 1 cup Cheddar cheese, shredded
- 4 garlic cloves, minced
- 18 oz. BBQ sauce

Directions:
1. Take your drip pan and add water; cover with aluminum foil.
2. Pre-heat your smoker to 225°F
3. Use water to fill the water pan halfway through and place it over the drip pan.
4. Add wood chips to the side tray.
5. Reserve about ½ a pound of your bacon for cooking later on.
6. Lay 2 strips of your remaining bacon on a clean surface in an X formation.
7. Alternate the horizontal and vertical bacon strips by waving them tightly in an over and under to create a lattice-like pattern.
8. Sprinkle 1 tsp. BBQ rub over the woven bacon.
9. Arrange ½ a pound of bacon in a large-sized skillet and cook them for 10 minutes over medium-high heat.
10. Drain the cooked slices on a kitchen towel and crumble them.
11. Place your sausages in a large-sized re-sealable bag.
12. While the links are still in the bag, roll them out to a square that has the same size as the woven bacon.
13. Cut off the load from the sausage and arrange the sausage over the woven bacon.
14. Toss away the bag.
15. Sprinkle some crumbled bacon, cheddar cheese, and garlic over the rolled sausages.
16. Pour about ¾ bottle of BBQ sauce over the sausage and season with more BBQ rub.
17. Roll up the woven bacon tightly around the link, forming a loaf.
18. Cook the bacon-sausage loaf in your smoker for about 1.5 hours.
19. Brush up the woven bacon with the remaining BBQ sauce and keep smoking for about 30 minutes until the center of the loaf is no longer pink.
20. Use an instant thermometer to check if the internal temperature is at least 165°F.
21. If yes, take it out and let it rest for 30 minutes.

22. Slice and serve!

Nutrition: Calories: 507 | Fat: 36 g. | Carbs: 20 g. | Fiber: 2 g.

106. Alabama Pulled Pig Pork

Preparation time: 1 hour
Cooking time: 12 hours
Servings: 8
Ingredients:
- 2 cups soy sauce
- 1 cup Worcestershire sauce
- 1 cup cranberry grape juice
- 1 cup Teriyaki sauce
- 1 tbsp. hot pepper sauce
- 2 tbsp. steak sauce
- 1 cup of light brown sugar
- ½ a tsp. ground black pepper
- 2 lb. flank steak cut up into ¼-inch slices
- 1/4 cup salt
- 3 cups apple cider vinegar

Directions:
1. Take a non-reactive saucepan and add apple cider vinegar, salt, brown sugar, cayenne pepper, black pepper, cranberry grape juice, and butter.
2. Bring the mix to a boil over medium-high heat.
3. Add in water and return the mixture to a boil.
4. Carefully rub the pork with the sauce.
5. Take your drip pan and add water. Cover with aluminum foil.
6. Pre-heat your smoker to 225°F.
7. Use water to fill the water pan halfway through and place it over the drip pan.
8. Add wood chips to the side tray.
9. Smoke meat for about 6–10 hours. Make sure to keep basting it with the sauce every hour or so.
10. After the first smoking is done, take an aluminum foil and wrap up the meat forming a watertight seal.
11. Place the meat in the middle of your foil and bring the edges to the top, cupping up the flesh completely.
12. Pour 1 cup of sauce over the meat and tighten it up.
13. Place the package back into your smoker and smoke for 2 hours until the meat easily pulls off from the bone.
14. Once done, remove it from the smoker, pull off the pork, and discard the bone and fat.
15. Place the meat chunks in a pan and pour 1 cup of sauce for every 4 lbs. of meat.
16. Heat until simmering, and serve immediately!

Nutrition: Calories: 1098 | Fat: 86 g. | Carbs: 38 g. | Fiber: 3 g.

107. Smoked Avocado Pork Ribs

Preparation time: 20 minutes
Cooking time: 3 hours
Servings: 5
Ingredients:
- 2 lbs. pork spare ribs
- 1 cup avocado oil
- 1 tsp. garlic powder
- 1 tsp. onion powder
- 1 tsp. sweet pepper flakes
- Salt and pepper to taste

Directions:
1. In a bowl, combine the avocado oil, garlic salt, garlic powder, onion powder, sweet pepper flakes, and salt and pepper.
2. Place pork chops in a shallow container and pour evenly avocado mixture.
3. Cover and refrigerate for at least 4 hours or overnight.
4. Start pellet grill on, lid open until the fire is established (4–5 minutes).
5. Increase the temperature to 225 and pre-heat for 10 to15 minutes.
6. Arrange pork chops on the grill rack and smoke for 3–4 hours.
7. Transfer pork chops to a serving plate, let them rest for 15 minutes, and serve.

Nutrition: Calories: 677 kcal | Carbohydrates: 0.9 g. | Fat: 64 g. | Fiber: 0.14 g. | Protein: 28.2 g.

108. Smoked Honey-Garlic Pork Chops

Preparation time: 15 minutes
Cooking time: 60 minutes
Servings: 4
Ingredients:
- ¼ cup lemon juice freshly squeezed
- ¼ cup honey (preferably a darker honey)
- 3 garlic cloves, minced
- 2 tbsp. soy sauce (or tamari sauce)
- Salt and pepper to taste
- 24 oz. center-cut pork chops boneless

Directions:
1. Combine honey, lemon juice, soy sauce, garlic, and salt and pepper in a bowl.
2. Place pork in a container and pour marinade over pork.
3. Cover and marinate in a fridge overnight.
4. Remove pork from marinade and pat dry on a kitchen paper towel. (Reserve marinade)
5. Start your pellet on Smoke with the lid open until the fire is established (4–5 minutes).
6. Increase temperature to 450°F and preheat, lid closed, for 10–15 minutes.
7. Arrange the pork chops on the grill racks and smoke for about one hour (depending on the thickness)
8. In the meantime, heat the remaining marinade in a small saucepan over medium heat to simmer.

9. Transfer pork chops to a serving plate, pour with the marinade and serve hot.

Nutrition: Calories: 301.5 kcal | Carbohydrates: 17 g. | Fat: 6.5 g. | Fiber: 0.2 g. | Protein: 41 g.

109. Smoked Pork Burgers

Preparation time: 15 minutes
Cooking time: 1 hour and 45 minutes
Servings: 4
Ingredients:
- 2 lb. ground pork
- ½ onion finely chopped
- 2 tbsp. fresh sage, chopped
- 1 tsp. garlic powder
- 1 tsp. cayenne pepper
- Salt and pepper to taste

Directions:
1. Start the pellet grill on SMOKE and wait until the fire is established.
2. Set the temperature to 225°F and preheat, lid closed, for 10–15 minutes.
3. In a bowl, combine ground pork with all remaining ingredients.
4. Use your hands to mix thoroughly—form the mixture into eight evenly burgers.
5. Place the hamburgers on the racks.
6. Smoke the burgers for 60 minutes until they reach an internal temperature of 150–160.
7. Serve hot.

Nutrition: Calories: 588.7 kcal | Carbohydrates: 1 g. | Fat: 48.2 g. | Fiber: 0.5 g. | Protein: 38.4 g.

110. Smoked Pork Cutlets in Citrus-Herbs Marinade

Preparation time: 4 hours
Cooking time: 1 hour and 45 minutes
Servings: 4
Ingredients:
• 4 pork cutlets
• 1 fresh orange juice
• 2 large lemons freshly squeezed
• 10 twigs of coriander chopped
• 2 tbsp. fresh parsley finely chopped
• 3 garlic cloves, minced
• 2 tbsp. olive oil
• Salt and ground black pepper
Directions:
1. Place the pork cutlets in a large container and all remaining ingredients; toss to cover well.
2. Refrigerate for at least 4 hours or overnight.
3. Remove the pork cutlets from the marinade and pat dry on a kitchen towel when ready.
4. Start pellet grill on, lid open until the fire is established (4–5 minutes). Increase the temperature to 250°F and allow to pre-heat, lid closed, for 10 to15 minutes.
5. Place pork cutlets on the grill grate and smoke for 1.5 hours.
6. Serve hot.
Nutrition: Calories: 260 | Carbohydrates: 5 g. | Fat: 12 g. | Fiber: 0.25 g. | Protein: 32.2 g.

Chapter 7. Lamb and Game Recipes

111. Lamb Skewers

Preparation time: 5 minutes
Cooking time: 8–12 minutes
Servings: 6
Ingredients:
- 1 lemon, juiced
- 2 garlic cloves, crushed
- 2 red onions, chopped
- 1 tsp. thyme, chopped
- Pepper and salt
- 1 tbsp. oregano
- ⅓ cup oil
- ½ t. cumin
- 2 lb. cubed lamb leg

Directions:
1. Refrigerate the chunked lamb.
2. The remaining ingredients should be mixed. Add in the meat. Refrigerate overnight.
3. Pat the meat dry and thread it onto some metal or wooden skewers. Wooden skewers should be soaked in water. Add wood pellets to your smoker and follow your cooker's startup procedure. Preheat your smoker with your lid closed until it reaches 450°F. Grill, covered, for 4–6 minutes on each side. Serve.

Nutrition: Calories: 201 Kcal │ Fat: 9 g. │ Carbohydrates: 3 g. │ Protein: 24 g. │ Fiber: 1 g.

112. Brown Sugar Lamb Chops

Preparation time: 2 hours
Cooking time: 10–15 minutes
Servings: 4
Ingredients:
- Pepper and salt
- 1 tsp. garlic powder
- 2 tsp. tarragon
- 1 tsp. cinnamon
- ¼ cup brown sugar
- 4 lamb chops
- 2 tsp. ginger

Directions:
1. Combine salt, garlic powder, pepper, cinnamon, tarragon, ginger, and sugar. Coat the lamb chops in the mixture and chill for 2 hours.
2. Add wood pellets to your smoker and follow your cooker's startup procedure. Preheat your smoker with your lid closed until it reaches 450°F.
3. Place the chops on the grill, cover, and smoke for 10–15 minutes per side. Serve.

Nutrition: Calories: 210 Kcal │ Fat: 11 g. │ Carbohydrates: 3 g. │ Protein: 25 g. │ Fiber: 1 g.

113. Traeger Smoked Lamb Chops

Preparation time: 10 minutes
Cooking time: 50 minutes
Servings: 4
Ingredients:
- 1 rack lamb
- 2 tbsp. rosemary, fresh
- 2 tbsp. sage, fresh
- 1 tbsp. thyme, fresh
- 2 garlic cloves, roughly chopped
- 1 tbsp. honey
- 2 tbsp. shallots, roughly chopped
- ½ tbsp. salt
- ½ tbsp. ground pepper
- ¼ cup olive oil

Directions:
1. Preheat the Traeger to 225°F
2. Trim any excess fat and silver skin from the lamb.
3. Combine the rest of the ingredients in the food processor and generously rub the lamb with the seasoning.
4. Place the seasoned lamb on the Traeger and cook for 45 minutes or until the internal temperature reaches 120°F.
5. Sear the lamb on the Traeger for 2 minutes per side or until the internal temperature reaches 125°F for medium-rare or 145°F for medium.
6. Let rest for 5 minutes beforehand, slicing it. Enjoy.

Nutrition: Calories: 916 │ Total Fat: 78.3 g. │ Total Carbs: 2.7 g. │ Protein: 47 g. │ Sugars: 0.1 g. │ Fiber: 0.5 g. │ Sodium: 1324 mg.

114. Traeger Smoked Lamb Shoulder

Preparation time: 20 minutes
Cooking time: 3 hours
Servings: 7
Ingredients:
- 5 lb. lamb shoulder
- 1 cup cider vinegar
- 2 tbsp. oil
- 2 tbsp. Kosher salt
- 2 tbsp. black pepper, freshly ground
- 1 tbsp. dried rosemary
For the spritz:
- 1 cup apple cider vinegar
- 1 cup apple juice

Directions:
1. Preheat the Traeger to 225°F with a pan of water for moisture.
2. Trim any extra fat from the lamb and rinse the meat in cold water.
3. Pat dry with a paper towel.
4. Inject the cider vinegar and apple juice into the meat, then pat dry with a clean paper towel.

5. Rub the meat with oil, salt, black pepper, and dried rosemary.

6. Tie the lamb shoulder with a twine.

7. Place in the smoker for an hour, then spritz every 15 minutes until the internal temperature reaches 165°F.

8. Remove from the Traeger and let rest for 1 hour before shredding.

9. Serve.

Nutrition: Calories 472 | Total Fat: 37 g. | Total Carbs: 3 g. | Protein: 31 g. | Sodium: 458 mg.

115.   Traeger Smoked Pulled Lamb Sliders

Preparation time: 10 minutes
Cooking time: 9 hours
Servings: 7
Ingredients:
• 5 lb. lamb shoulder, boneless
• ½ cup olive oil
• ⅓ cup Kosher salt
• ⅓ cup pepper, coarsely ground
• ⅓ cup granulated garlic
For the spritz:
10. 4 oz. Worcestershire sauce
11. 6 oz. apple cider vinegar
Directions:
1. Preheat the Traeger to 225°F with a pan of water for moisture.

2. Trim any excess fat from the lamb, then pat it dry with a paper towel. Rub with oil, salt, pepper, and garlic.

3. Place the lamb in the Traeger smoker for 90 minutes, then spritz every 30 minutes until the internal temperature reaches 165°F.

4. Transfer the lamb to a foil pan, then add the remaining spritz liquid. Cover with a foil and place back in the Traeger.

5. Smoke until the internal temperature reaches 205°F.

6. Remove from the smoker and rest in a cooler without ice for 30 minutes before pulling it. Serve with slaw or bun, and enjoy.

Nutrition: Calories 235 | Total Fat: 6 g. | Total Carbs: 22 g. | Protein: 20 g. | Sugars: 7 g. | Fiber: 1 g. | Sodium: 592 mg. | Potassium: 318 mg.

116.   Traeger Smoked Lamb Meatballs

Preparation time: 10 minutes
Cooking time: 1 hour
Servings: 20 meatballs
Ingredients:
7. 1 lb. lamb shoulder, ground
8. 3 garlic cloves, finely diced
9. 3 tbsp. shallot, diced
10. 1 tbsp. salt
11. 1 egg
12. ½ tbsp. pepper
13. ½ tbsp. cumin
14. ½ tbsp. smoked paprika
15. ¼ tbsp. red pepper flakes
16. ¼ tbsp. cinnamon
17. ¼ cup panko breadcrumbs

Directions:
1. Set your Traeger to 250°F.

2. Combine all the ingredients in a small bowl, then mix thoroughly using your hands.

3. Form golf ball-sized meatballs and place them on a baking sheet.

4. Place the baking sheet in the smoker and smoke until the internal temperature reaches 1600°F.

5. Remove the meatballs from the smoker and serve when hot.

Nutrition: Calories: 93 | Total Fat: 5.9 g. | Total Carbs: 4.8 g. | Protein: 5 g. | Sugars: 0.3 g. | Fiber: 0.3 g. | Sodium: 174.1 mg. | Potassium: 82.8 mg.

117.   Traeger Crown Rack of Lamb

Preparation time: 30 minutes
Cooking time: 30 minutes
Servings: 6
Ingredients:
6. 2 lamb racks, French style
7. 1 tbsp. garlic, crushed
8. 1 tbsp. rosemary
9. ½ cup olive oil
10. Kitchen wine
Directions:
1. Preheat your Traeger to 450°F.

2. Rinse the lab with clean cold water and then dry it with a paper towel.

3. Lay the lamb on a chopping board and score a ¼ inch between the bones. Repeat the process between the bones on each lamb rack. Set aside.

4. In a small mixing bowl, combine garlic, rosemary, and oil. Brush the lamb rack generously with the mixture.

5. Bend the lamb rack into a semicircle, then place the racks together so the bones will be up and form a crown shape.

6. Wrap around 4 times, starting from the base and moving upward. Tie tightly to keep the racks together.

7. Place the lambs on a baking sheet and set them in the Traeger. Cook on high heat for 10 minutes. Reduce the temperature to 300°F and cook for 20 more minutes or until the internal temperature reaches 1300°F.

8. Remove the lamb rack from the Traeger and let rest while wrapped in a foil for 15 minutes. Serve when hot.

Nutrition: Calories 390 | Total Fat: 35 g. | Total Carbs: 0 g. | Protein: 17 g. | Sodium: 65 mg.

118. Traeger Smoked Leg

Preparation time: 15 minutes
Cooking time: 3 hours
Servings: 6
Ingredients:
• 1 leg of lamb, boneless
• 2 tbsp. oil
• 4 garlic cloves, minced
• 2 tbsp. oregano
• 1 tbsp. thyme
• 2 tbsp. salt
• 1 tbsp. black pepper, freshly ground
Directions:
1. Trim excess fat from the lamb, ensuring you keep the meat even thick for cooking.
2. In a mixing bowl, mix oil, garlic, and all spices. Rub the mixture all over the lamb, then cover with a plastic wrap.
3. Place the lamb in a fridge and let it marinate for an hour.
4. Transfer the lamb to a smoker rack and set the Traeger to smoke at 250°F.
5. Smoke the meat for 4 hours or until the internal temperature reaches 145°F
6. Remove from the Traeger and serve immediately.
Nutrition: Calories 356 | Total Fat: 16 g. | Total Carbs: 3 g. | Protein: 49 g. | Sugars: 1 g. | Fiber: 1 g. | Sodium: 2474 mg.

119. Traeger Grilled Aussie Leg of Lamb

Preparation time: 30 minutes
Cooking time: 2 hours
Servings: 8
Ingredients:
• 5 lb. Aussie boneless leg of lamb
Smoked paprika rub:
• 1 tbsp. raw sugar
• 1 tbsp. salt
• 1 tbsp. black pepper
• 1 tbsp. smoked paprika
• 1 tbsp. garlic powder
• 1 tbsp. rosemary
• 1 tbsp. onion powder
• 1 tbsp. cumin
• ½ tbsp. cayenne pepper
Roasted carrots:
• 1 rainbow carrot bunch
• Olive oil
• Salt and pepper
Directions:
1. Preheat your Traeger to 350°F and trim any excess fat from the meat.
2. Combine the paprika rub ingredients and generously rub all over the meat.
3. Place the lamb on the preheated Traeger over indirect heat and smoke for 2 hours.

4. Meanwhile, toss the carrots in oil, salt, and pepper. Add the carrots to the grill after 1 ½ hour or until the internal temperature has reached 90°F. Cook until the internal meat temperature reaches 135°F. Remove the lamb from the Traeger and cover it with foil for 30 minutes. Once the carrots are cooked, serve with the meat and enjoy it.
Nutrition: Calories: 257 | Total Fat: 8 g. | Total Carbs: 6 g. | Protein: 37 g. | Sugars: 3 g. | Fiber: 1 g. | Sodium: 431 mg. | Potassium: 666 mg.

120. Simple Traeger Grilled Lamb Chops

Preparation time: 10 minutes
Cooking time: 20 minutes
Servings: 6
Ingredients:
• ¼ cup white vinegar, distilled
• 2 tbsp. olive oil
• 2 tbsp. salt
• ½ tbsp. black pepper
• 1 tbsp. minced garlic
• 1 onion, thinly sliced
• 2 lb. lamb chops
Directions:
5. Mix vinegar, oil, salt, black pepper, garlic, and sliced onions in a resealable bag until all salt has dissolved.
6. Add the lamb and toss until evenly coated. Place in a fridge to marinate for 2 hours.
7. Preheat your Traeger.
8. Remove the lamb from the resealable bag and leave any onion stuck on the meat. Use aluminum foil to cover any exposed bone ends.
9. Grill until the desired doneness is achieved. Serve and enjoy when hot.
Nutrition: Calories: 519 | Total Fat: 44.8 g. | Total Carbs: 2.3 g. | Protein: 25 g. | Sugars: 0.8 g. | Fiber: 0.4 g. | Sodium: 861 mg. | Potassium: 358.6 mg.

121. Traeger Grilled Lamb With Sugar Glaze

Preparation time: 15 minutes
Cooking time: 20 minutes
Servings: 4
Ingredients:
• ¼ cup sugar
• 2 tbsp. ginger, grounded
• 2 tbsp. dried tarragon
• ½ tbsp. salt
• 1 tbsp. black pepper, grounded
• 1 tbsp. cinnamon, grounded
• 1 tbsp. garlic powder
• 4 lamb chops
Directions:
1. Mix sugar, ground ginger, tarragon, salt, pepper, cinnamon, and garlic in a mixing bowl.

2. Rub the lamb chops with the mixture and refrigerate for an hour.

3. Meanwhile, preheat your Traeger.

4. Brush the grill grates with oil and place the marinated lamb chops on it—Cook for 5 minutes on each side.

5. Serve and enjoy.

Nutrition: Calories: 241 | Total Fat: 13.1 g. | Total Carbs: 15.8 g. | Protein: 14.6 g. | Sugars: 13.6 g. | Fiber: 0.7 g. | Sodium: 339.2 mg. | Potassium: 256.7 mg.

122. Roasted Leg of Lamb

Preparation time: 30 minutes
Cooking time: 2 hours
Servings: 12
Ingredients:
- 8 lb. lamb leg, bone-in, fat trimmed
- 2 lemons, juiced, zested
- 1 tbsp. minced garlic
- 4 sprigs of rosemary, 1-inch diced
- 4 garlic cloves, peeled, sliced lengthwise
- Salt as needed
- Ground black pepper as needed
- 2 tsp. olive oil

Directions:

1. Switch on the Traeger grill, fill the grill hopper with cherry-flavored wood pellets, power the grill on by using the control panel, select 'smoke' on the temperature dial, or set the temperature to 450°F and let it preheat for a minimum of 15 minutes.

2. Meanwhile, take a small bowl, place the minced garlic, stir in oil and then rub this mixture on all sides of the lamb leg.

3. Then make ¾-inch deep cuts into the lamb meat, about 2 dozen, stuff each cut with garlic slices and rosemary, sprinkle with lemon zest, drizzle with lemon juice, and then season well with salt and black pepper.

4. When the grill has preheated, open the lid, place the leg of lamb on the grill grate, shut the grill, and smoke for 30 minutes.

5. Change the smoking temperature to 350°F and then continue smoking for 1 hour and 30 minutes until the internal temperature reaches 130°F.

6. Transfer lamb to a cutting board, let it rest for 15 minutes, then cut it into slices and serve.

Nutrition: Calories: 219 Kcal | Fat: 14 g. | Carbs: 1 g. | Protein: 22 g. | Fiber: 0 g.

123. Greek-Style Roast Lamb Leg

Preparation time: 25 minutes
Cooking time: 1 hour and 30 minutes
Servings: 12
Ingredients:
- 7 lb. lamb leg, bone-in, fat trimmed
- 2 lemons, juiced
- 8 garlic cloves, peeled, minced
- Salt as needed
- Ground black pepper as needed

- 1 tsp. dried oregano
- 1 tsp. dried rosemary
- 6 tbsp. olive oil

Directions:

1. Make a small cut into the meat of lamb by using a paring knife, then stir together garlic, oregano, and rosemary and stuff this paste into the slits of the lamb meat.

2. Take a roasting pan, place lamb in it, then rub with lemon juice and olive oil, cover with a plastic wrap and let marinate for a minimum of 8 hours in the refrigerator.

3. When ready to cook, switch on the Traeger grill, fill the grill hopper with oak-flavored wood pellets, power the grill on by using the control panel, select 'smoke' on the temperature dial, or set the temperature to 400°F and let it preheat for a minimum of 15 minutes.

4. Meanwhile, remove the lamb from the refrigerator, bring it to room temperature, uncover it and then season well with salt and black pepper.

5. When the grill has preheated, open the lid, place food on the grill grate, shut the grill, and smoke for 30 minutes.

6. Change the smoking temperature to 350°F and then continue smoking for 1 hour until the internal temperature reaches 140°F.

7. Transfer lamb to a cutting board, let it rest for 15 minutes, then cut it into slices and serve.

Nutrition: Calories: 168 Kcal | Fat: 10 g. | Carbs: 2 g. | Protein: 17 g. | Fiber: 0.7 g.

124. Lamb Chops

Preparation time: 10 minutes
Cooking time: 10 minutes
Servings: 8
Ingredients:
For the lamb:
- 16 lamb chops, fat trimmed
- 2 tbsp. Greek Freak seasoning
For the mint sauce:
- 1 tbsp. parsley, chopped
- 12 garlic cloves, peeled
- 1 tbsp. mint, chopped
- ¼ tsp. dried oregano
- 1 tsp. salt
- ¼ tsp. ground black pepper
- ¾ cup lemon juice
- 1 cup olive oil

Directions:

1. To make the mint sauce, combine all ingredients in a food processor and pulse for 1 minute, or until smooth.

2. Pour 1/3 cup of the mint sauce into a plastic bag, add the lamb chops, seal the bag, flip it upside down to coat the lamb chops with the sauce, and refrigerate for at least 30 minutes.

3. When ready to cook, switch on the Traeger grill, fill the grill hopper with apple-flavored wood pellets, power the grill on by using the control panel, select 'smoke' on the

temperature dial, or set the temperature to 450°F and let it preheat for a minimum of 15 minutes.

4. Meanwhile, remove the marinated lamb chops from the marinade and season with Greek spice.

5. When the grill is hot, open the cover, set the lamb chops on the grill grate, close the lid, and smoke for 4–5 minutes per side, or until cooked to your liking.

6. When the lamb chops are done, transfer them to a serving plate and serve.

Nutrition: Calories: 362 Kcal | Fat: 26 g. | Carbs: 0 g. | Protein: 31 g. | Fiber: 0 g.

125. Smoked Lamb Rack

Preparation time: 10 minutes
Cooking time: 1 hour and 15 minutes
Servings: 4
Ingredients:
• 1 lamb rib rack, membrane removed
For the marinade:
• 1 lemon, juiced
• 2 tsp. garlic, minced
• 1 tsp. salt
• 1 tsp. ground black pepper
• 1 tsp. thyme, dried
• ¼ cup balsamic vinegar
• 1 tsp. basil, dried
For the glaze:
• 2 tbsp. soy sauce
• ¼ cup Dijon mustard
• 2 tbsp. Worcestershire sauce
• ¼ cup red wine
Directions:
1. Prepare the marinade and for this, take a small bowl, place all the ingredients in it and whisk until combined.

2. Place the rack of lamb into a large plastic bag, pour in marinade, seal the bag, turn it upside down to coat the lamb with the marinade, and let it marinate for a minimum of 8 hours in the refrigerator.

3. When ready to cook, switch on the Traeger grill, fill the grill hopper with flavored wood pellets, power the grill on by using the control panel, select 'smoke' on the temperature dial, or set the temperature to 300°F and let it preheat for a minimum of 5 minutes.

4. Meanwhile, prepare the glaze and take a small bowl, place all of its ingredients in it and whisk until combined.

5. When the grill has preheated, open the lid, place the lamb rack on the grill grate, shut the grill, and smoke for 15 minutes.

6. Brush with glaze, flip the lamb and then continue smoking for 1 hour and 15 minutes until the internal temperature reaches 145°F, basting with the glaze every 30 minutes.

7. Transfer the lamb rack to a cutting board, let it rest for 15 minutes, cut it into slices, and then serve.

Nutrition: Calories: 323 Kcal | Fat: 18 g. | Carbs: 13 g. | Protein: 25 g. | Fiber: 1 g.

126. Rosemary Lamb

Preparation time: 10 minutes
Cooking time: 3 hours
Servings: 2
Ingredients:
• 1 lamb rib rack, membrane removed
• 12 baby potatoes
• 1 asparagus bunch, ends trimmed
• Ground black pepper, as needed
• Salt, as needed
• 1 tsp. dried rosemary
• 2 tbsp. olive oil
• ½ cup butter, unsalted
Directions:
1. Switch on the Traeger grill, fill the grill hopper with flavored wood pellets, power the grill on by using the control panel, select 'smoke' on the temperature dial, or set the temperature to 225°F and let it preheat for a minimum of 5 minutes.

2. Meanwhile, drizzle oil on both sides of lamb ribs and then sprinkle with rosemary.

3. Take a deep baking dish, place potatoes in it, add butter and mix until coated.

4. When the grill has been preheated, open the lid, place lamb ribs on the grill grate and potatoes in the baking dish, shut the grill, and smoke for 3 hours until the internal temperature reaches 145°F.

5. Add asparagus into the baking dish in the last 20 minutes and, when done, remove the baking dish from the grill and transfer the lamb to a cutting board.

6. Let lamb rest for 15 minutes, cut it into slices, and then serve with potatoes and asparagus.

Nutrition: Calories: 355 Kcal | Fat: 12.5 g. | Carbs: 25 g. | Protein: 35 g. | Fiber: 6 g.

127. Lamb Chops With Rosemary and Olive Oil

Preparation time: 10 minutes
Cooking time: 50 minutes
Servings: 4
Ingredients:
• 12 lamb loin chops, fat trimmed
• 1 tbsp. rosemary leaves, chopped
• Salt as needed for dry brining
• Jeff's Original rub as needed
• ¼ cup olive oil
Directions:
1. Take a cookie sheet, place lamb chops on it, sprinkle with salt, and then refrigerate for 2 hours.
2. Meanwhile, take a small bowl, place rosemary leaves in it, stir in oil and let the mixture stand for 1 hour.
3. When ready to cook, switch on the Traeger grill, fill the grill hopper with apple-flavored wood pellets, power the grill on by using the control panel, select 'smoke' on the temperature dial, or set the temperature to 225°F and let it preheat for a minimum of 5 minutes.
4. Meanwhile, brush rosemary-oil mixture on all sides of lamb chops and then sprinkle with Jeff's original rub.
5. When the grill has preheated, open the lid, place lamb chops on the grill grate, shut the grill, and smoke for 50 minutes until the internal temperature of lamb chops reaches 138°F.
6. When done, wrap lamb chops in foil, let them rest for 7 minutes and then serve.
Nutrition: Calories: 171.5 Kcal | Fat: 7.8 g. | Carbs: 0.4 g. | Protein: 23.2 g. | Fiber: 0.1 g.

128. Boneless Lamb Leg

Preparation time: 10 minutes
Cooking time: 4 hours
Servings: 4
Ingredients:
• 2 ½ ob. lamb leg, boneless, fat trimmed
For the marinade:
• 2 tsp. garlic, minced
• 1 tbsp. ground black pepper
• 2 tbsp. salt
• 1 tsp. thyme
• 2 tbsp. oregano
• 2 tbsp. olive oil
Directions:
1. Take a small bowl, place all the ingredients for the marinade, and then stir until combined.
2. Rub the marinade on all sides of the lamb, then place it on a large sheet, cover it with plastic wrap and marinate for a minimum of 1 hour in the refrigerator.
3. When ready to cook, switch on the Traeger grill, fill the grill hopper with apple-flavored wood pellets, power the grill on by using the control panel, select 'smoke' on the

temperature dial, or set the temperature to 250°F and let it preheat for a minimum of 5 minutes.
4. Meanwhile,
5. When the grill has preheated, open the lid, place the lamb on the grill grate, shut the grill, and smoke for 4 hours until the internal temperature reaches 145°F.
6. Transfer lamb to a cutting board, let it stand for 10 minutes, then carve it into slices and serve.
Nutrition: Calories: 213 Kcal | Fat: 9 g. | Carbs: 1 g. | Protein: 29 g. | Fiber: 0 g.

129. Smoked Lamb Shoulder

Preparation time: 10 minutes
Cooking time: 4 hours
Servings: 6
Ingredients:
• 8 lb. lamb shoulder, fat trimmed
• 2 tbsp. olive oil
• Salt as needed
For the rub:
• 1 tbsp. oregano, dried
• 2 tbsp. salt
• 1 tbsp. crushed dried bay leaf
• 1 tbsp. sugar
• 2 tbsp. crushed sage, dried
• 1 tbsp. thyme, dried
• 1 tbsp. ground black pepper
• 1 tbsp. basil, dried
• 1 tbsp. rosemary, dried
• 1 tbsp. parsley, dried
Directions:
1. Switch on the Traeger grill, fill the grill hopper with cherry-flavored wood pellets, power the grill on by using the control panel, select 'smoke' on the temperature dial, or set the temperature to 250°F and let it preheat for a minimum of 5 minutes.
2. Meanwhile, prepare the rub and take a small bowl, place all of its ingredients in it and stir until mixed.
3. Brush lamb with oil and then sprinkle with prepared rub until evenly coated.
4. When the grill has preheated, open the lid, place lamb should go on the grill, grate fat-side up, shut the grill, and smoke for 3 hours.
5. Then change the smoking temperature to 325°F and continue smoking for 1 hour until fat renders and the internal temperature reaches 195°F.
6. When finished, you should wrap the lamb in aluminum foil and let it rest for 20 minutes.
7. Pull lamb shoulder by using 2 forks, and then serve.
Nutrition: Calories: 300 Kcal | Fat: 24 g. | Carbs: 0 g. | Protein: 19 g. | Fiber: 0 g.

130. Herby Lamb Chops

Preparation time: 10 minutes
Cooking time: 2 hours
Servings: 4
Ingredients:
• 8 lamb chops, each about ¾-inch thick, fat trimmed
For the marinade:
• 1 tsp. garlic, minced
• Salt as needed
• 1 tbsp. rosemary, dried
• Ground black pepper as needed
• ½ tbsp. thyme, dried
• 3 tbsp. balsamic vinegar
• 1 tbsp. Dijon mustard
• ½ cup olive oil
Directions:
1. Prepare the marinade and for this, take a small bowl, place all its ingredients in it and stir until well combined.
2. Place lamb chops in a large plastic bag, pour in marinade, seal the bag, turn it upside down to coat lamb chops with the marinade and let it marinate for a minimum of 4 hours in the refrigerator.
3. When ready to cook, switch on the Traeger grill, fill the grill hopper with flavored wood pellets, power the grill on by using the control panel, select 'smoke' on the temperature dial, or set the temperature to 450°F and let it preheat for a minimum of 5 minutes.
4. Meanwhile, remove lamb chops from the refrigerator and bring them to room temperature.
5. When the grill has preheated, open the lid, place lamb chops on the grill grate, shut the grill, and smoke for 5 minutes per side until seared.
6. Transfer lamb chops to a dish, let them rest for 5 minutes, and then serve.
Nutrition: Calories: 280 Kcal │ Fat: 12.3 g. │ Carbs: 8.3 g. │ Protein: 32.7 g. │ Fiber: 1.2 g.

131. Garlic Rack of Lamb

Preparation time: 10 minutes
Cooking time: 3 hours
Servings: 4
Ingredients:
• 1 rack of lamb, membrane removed
For the marinade:
• 2 tsp. garlic, minced
• 1 tsp. basil, dried
• ⅓ cup cream sherry
• 1 tsp. oregano, dried
• ⅓ cup Marsala wine
• 1 tsp. rosemary, dried
• ½ tsp. ground black pepper
• ⅓ cup balsamic vinegar
• 2 tbsp. olive oil
Directions:

1. Prepare the marinade and for this, take a small bowl, place all its ingredients in it and stir until well combined.
2. Place lamb rack in a large plastic bag, pour in marinade, seal the bag, turn it upside down to coat the lamb with the marinade, and let it marinate for a minimum of 45 minutes in the refrigerator.
3. When ready to cook, switch on the Traeger grill, fill the grill hopper with flavored wood pellets, power the grill on by using the control panel, select 'smoke' on the temperature dial, or set the temperature to 250°F and let it preheat for a minimum of 5 minutes.
4. Meanwhile,
5. When the grill has preheated, open the lid, place the lamb rack on the grill grate, shut the grill, and smoke for 3 hours until the internal temperature reaches 165°F.
6. Transfer the lamb rack to a cutting board, let it rest for 10 minutes, then cut into slices and serve.
Nutrition: Calories: 210 Kcal │ Fat: 11 g. │ Carbs: 3 g. │ Protein: 25 g. │ Fiber: 1 g.

132. Traeger Grilled Leg of Lamb Steak

Preparation time: 10 minutes
Cooking time: 10 minutes
Servings: 4
Ingredients:
• 4 reaches lamb steaks, bone-in
• ¼ cup olive oil
• 4 garlic cloves, minced
• 1 tbsp. rosemary, freshly chopped
• Salt and pepper to taste
Directions:
1. Arrange the steak in a dish in a single layer. Cover the meat with oil, garlic, fresh rosemary, salt, and pepper.
2. Flip the meat to coat on all sides and let it marinate for 30 minutes.
3. Preheat your Traeger and lightly oil the grates. Cook the meat on the grill until well browned on both sides and the internal temperature reaches 1400°F. Serve and enjoy.
Nutrition: Calories 327.3 │ Total Fat: 21.9 g. │ Total Carbs: 1.7 g. │ Protein: 29.6 g. │ Sugars: 0.1 g. │ Fiber: 0.2 g. │ Sodium: 112.1 mg. │ Potassium: 409.8 mg.

133. Traeger Garlic Rack Lamb

Preparation time: 45 minutes
Cooking time: 3 hours
Servings: 4
Ingredients:
• 1 tsp. Lamb Rack
• Basil
• 1 tsp. oregano
• 10 cranks peppermill
• 3 oz. Marsala wine
• 3 oz. cram sherry
• 3 oz. olive oil; Madeira wine
• 3 oz. balsamic vinegar
• 1 tsp. rosemary

Directions:

1. Add all the ingredients into a zip bag to mix well to form an emulsion.

2. Place the rack lamb into the bag to release the air as you rub the marinade all over the lamb.

3. Let it stay in the bag for about 45 minutes

4. Get the wood pellet grill preheated to 250°F, then cook the lamb for 3 hours as you turn on both sides.

5. Ensure the internal temperature is at 165°F before removing it from the grill.

6. Allow to cool for a few minutes, then serve and enjoy.

Nutrition: Calories: 291 Cal | Protein: 26 g. | Fat: 21 g.

134. Traeger Braised Lamb Shank

Preparation time: 20 minutes
Cooking time: 4 hours
Servings: 6
Ingredients:
• 4 lamb shanks
• Olive oil as required
• 1 cup beef broth
• 1 cup red wine
• 4 fresh thyme and sprigs

Directions:

1. Season lamb shanks with prime rib rub, then allow resting.

2. Get the wood pellet grill temperature set to high, then cook the lamb shanks for about 30 minutes.

3. Place the shanks directly on the grill grate, then cook for another 20 minutes until browned on the outside.

4. Transfer the cooked lamb shanks into a Dutch oven, then pour beef broth, herbs, and wine. Cover it with a fitting lid, then place it back on the grill grate and allow it to cook at a reduced temperature of 325°F.

5. Brace the lamb shanks for about 3 hours or until the internal temperature gets to 180°F.

6. Remove the lid once ready, then serve on a platter with the accumulated juices and enjoy.

Nutrition: Calories: 312 Cal | Protein: 27 g. | Fat: 24 g.

135. Cornish Game Hens

Preparation time: 10 minutes
Cooking time: 1 hour
Servings: 6
Ingredients:
• 4 Cornish game hens, giblets removed
• 4 tsp. chicken rub
• 4 rosemary sprigs
• 4 tbsp. butter, unsalted, melted

Directions:

1. Switch on the Traeger grill, fill the grill hopper with mesquite-flavored wood pellets, power the grill on by using the control panel, select 'smoke' on the temperature dial, or set the temperature to 375°F and let it preheat for a minimum of 15 minutes.

2. Meanwhile, rinse the hens, pat dry with paper towels, tie the wings using a butcher's strong, then rub evenly with melted butter, sprinkle with chicken rub, and stuff the cavity of each hen with a rosemary sprig.

3. When the grill has preheated, open the lid, place hens on the grill grate, shut the grill, and smoke for 1 hour until thoroughly cooked and internal temperature reaches 165°F.

4. When done, transfer hens to a dish, let rest for 5 minutes, and then serve.

Nutrition: Calories: 173 Kcal | Fat: 7.4 g. | Carbs: 1 g. | Protein: 24.1 g. | Fiber: 0.2 g.

136. BBQ Elk Short Ribs

Preparation time: 10 minutes
Cooking time: 1 hour
Servings: 6
Ingredients:
• ½ lb. green beans
• 3 lbs. elk short ribs
• ½ lb. Chanterelle mushrooms
• 6 oz. rib rub
• Salt as needed
• Ground black pepper as needed
• 4 tbsp. unsalted butter

Directions:

1. Switch on the Traeger grill, fill the grill hopper with cherry-flavored wood pellets, power the grill on by using the control panel, select 'smoke' on the temperature dial, or set the temperature to 275°F and let it preheat for a minimum of 15 minutes.

2. Meanwhile, prepare the ribs, season them with salt, and rib rub until well coated.

3. When the grill has preheated, open the lid, place ribs on the grill rib-side down, shut the grill, and smoke for 30 minutes.

4. Then wrap ribs in foil in the double layer, return to the grill grate and continue smoking for 15 minutes or until the internal temperature reaches 125°F.

5. Transfer ribs to a dish and lets them rest until required.

6. Change the smoking temperature to 450°F, shut with the lid, and let it preheat for 15 minutes.

7. Then place a skillet pan on the grill grate and when hot, add butter when it melts, add mushrooms and beans, toss until mixed, shut with lid, and cook for 15 minutes until vegetables have turned tender golden brown.

8. Serve grilled vegetables with elk ribs.

Nutrition: Calories: 393 Kcal | Fat: 16.6 g. | Carbs: 25 g. | Protein: 36 g. | Fiber: 0.9 g.

Chapter 8. Burgers Recipes

137. Mini Portobello Burgers

Preparation time: 15 minutes
Cooking time: 15 minutes
Servings: 4
Ingredients:
- 4 Portobello mushroom caps
- 4 slices Mozzarella cheese
- 4 buns, brioche-like

For the marinade:
- ¼ cup balsamic vinegar
- 2 tbsp. olive oil
- 1 tsp. dried basil
- 1 tsp. dried oregano
- 1 tsp. garlic powder
- ¼ tsp. sea salt
- ¼ tsp. black pepper

Directions:
1. Whisk together marinade ingredients in a large mixing bowl. Add mushroom caps and toss to coat.
2. Fire up the grill for medium-high heat.
3. Place mushrooms on the grill; reserve marinade for basting.
4. Grill for 5–8 minutes on each side
5. Brush with marinade frequently.
6. Top with mozzarella cheese during the last 2 minutes of grilling.
7. Remove from grill and serve on brioche buns.

Nutrition: Energy (calories): 372 kcal | Protein: 3.18 g. | Fat: 24.08 g. | Carbohydrates: 35.24 g. | Calcium: 133 mg. | Magnesium: 14 mg. | Phosphorus: 93 mg. | Iron: 1.35 mg.

138. Layered Beef & Corn Burger

Preparation time: 20 minutes
Cooking time: 30 minutes
Servings: 6
Ingredients:
- 1 large egg, lightly beaten
- 1 cup whole kernel corn, cooked
- ½ cup bread crumbs
- 2 tbsp. shallots, minced
- 1 tsp. Worcestershire sauce
- 2 lb. ground beef
- 1 tsp. salt
- ½ tsp. pepper
- ½ tsp. ground sage

Directions:
1. Combine the egg, corn, bread crumbs, shallots, and Worcestershire sauce in a mixing bowl and set aside.
2. Combine ground beef and seasonings in a separate bowl.

3. Roll beef mixture into 12 thin burger patties.
4. Spoon corn mixture into the center of 6 patties and spread evenly across within an inch of the edge
5. Top each with a second circle of meat and press edges to seal the corn mixture in the middle of each burger.
6. Grill into your Traeger smoker over medium heat for 12–15 minutes on each side.

Nutrition: Energy (calories): 433 kcal | Protein: 40.16 g. | Fat: 25.53 g. | Carbohydrates: 8.62 g. | Calcium: 52 mg. | Magnesium: 40 mg. | Phosphorus: 312 mg. | Iron: 4.47 mg. | Potassium: 518 mg.

139. Grilled Ultimate Game Burger

Preparation time: 10 minutes
Cooking time: 15 minutes
Servings: 4
Ingredients:
- ¾ lb. wild boar, ground
- ¾ lb. venison, ground
- Pepper to taste
- Salt to taste
- 2 tbsp. mayonnaise
- 1 tbsp. ketchup
- 2 tbsp. sweet pickle relish
- ½ tbsp. sugar
- ½ tbsp. white vinegar
- 1 white onion, sliced
- 4 buns
- 4 American cheese pieces
- 4 lettuce pieces
- 1 tomato, sliced

Directions:
1. Place and combine venison and boar in a bowl. Mix, but do not overwork.
2. Form 4 patties from the meat mixture and generously splash with pepper and salt.
3. Mix all sauce ingredients in a bowl and set aside.
4. Start your Traeger to smoke for about 5 minutes with the lid open.
5. Preheat the Traeger to 400°F while the lid is closed for 10–15 minutes.
6. Arrange the patties on the grill grate.
7. Cook until the internal temperature reaches 160°F. Flip once.
8. Place the sliced onion on the grill for 5 minutes before cooking is over.
9. During the last minutes, place cheese on your burgers and your buns on the grill
10. Build the burgers and serve.

Nutrition: Calories: 256 | Fat: 6 g. | Carbs: 9.4 g. | Protein: 37.2 g.

140.   Cheesy Lamb Burgers

Preparation time: 15 minutes
Cooking time: 20 minutes
Servings: 4
Ingredients:
• 2 lb. ground lamb
• 1 cup Parmigiano-Reggiano cheese, grated
• Salt and ground black pepper to taste
Directions:
1. Set the temperature of Traeger to 425°F and preheat with a closed lid for 15 minutes.
2. In a bowl, add all the ingredients and mix well.
3. Make 4 patties from the mixture.
4. Make a shallow but wide depression in each patty with your thumbs.
5. Arrange the patties onto the grill, depression-side down, and cook for about 8 minutes.
6. Flip and cook for 8–10 minutes. Serve.
Nutrition: Calories: 502 | Fat: 22.6 g. | Carbs: 0 g. | Protein: 71.7 g.

141.   Tuna Burgers

Preparation time: 15 minutes
Cooking time: 15 minutes
Servings: 6
Ingredients:
• 2 lb. tuna steak
• 1 green bell pepper, seeded and chopped
• 1 white onion, chopped
• 2 eggs
• 1 tsp. soy sauce
• 1 tbsp. blackened Saskatchewan rub
• Salt and ground black pepper to taste
Directions:
1. Set the grill's temperature to 500°F and preheat with a closed lid for 15 minutes.
2. In a bowl, add all the ingredients and mix well.
3. Make patties from this mixture.
4. Place the patties onto the grill close to the edges and cook for 10–15 minutes. Flip once.
5. Serve.
Nutrition: Calories: 313 | Fat: 11 g. | Carbs: 3.4 g. | Protein: 47.5 g.

142.   Veggie Lover's Burgers

Preparation time: 20 minutes
Cooking time: 51 minutes
Servings: 6
Ingredients:
• ¾ cup lentils
• 1 tbsp. ground flaxseed
• 2 tbsp. extra-virgin olive oil
• 1 onion, chopped
• 2 garlic cloves, minced
• Salt and ground black pepper to taste
• 1 cup walnuts, toasted
• ¾ cup breadcrumbs
• 1 tsp. ground cumin
• 1 tsp. paprika
Directions:
1. Add the lentils to a pan of boiling water and cook for 15 minutes or until soft.
2. Drain lentils and set them aside.
3. In a bowl, mix the flaxseed with 4 tbsp. water. Set aside for 5 minutes.
4. Heat the oil and sauté the onion in a skillet for 5 minutes.
5. Add the garlic, salt, and pepper, and cook for 30 seconds more.
6. Remove from the heat and place the onion mixture into a food processor.
7. Add ¾ of the lentils, flaxseed mixture, walnuts, breadcrumbs, and spices, and pulse until smooth.
8. Transfer the mixture into a bowl and fold in the remaining lentils.
9. Make 6 patties from the mixture.
10. Place the patties onto a parchment paper-lined plate and refrigerate for at least 30 minutes.
11. Set the temperature of Traeger to 425°F and preheat with a closed lid for 15 minutes.
12. Place the burgers onto the grill and cook for 8–10 minutes. Flipping once.
13. Serve.
Nutrition: Calories: 324 | Fat: 18.5 g. | Carbs: 28.9 g. | Protein: 13.6 g.

143.   Cheesy Turkey Burger

Preparation time: 20 minutes
Cooking time: 3 hours
Servings: 8
Ingredients:
14. 3 lb. ground turkey
15. Burger seasoning
16. 7 oz. brie cheese, sliced into cubes
17. 8 burger buns, sliced
18. Blueberry jam
19. 2 roasted bell peppers, sliced
Directions:
1. Season the turkey with burger seasoning and mix well.
2. Form 8 patties from the mixture.
3. Press the cheese into the patties and cover the top with more turkey.
4. Preheat the grill to 350°F
5. Cook turkey burgers for 30–40 minutes per side.
6. Spread the burger buns with blueberry jam.
7. Add the turkey burger on top.
8. Top with the bell peppers and serve.
Nutrition: Calories: 935 | Fat: 53 g. | Carbs: 22 g. | Protein: 57 g.

144.   Buffalo Chicken Burgers

Preparation time: 15 minutes
Cooking time: 35 minutes
Servings: 4
Ingredients:
9. 1 lb. ground chicken breast
10. 4 slices Mozzarella cheese
11. 4 tbsp. bread crumbs
12. Ranch dressing (or blue cheese)
13. 2 tbsp. parmesan cheese
14. More wing sauce to drizzle
15. 2 tbsp. buffalo wing sauce
16. 4 wheat buns
17. 1 tsp. Kosher salt
18. Lettuce leaves
19. 1 tsp. ground black pepper
20. Fresh tomato, sliced
Directions:
1. Preheat the grill to 350°F
2. Combine the ground chicken, bread crumbs, salt, pepper, parmesan cheese, and wing sauce in a bowl. Mix well.
3. Form 4 burger patties.
4. Place the patties on the grill and cook for 10 minutes. Flip once.
5. Put mozzarella cheese slices on the burgers for the last minute to melt.
6. Remove from the grill when done.
7. Rest for 10 minutes. Arrange and serve.
Nutrition: Calories: 430 | Fat: 33 g. | Carbs: 2.1 g. | Protein: 25.4 g.

145.   Stuffed Burgers

Preparation time: 20 minutes
Cooking time: 15 minutes
Servings: 6
Ingredients:
• 3 lb. ground beef
• ½ tbsp. onion powder
• ¼ tbsp. garlic powder
• 1 tbsp. salt
• ½ tbsp. pepper
• 1-½ cups Colby's Jack cheese, shredded
• Seasoning salt
• 6 slices Colby Jack cheese
Directions:
1. Preheat the grill to 375°F.
2. Mix beef, onion powder, garlic powder, salt, and pepper. Make 12 patties.
3. Place cheese on the burger patty and cover with another patty, then seal the edges.
4. Season with salt, then place the patties on the grill. Cook the patties on the grill for 8 minutes. Then flip and cook for 5 minutes more.
5. Place a slice of cheese on each patty and grill with the lid closed to melt the cheese.

6. Remove the patties from the grill and rest for 10 minutes. Serve.
Nutrition: Calories: 436 | Fat: 29 g. | Carbs: 1 g. | Protein: 67 g.

146.   Grilled Steak With American Cheese Sandwich

Preparation time: 10 minutes
Cooking time: 55 minutes
Servings: 4
Ingredients:
• 1 lb. beef steak
• ½ tsp. salt to taste
• ½ tsp. pepper to taste
• 1 tbsp. Worcestershire sauce
• 2 tbsp. butter
• 1 onion, chopped
• ½ green bell pepper, chopped
• Salt and pepper to taste
• 8 slices American cheese
• 8 slices white bread
• 4 tbsp. butter
Directions:
1. Turn your Wood Pellet Smoker and Grill to smoke and fire up for about 4–5 minutes. Set the grill's temperature to 450°F and let it preheat for about 10–15 minutes with its lid closed.
2. Next, place a non-stick skillet on the grill and preheat for about 15 minutes until it becomes hot. Once hot, add in the butter and let melt. Once the butter melts, add in the onions and green bell pepper, then cook for about 5 minutes until they become brown; set aside.
3. Next, still using the same pan on the grill, add the steak, Worcestershire sauce, salt, and pepper to taste, then cook for about 5–6 minutes until it is cooked through. Add in the cooked bell pepper mixture; stir to combine, then heat for another 3 minutes, set aside.
4. Use a sharp knife to slice the bread in half, butter each side, then grill for about 3–4 minutes with its sides down. To assemble, add cheese slices to each bread slice, top with the steak mixture, then your favorite toppings, close the sandwich with another bread slice, then serve.
Nutrition: Calories 589 kcal | Carbohydrates: 28 g. | Protein: 24 g. | Fat: 41 g. | Fiber: 2 g.

147. Ground Turkey Burgers

Preparation time: 15 minutes
Cooking time: 50 minutes
Servings: 6
Ingredients:
- Some beaten egg
- ⅔ cup bread crumbs
- ½ cup celery, chopped
- ¼ cup onion, chopped
- 1 tbsp. parsley, minced
- 1 tsp. Worcestershire sauce
- 1 tsp. oregano, dried
- ½ tsp. salt to taste
- ¼ tsp. pepper
- 1-¼ lb. lean ground turkey
- 6 hamburger buns
- Optional topping:
- 1 tomato, sliced
- 1 onion, sliced
- Lettuce leaves

Directions:
1. Using a small mixing bowl, add all the ingredients on the list aside from the turkey and buns, then mix properly to combine.
2. Add in the ground turkey, then mix everything to combine. Feel free to use clean hands for this. Make about 6 patties of the mixture and set aside.
3. Preheat your Wood Pellet Smoker and Grill to 375°F, place the turkey patties on the grill, and grill for about 45 minutes until its internal temperature reads 165°F. To assemble, use a knife to split the bun into 2, top with the prepared burger and your favorite topping, then close with another half of the buns, and serve.

Nutrition: Calories 293 kcal | Fat: 11 g. | Carbohydrate: 27 g. | Fiber: 4 g. | Protein: 22 g.

148. BBQ Shredded Beef Burger

Preparation time: 10 minutes
Cooking time: 5 hours 10 minutes
Servings: 4
Ingredients:
- 3 lb. boneless chuck roast.
- Salt to taste
- Pepper to taste
- 2 tbsp. garlic, minced
- 1 cup onion, chopped
- 28 oz. barbeque sauce
- 6 buns

Directions:
1. Set the temperature of the Wood Pellet Smoker and Grill to 250°F, then preheat for about 15 minutes with its lid closed.
2. Use a knife to trim off the excess fat on the roast, then place the meat on the preheated grill.

3. Grill the roast for about 3 and a half hours until it attains an internal temperature of 160°F.
4. Next, place the chuck roast in aluminum foil, add garlic, onion, barbeque sauce, salt, and pepper, and stir to coat.
5. Place the roast bake on the grill and cook for another 1.5 hours until an inserted thermometer reads 204°F.
6. Once cooked, let the meat cool for a few minutes and shred with a fork. Fill the buns with shredded beef.
7. Serve.

Nutrition: Calories 593 kcal | Fat: 31 g. | Carbohydrates: 34 g. | Fiber: 1 g. | Protein: 44 g.

149. Grilled Pork Burgers

Preparation time: 15 minutes
Cooking time: 1 hour
Servings: 4 - 6
Ingredients:
- 1 beaten egg
- ¾ cup soft breadcrumbs
- ¾ cup grated parmesan cheese
- 1 tbsp. dried parsley
- 1 tsp. basil, dried
- ½ tsp. salt to taste
- ½ tsp. garlic powder
- ¼ tsp. pepper to taste
- 2 lb. ground pork
- 6 hamburger buns
Toppings:
- Lettuce leaves
- Sliced tomato
- Sliced sweet onion

Directions:
1. Using a large mixing bowl, add the egg, bread crumbs, cheese, parsley, basil, garlic powder, salt, and pepper to taste, then mix properly to combine.
2. Add in the ground pork, then mix properly to combine using clean hands. Form about 6 patties with the mixture, then set aside.
3. Next, set a Wood Pellet smoker and grill to smoke (250°F), then let it fire up for about 5 minutes. Place the patties on the grill and smoke for about 30 minutes.
4. Flip the patties over, increase the grill's temperature to 300°F, then grill the patties for a few minutes until an inserted thermometer reads 160°F.
5. Serve the pork burgers with lettuce, tomato, and onion on the buns.

Nutrition: Calories 522 kcal | Fat: 28 g. | Carbohydrate: 28 g. | Fiber: 2 g. | Protein: 38 g.

150.   Delicious BLT Sandwich

Preparation time: 15 minutes
Cooking time: 35 minutes
Servings: 4–6
Ingredients:
• 8 bacon slices
• ½ romaine heart
• 1 sliced tomato
• 4 slices sandwich bread
• 3 tbsp. mayonnaise
• Salted butter
• Sea salt to taste
• Pepper to taste
Directions:
1. Preheat a Wood Pellet Smoker and Grill to 350°F for about 15 minutes with its lid closed.
2. Place the bacon slices on the preheated grill and cook for about 15–20 minutes until they become crispy.
3. Next, butter both sides of the bread, place a grill pan on the griddle of the Pellet, and toast the bread for a few minutes until they become brown on both sides; set aside.
4. Using a small mixing bowl, add the sliced tomatoes, season with salt and pepper to taste, then mix to coat.
5. Next, spread mayo on both sides of the toasted bread, top with the lettuce, tomato, and bacon, then enjoy.
Nutrition: Calories 284 kcal │ Protein: 19 g. │ Fat: 19 g. │ Carbohydrates: 11 g. │ Fiber: 2 g.

151.   Delicious Grilled Chicken Sandwich

Preparation time: 15 minutes
Cooking time: 50 minutes
Servings: 4
Ingredients:
• ¼ cup mayonnaise
• 1 tbsp. Dijon mustard
• 1 tbsp. honey
• 4 boneless and skinless chicken breasts
• ½ tsp. steak seasoning
• 4 slices American Swiss cheese
• 4 hamburger buns
• 2 bacon strips
• Lettuce leaves and tomato slices
Directions:
1. Using a small mixing bowl, add the mayonnaise, mustard, and honey, then mix properly to combine.
2. Use a meat mallet to pound the chicken into even thickness, then slice it into four parts. Season the chicken with the steak seasoning, then set aside.
3. Preheat a Wood Pellet Smoker and Grill to 350°F for about 10–15 minutes with its lid closed.
4. Place the seasoned chicken on the grill and grill for about 25–30 minutes until it reads an internal temperature of 165°F. Grill the bacon until crispy, then crumble.

5. Add the cheese to the chicken and cook for about one minute until it melts completely. At the same time, grill the buns for about 1–2 minutes until it is toasted as desired.
6. Place the chicken on the buns, top with the grilled bacon, mayonnaise mixture, lettuce, and tomato, then serve.
Nutrition: Calories 410 kcal │ Fat: 17 g. │ Carbohydrate: 29 g. │ Fiber: 3 g. │ Protein: 34 g.

152.   Bacon, Egg, and Cheese Sandwich

Preparation time: 15 minutes
Cooking time: 20 minutes
Servings: 4
Ingredients:
• 2 large eggs
• 2 tbsp. milk or water
• Salt to taste
• Pepper to taste
• 3 tsp. butter
• 4 white bread slices
• 2 Jack cheese slices
• 4 bacon slices
Directions:
1. Using a small mixing bowl, add the eggs, milk, salt, and pepper to taste, then mix properly.
2. Preheat a Wood Pellet Smoker and Grill to 400°F for about 10–15 minutes with its lid closed.
3. Place the bacon slices on the preheated grill and grill for about eight to 10 minutes, flipping once until it becomes crispy. Set the bacon aside on a paper-lined towel.
4. Decrease the grill's temperature to 350°F, place a grill pan on it, and let it heat for about 10 minutes.
5. Spread 2 tbsp. butter on the cut side of the bread, place the bread on the skillet pan and toast for about 2 minutes until brown.
6. Place the cheese on the toasted bread, close the grill lid, then cook for about one minute until the cheese melts completely; set aside. Still using the same grill pan, add the rest of the butter, then let it melt. Pour in the egg mixture and cook for a few minutes until it is cooked as desired.
7. Assemble the sandwich as desired, then serve.
Nutrition: Calories 401 kcal │ Fat: 23 g. │ Carbohydrates: 26 g. │ Fiber: 3 g. │ Protein: 23 g.

153. Grilled Lamb Burgers

Preparation time: 15 minutes
Cooking time: 25 minutes
Servings: 5
Ingredients:
- ¼ lb. ground lamb
- 1 egg
- 1 tsp. oregano, dried
- 1 tsp. dry sherry
- 1 tsp. white wine vinegar
- ½ tsp. red pepper flakes, crushed
- 4 minced garlic cloves
- ½ cup green onions, chopped
- 1 tbsp. mint, chopped
- 2 tbsp. cilantro, chopped
- 2 tbsp. dry bread crumbs
- ⅛ tsp. salt to taste
- ¼ tsp. ground black pepper to taste
- 1 hamburger buns

Directions:
1. Preheat a Wood Pellet Smoker or Grill to 350–450°F, then grease its grates.
2. Using a large mixing bowl, add all the ingredients on the list aside from the buns, then mix properly to combine with clean hands.
3. Make about 5 patties out of the mixture, then set aside.
4. Place the lamb patties on the preheated grill and cook for about seven to nine minutes, turning only once until an inserted thermometer reads 160°F.
5. Serve the lamb burgers on the hamburger, add your favorite toppings and enjoy.

Nutrition: Calories: 376 kcal | Fat: 18.5 g. | Fiber: 1.6 g. Carbohydrates 25.4 g. | Protein: 25.5 g.

154. Grilled Lamb Sandwiches

Preparation time: 15 minutes
Cooking time: 55 minutes
Servings: 6
Ingredients:
- 1 (4 lb.) boneless lamb
- 1 cup raspberry vinegar
- 2 tbsp. olive oil
- 1 tbsp. fresh thyme, chopped
- 2 pressed garlic cloves
- ¼ tsp. salt to taste
- ¼ tsp. ground pepper
- Sliced bread

Directions:
1. Using a large mixing bowl, add the raspberry vinegar, oil, and thyme, then mix properly to combine. Add in the lamb, toss to combine, then let it sit in the refrigerator for about eight hours or overnight.
2. Next, discard the marinade the season the lamb with salt and pepper to taste. Preheat a Wood Pellet Smoker and grill

to 400–500°F; add in the seasoned lamb, and grill for about 30–40 minutes until it attains a temperature of 150°F.
3. Once cooked, let the lamb cool for a few minutes, slice as desired, then serve on the bread with your favorite topping.
Nutrition: Calories 407 kcal | Fat: 23 g. | Carbohydrates: 26 g. | Fiber: 2.3 g. | Protein: 72 g.

155. Grilled Chicken Quesadilla Sandwich

Preparation time: 15 minutes
Cooking time: 55 minutes
Servings: 6
Ingredients:
- 4 chicken breasts
- 1 package taco seasoning
- 1 green bell pepper
- 1 red bell pepper
- 1 red onion
- 2 cups Monterey Jack Cheese
- 4 ciabatta buns, sliced in half
- ½ cup margarine
- 1 tbsp. Croix Valley Garlic Barbecue Booster
- 1 cup sour cream
- 2 tbsp. chipotle in Adobo sauce
- 1 cup Ajvar Relish (Eastern European relish of garlic, peppers, and eggplant)
- 1 tbsp. olive oil
- 1 head iceberg lettuce, shredded
- 1 medium tomato, diced

Directions:
1. Lightly oil hen breasts and coast generously with Taco Seasoning.
2. Grill cook over the medium grill (about 350°F) until internal temperature reaches 165°F. Let relaxation for 5 minutes, then slice into strips.
3. Julienne peppers and onion. Fry in oil until greens begin to brown. Cover and set aside.
4. Make 4 piles of chook (as flat as possible) on the baking sheet. Then, put the fried vegetables, ½ cup of cheese, and a sprint of taco seasoning on the top. Transfer to blanketed grill and cook till cheese begins to brown.
5. Combine margarine and garlic seasoning. Blend properly.
6. Spread margarine garlic mixture on the internal ciabatta buns. Grill till they begin to brown.
7. Combine buttercream and chipotle in adobo sauce. Blend well.
8. Spread Ajvar savor on the inner of the backside bun.
9. Place chicken/vegetable/cheese stacks on top of Ajvar delight.
10. Top with shredded lettuce and diced tomato.
11. Spread the chipotle mixture on the pinnacle bun's internal and of the sandwich.
12. Serve and enjoy!
Nutrition: Calories 407 kcal | Fat: 23 g. | Carbohydrates: 26 g. | Fiber: 2.3 g. | Protein: 72 g.

156.   Turkey Apple Burgers

Preparation time: 150minutes
Cooking time: 45 minutes
Servings: 6
Ingredients:
- 3 ½ lb. ground turkey
- 1 apple, finely minced
- 1 tsp. garlic powder
- 1 ½ tsp. onion powder
- 1 tsp. oregano
- 1 tsp. salt
- 1 tsp. pepper

Directions:
1. Preheat grill to 450°F.
2. Meanwhile, make patties by combining turkey, apple, and spices in a mixing bowl. Mix very well together with your hands. Use a 1½ cup as your guide and shape meat patties.
3. Grill on direct warmness at 450°F for around 30 minutes, flipping ½ way through. Grill till internal meat temperature reaches 165°F.
4. Remove patties and permit relaxation 5 minutes earlier than serving.
Nutrition: Calories 207 kcal │Fat: 20 g. │Carbohydrates: 16 g.│ Fiber: 2.3 g.│ Protein: 72 g.

Chapter 9. Sausages Recipes

157. Smoked Pork Sausages

Preparation time: 10 minutes
Cooking time: 1 hour
Servings: 6
Ingredients:
- 3 lb. ground pork
- ½ tbsp. ground mustard
- 1 tbsp. onion powder
- 1 tbsp. garlic powder
- 1 tsp. pink curing salt
- 1 tsp. salt
- 1 tsp. black pepper
- ¼ cup ice water
- Hog casings, soaked and rinsed in cold water

Directions:
1. In a bowl, combine all ingredients except for the hog casings. Using your hands, mix them well.
2. Using a sausage stuffer, stuff the hog casings using the pork mixture.
3. Measure 4 inches of the stuffed hog casing and twist it to form a sausage. Repeat the process until you create sausage links.
4. When ready to cook, fire the Traeger Grill to 225°F. Use apple wood pellets when cooking. Close the lid and preheat for 15 minutes.
5. Put the sausage links on the grill grate and cook for 1 hour or until the internal temperature of the sausage reaches 155°F.
6. Allow resting before slicing.
Nutrition: Calories: 688 | Protein: 58.9 g. | Carbs: 2.7 g. | Fat: 47.3 g. | Sugar: 0.2 g.

158. Grilled Sausage Ala Carte

Preparation time: 5 minutes
Cooking time: 30–45 minutes
Servings: 1
Ingredients:
- 3 lbs. hot Italian sausage
- 2 bottles (18 oz. each) barbecue sauce
- 2 cups packed brown sugar

Directions:
7. Divide the sausages between 2 ungreased 13" x 9" baking dishes.
8. Combine the barbecue sauce and brown sugar.
9. Pour over the sausages, and make sure to coat thoroughly.
10. Bake uncovered at 350°F for 35–40 minutes or until the sauce has thickened.
11. Stir gently for 1 minute, and then let it rest.
Nutrition: Calories: 439 | Fat: 31 g. | Carbohydrates: 23 g. | Protein: 16 g. | Fiber: 0 g.

159. Smoked Pork Sausage

Preparation time: 10 minutes
Cooking time: 1 hour
Servings: 6
Ingredients:
- 3 lbs. ground pork
- ½ tbsp. ground mustard
- 1 tbsp. onion powder
- 1 tbsp. garlic powder
- 1 tsp. pink curing salt
- 1 tsp. salt
- 1 tsp. black pepper
- ¼ cup ice water
- Hog casings, soaked and rinsed in cold water

Directions:
12. Mix all ingredients except the hog casings in a bowl. Mix well.
13. Using a sausage stuffer, stuff the hog casings with pork mixture.
14. Measure 4 inches of the stuffed hog casing and twist it to form a sausage. Repeat the process until you create sausage links.
15. Fire the Traeger to 225°F. Close the lid and preheat for 15 minutes.
16. Place the sausage links on the grill and cook for 1 hour or until the internal temperature of the sausage reads 155°F.
17. Rest. Slice and serve.
Nutrition: Calories: 688 | Fat: 47.3 g. | Carbs: 2.7 g. | Protein: 58.9 g.

160. Breakfast Sausage

Preparation time: 60 minutes
Cooking time: 9 hours
Servings: 6
Ingredients:
• 20/22-millimeter natural sheep casings, rinsed
• Warm water
• 2 lb. ground pork
• Apple butter rub
• Pinch dried marjoram
• ½ tsp. ground cloves
• 1 tbsp. brown sugar
• ⅓ cup ice water
• Pepper to taste
Directions:
18. Soak the sheep casting in warm water for 1 hour.
19. Mix everything in a bowl.
20. Combine the ingredients in a mixture at low speed.
21. Cover and refrigerate the mixture for 15 minutes.
22. Insert the casings into the sausage stuffer.
23. Stuff the casings with the ground pork mixture.
24. Twist into 5 links and remove bubbles using a pricker.
25. Put the sausage on a baking pan and refrigerate for 24 hours.
26. Set the grill to smoke.
27. Hang the sausages on hooks and put them in the smoking cabinet.
28. Set the grill temperature to 350°F and smoke the sausage for 1 hour.
29. Increase the temperature to 425°F and cook for 30 minutes more.
30. Serve.
Nutrition: Calories: 220 | Fat: 19 g. | Carbs: 1 g. | Protein: 11 g.

161. Backyard Cookout Sausages

Preparation time: 15 minutes
Cooking time: 23 minutes
Servings: 6
Ingredients:
• ½ cup apricot jam
• 1 tbsp. Dijon mustard
• 12 breakfast sausage links
Directions:
31. Set the grill's temperature to 350°F and preheat with a closed lid for 15 minutes.
32. Add jam and mustard over low heat in a pan and cook until warm.
33. Reduce the heat to low and keep the glaze warm.
34. Arrange the sausage links onto the grill and cook for 10–15 minutes, flipping twice.
35. Coat the sausage links with jam glaze evenly and cook for 2–3 minutes.
36. Remove the sausage links from the grill and serve with the remaining glaze.

Nutrition: Calories: 575 | Fat: 42.7 g. | Carbs: 17.3 g. | Protein: 29.5 g.

162. Traeger Smoked Sausage

Preparation time: 35 minutes
Cooking time: 3 hours 10 minutes
Servings: 6
Ingredients:
• 3 lb. ground pork
• 1 tbsp. onion powder
• ½ tbsp. ground mustard
• 1 tsp. pink curing salt
• 1 tbsp. garlic powder
• 1 tbsp. salt
• ½ cup ice water
• 4 tsp. black pepper
• Hog casings, soaked and rinsed in cold water
Directions:
37. In a bowl, combine meat and all the seasonings and mix well. Add the ice water and mix well.
38. Place this mixture in a sausage stuffer and follow the manufacturer's instructions. Once the whole meat gets stuffed, choose your desired length to pinch and twist.
39. Set the grill temperature to 225°F and preheat for 15 minutes.
40. Cook the sausage for 1–2 hours or until the internal temperature reaches 155°F.
41. Rest and serve.
Nutrition: Calories: 341 | Fat: 8.3 g. | Carbs: 3.2 g. | Protein: 60.1 g.

Chapter 10. Poultry Recipes

163. Traeger Chili Lime Chicken

Preparation time: 2 minutes
Cooking time: 15 minutes
Servings: 1
Ingredients:
• 1 chicken breast
• 1 tbsp. oil
• 1 tbsp. spice Chili Lime Seasoning
Directions:
1. Preheat your Traeger to 400°F.
2. Brush the chicken breast with oil, then sprinkle the chili-lime seasoning and salt.
3. Place the chicken breast on the grill and cook for 7 minutes on each side until the internal temperature reaches 165°F.
4. Serve when hot and enjoy.
Nutrition: Calories 131 │ Total Fat: 5 g. │ Saturated Fat: 1 g. │ Total Carbs: 4 g. │ Net Carbs: 3 g. │ Protein: 19 g. │ Sugar: 1 g. │ Fiber: 1 g. │ Sodium: 235 mg.

164. Traeger Grilled Buffalo Chicken

Preparation time: 5 minutes
Cooking time: 10 minutes
Servings: 6
Ingredients:
• 5 chicken breasts, boneless and skinless
• 2 tbsp. homemade BBQ rub
• 1 cup homemade Cholula Buffalo sauce
Directions:
1. Preheat the Traeger to 400°F.
2. Slice the chicken breast lengthwise into strips. Season the slices with BBQ rub.
3. Place the chicken slices on the grill and paint both sides with buffalo sauce.
4. Cook for 4 minutes with the lid closed. Flip the breasts, paint with sauce, and cook until the internal temperature reaches 165°F.
5. Remove the chicken from the Traeger and serve when warm.
Nutrition: Calories: 176 │ Total Fat: 4 g. │ Saturated Fat: 1 g. │ Total Carbs: 1 g. │ Net Carbs: 1 g. │ Protein: 32 g. │ Sugars: 1 g. │ Fiber: 0 g. │ Sodium 631 mg.

165. Traeger Sheet Pan Chicken Fajitas

Preparation time: 10 minutes
Cooking time: 10 minutes
Servings: 10
Ingredients:
• 2 lb. chicken breast
• 1 onion, sliced.
• 1 red bell pepper seeded and sliced.
• 1 orange-red bell pepper seeded and sliced.
• 1 tbsp. salt
• ½ tbsp. onion powder
• ½ tbsp. granulated garlic
• 2 tbsp. Spiceologist Chile Margarita seasoning
• 2 tbsp. oil
Directions:
1. Preheat the Traeger to 450 degrees Fahrenheit and line a baking sheet with parchment paper.
2. Toss the peppers and chicken with the seasonings and oil in a mixing bowl.
3. Place the baking sheet in the Traeger and close the lid for 10 minutes.
4. Remove the lid and arrange the vegetables and chicken in a single layer.
5. Cook and cover for 10 minutes until the chicken is no longer pink.
6. Serve with warm tortillas and your preferred toppings.
Nutrition: Calories 211 │ Total Fat: 6 g. │ Saturated Fat: 1 g. │ Total Carbs: 5 g. │ Net Carbs: 4 g.│ Protein: 29 g. │ Sugars: 4 g. │ Fiber: 1 g. │ Sodium: 360 mg.

166. Traeger Asian Miso Chicken Wings

Preparation time: 15 minutes
Cooking time: 25 minutes
Servings: 6
Ingredients:
• 2 lb. chicken wings
• ¾ cup soy
• ½ cup pineapple juice
• 1 tbsp. sriracha
• ⅛ cup miso
• ⅛ cup gochujang
• ½ cup water
• ½ cup oil
• Togarashi
Directions:
1. Preheat the Traeger to 375°F
2. Combine all the ingredients except togarashi in a zip lock bag. Toss until the chicken wings are well coated. Refrigerate for 12 hours.
3. Pace the wings on the grill grates and close the lid. Cook for 25 minutes or until the internal temperature reaches 165°F.
4. Remove the wings from the Traeger and sprinkle Togarashi.
5. Serve when hot and enjoy.
Nutrition: Calories: 703 │ Total Fat: 56 g. │ Saturated Fat: 14 g. │ Total Carbs: 24 g. │ Net Carbs: 23 g. │ Protein: 27 g.│ Sugars: 6 g. │ Fiber: 1 g.│ Sodium: 1156 mg.

167. Yan's Grilled Quarters

Preparation time: 20 minutes (additional 2–4 hours marinade)
Cooking time: 1–1.5 hours
Servings: 4
Ingredients:
• 4 fresh or thawed frozen chicken quarters
• 4–6 glasses extra-virgin olive oil
• 4 tbsp. Yang's original dry lab
Directions:
1. Configure a wood pellet smoker grill for indirect cooking and use the pellets to preheat to 325°F.
2. Place chicken on the grill and cook at 325°F for 1 hour.
3. After one hour, raise the pit temperature to 400°F to finish the chicken and crisp the skin.
4. When the inside temperature of the thickest part of the thighs and feet reaches 180°F, and the juice becomes clear, pull the crispy chicken out of the grill.
5. Let the crispy grilled chicken rest under a loose foil tent for 15 minutes before eating.
Nutrition: Calories: 956 | Total Fat: 47 g. | Saturated Fat: 13 g. | Total Carbs: 1 g. | Net Carbs: 1 g. | Protein: 124 g. | Sugars: 0 g. | Fiber: 0 g. | Sodium: 1750 mg.

168. Cajun Patch Cock Chicken

Preparation time: 30 minutes (additional 3 hours marinade)
Cooking time: 2.5 hours
Servings: 4
Ingredients:
• 4–5 lb. fresh or thawed frozen chicken
• 4–6 glasses extra-virgin olive oil
• Cajun Spice Lab 4 tbsp. or Lucile Bloody Mary Mix Cajun Hot Dry Herb Mix Seasoning
Directions:
1. Use hickory, pecan pellets, or blend to configure a wood pellet smoker grill for indirect cooking and preheat to 225°F.
2. If the unit has a temperature meat probe input, such as a MAK Grills 2 Star, insert the probe into the thickest part of the breast.
3. Make chicken for 1.5 hours.
4. After one and a half hours at 225°F, raise the pit temperature to 375°F and roast until the inside temperature of the thickest part of the chest reaches 170°F, and the thighs are at least 180°F.
5. Place the chicken under a loose foil tent for 15 minutes before carving.
Nutrition: Calories: 956 | Total Fat: 47 g. | Saturated Fat: 13 g. | Total Carbs: 1 g. | Net Carbs: 1 g. | Protein: 124 g. | Sugars: 0 g. | Fiber: 0 g. | Sodium: 1750 mg.

169. Roasted Tuscan Thighs

Preparation time: 20 minutes (plus 1–2 hours marinade)
Cooking time: 40–60 minutes
Servings: 4
Ingredients:
• 8 chicken thighs, with bone, with skin
• 3 extra-virgin olive oils with roasted garlic flavor
• 3 cups Tuscan seasoning per thigh
Directions:
1. Set the wood pellet smoker grill for indirect cooking and use the pellets to preheat to 375°Fahrenheit.
2. Depending on the grill of the wood pellet smoker, roast for 40–60 minutes until the internal temperature of the thick part of the chicken thigh reaches 180°F. Place the roasted Tuscan thighs under a loose foil tent for 15 minutes before serving.
Nutrition: Calories: 956 | Total Fat: 47 g. | Saturated Fat: 13 g. | Total Carbs: 1 g. | Net Carbs: 1 g. | Protein: 124 g. | Sugars: 0 g. | Fiber: 0 g. | Sodium: 1750 mg.

170. Bone In-Turkey Breast

Preparation time: 20 minutes
Cooking time: 3–4 hours
Servings: 6–8
Ingredients:
• 1 (8–10 lb.) boned turkey breast
• 6 tbsp. extra virgin olive oil
• 5 Yang original dry lab or poultry seasonings
Directions:
1. Configure a wood pellet smoker grill for indirect cooking and preheat to 225°F using hickory or pecan pellets.
2. Smoke the boned turkey breast directly in a V rack or grill at 225°F for 2 hours.
3. After 2 hours of hickory smoke, raise the pit temperature to 325°F. Roast until the thickest part of the turkey breast reaches an internal temperature of 170°F, and the juice is clear.
4. Place the hickory-smoked turkey breast under a loose foil tent for 20 minutes, then scrape the grain.
Nutrition: Calories: 956 | Total Fat: 47 g. | Saturated Fat: 13 g. | Total Carbs: 1 g. | Net Carbs: 1 g. | Protein: 124 g. | Sugars: 0 g. | Fiber: 0 g. | Sodium: 1750 mg.

171. Teriyaki Smoked Drumstick

Preparation time: 15 minutes (more marinade overnight)
Cooking time: 1.5 hours to 2 hours
Servings: 4
Ingredients:
• 3 cup teriyaki marinade and cooking sauce like Yoshida's original gourmet
• 3 tsp. poultry seasoning
• 1 tsp. garlic powder
• 10 chicken drumsticks
Directions:
1. Configure a wood pellet smoking grill for indirect cooking.
2. Place the skin on the drumstick and, while the grill is preheating, hang the drumstick on a poultry leg and wing rack to drain the cooking sheet on the counter. If you do not have a poultry leg and feather rack, you can dry the drumstick by tapping it with a paper towel.

3. Preheat the wood pellet smoker grill to 180°F using hickory or maple pellets.

4. Make marinated chicken leg for 1 hour.

5. After 1 hour, raise the temperature to 350°F and cook the drumstick for another 30–45 minutes until the thickest part of the stick reaches an internal temperature of 180°F.

6. Place the chicken drumstick under the loose foil tent for 15 minutes before serving.

Nutrition: Calories: 956 | Total Fat: 47 g. | Saturated Fat: 13 g. | Total Carbs: 1 g. | Net Carbs: 1 g. | Protein: 124 g. | Sugars: 0 g. | Fiber: 0 g. | Sodium: 1750 mg.

172.   Hickory Spatchcock Turkey

Preparation time: 20 minutes

Cooking time: 3–4 hours

Servings: 8–10

Ingredients:
• 1 (14 lb.) fresh or thawed frozen young turkey
• ¼ extra-virgin olive oil with 1 cup of roasted garlic flavor
• 6 poultry seasonings or original dry lab in January
• **Directions:**

1. Configure a wood pellet smoking grill for indirect cooking and preheat to 225°F using hickory pellets.

2. Place the turkey skin on a non-stick grill mat made of Teflon-coated fiberglass.

3. Suck the turkey at 225°F for 2 hours.

4. After 2 hours, raise the pit temperature to 350°F.

5. Roast turkey until the thickest part of the chest reaches an internal temperature of 170°F, and the juice is clear.

6. Place the Hickory smoked roast turkey under a loose foil tent for 20 minutes before engraving.

Nutrition: Calories: 956 | Total Fat: 47 g. | Saturated Fat: 13 g. | Total Carbs: 1 g. | Net Carbs: 1 g. | Protein: 124 g. | Sugars: 0 g. | Fiber: 0 g. | Sodium: 1750 mg.

173.   Lemon Cornish Chicken Stuffed With Crab

Preparation time: 30 minutes (additional 2–3 hours marinade)

Cooking time: 1 hour 30 minutes

Servings: 2–4

Ingredients:
• 2 Cornish chickens (about 1¾ pound each)
• 1/2 lemon
• 4 tbsp. western rub or poultry rub
• 2 cups stuffed with crab meat

Directions:

1. Set wood pellet smoker grill for indirect cooking and preheat to 375°F with pellets.

2. Place the stuffed animal on the rack in the baking dish. If you do not have a small enough rack to fit, you can place the chicken directly on the baking dish.

3. Roast the chicken at 375°F until the inside temperature of the thickest part of the chicken breast reaches 170°F, the thigh reaches 180°F, and the juice is clear.

4. Test the crab meat stuffing to see if the temperature has reached 165°F.

5. Place the roasted chicken under a loose foil tent for 15 minutes before serving.

Nutrition: Calories: 956 | Total Fat: 47 g. | Saturated Fat: 13 g. | Total Carbs: 1 g. | Net Carbs: 1 g. | Protein: 124 g. | Sugars: 0 g. | Fiber: 0 g. | Sodium: 1750 mg.

174.   Bacon Cordon Blue

Preparation time: 30 minutes

Cooking time: 30 minutes

Servings: 4

Ingredients:
• 4 (4-5 oz) boneless, skinless chicken breasts
• 8 slices prosciutto or ham
• 8 slices Swiss cheese
• 1/3 cup all-purpose flour
• A pinch salt
• Freshly ground black pepper to taste
• 1 cup breadcrumbs, preferably panko
• 1/4 cup Parmesan cheese, grated
• 2 tbsp butter, melted
• 2 tsp fresh thyme leaves
• 2 eggs

Directions:

1. Line a baking sheet with parchment paper or spray with nonstick cooking spray. Set aside.

2. Butterfly each chicken breast and place it between two pieces of plastic wrap.

3. Evenly pound with the flat side of a meat mallet, being careful not to tear the chicken until the chicken is 1/4-inch thick.

4. Lay each chicken breast on a fresh piece of plastic wrap. Season chicken with salt and lay 1 to 2 slices of cheese on each breast, followed by prosciutto or ham, then 1 to 2 more slices of cheese.

5. Roll the chicken breast up like you would roll a burrito. Using the bottom piece of plastic wrap as an aid, fold the bottom of the breast up about an inch, then fold in the sides. Roll tightly. Wrap the plastic wrap and tightly twist the ends to shape and compress the chicken. Repeat with the remaining chicken breasts.

6. Chill in the refrigerator for 1 hour.

7. While chicken chills, season the flour with salt and pepper and put in a shallow dish.

8. Combine the breadcrumbs, Parmesan cheese, butter, and thyme. Season with salt and pepper and put in a second shallow dish.

9. Whisk the eggs in a separate third dish.

10. Arrange your workspace in this order: flour, eggs, breadcrumbs. Put the prepared baking sheet next to the breadcrumbs.

11. Remove the plastic wrap from the chicken breasts. Coat each lightly with flour, then dip in the egg. Finally, roll in

breadcrumbs, patting them to make them adhere. Arrange on the baking sheet.

12. When ready to cook, set Traeger temperature to 375°F and preheat, lid closed for 15 minutes.

13. Place the baking sheet with the chicken on the grill. Bake for 30 to 40 minutes until the coating is golden brown and the chicken is cooked.

14. Serve whole or slice crosswise into pinwheels with a sharp serrated knife. Enjoy!

Nutrition: Calories: 956 | Total Fat: 47 g. | Saturated Fat: 13 g. | Total Carbs: 1 g. | Net Carbs: 1 g. | Protein: 124 g. | Sugars: 0 g. | Fiber: 0 g. | Sodium: 1750 mg.

175. Roast Duck à I Orange

Preparation time: 30 minutes
Cooking time: 2–2.5 hours
Servings: 3–4
Ingredients:
- 1 (5–6 lb.) Frozen Long Island, Beijing, or Canadian ducks
- 3 tbsp. west
- 1 large orange, cut into wedges
- 3 celery stems chopped into large chunks
- 1/2 small red onion
- Orange sauce:
- 2 cups orange
- 2 tbsp. soy sauce
- 2 tbsp. orange marmalade
- 2 tbsp. honey
- 3 tsp. grated raw

Directions:

1. Set the wood pellet smoker grill for indirect cooking and use the pellets to preheat to 350°F.

2. Roast the ducks at 350°F for 2 hours.

3. After 2 hours, brush the duck freely with orange sauce.

4. Roast the orange glass duck for another 30 minutes, ensuring that the inside temperature of the thickest part of the leg reaches 165°F.

5. Place duck under a loose foil tent for 20 minutes before serving.

6. Discard the orange wedge, celery, and onion. Serve with a quarter of duck with poultry scissors.

Nutrition: Calories: 956 | Total Fat: 47 g. | Saturated Fat: 13 g. | Total Carbs: 1 g. | Net Carbs: 1 g. | Protein: 124 g. | Sugars: 0 g. | Fiber: 0 g. | Sodium: 1750 mg.

176. Bourbon & Orange Brined Turkey

Preparation time: 30 minutes
Cooking time: 1 hour 30 minutes
Servings: 2–4
Ingredients:
- Traeger orange brine (from Kit)
- Traeger turkey rub (from Kit)
- 1.25–2.5 gallons cold water
- 1 cup Bourbon
- 1 tbsp. butter, melted

Directions:

1. Mix Traeger orange brine seasoning (from Orange Brine & Turkey rub Kit) with ¼ water. Boil for 5 minutes. Remove from heat, and add 1 gallon of cold water and bourbon.

2. Place turkey breast side down in a large container. Pour the cooled brine mixture over the bird. Add cold water until the bird is submerged. Refrigerate for 24 hours.

3. Remove turkey and disregard brine. Blot turkeys dry with paper towels. Combine butter and Grand Marnier and coat outside of turkey.

4. Season outside of turkey with Traeger Turkey rub (from Orange Brine & Turkey rub Kit).

5. When ready to cook, set temperature to 225°F and preheat, lid closed for 15 minutes.

Nutrition: Calories: 956 | Total Fat: 47 g. | Saturated Fat: 13 g. | Total Carbs: 1 g. | Net Carbs: 1 g. | Protein: 124 g. | Sugars: 0 g. | Fiber: 0 g. | Sodium: 1750 mg.

177. Traeger Leftover Turkey Soup

Preparation time: 30 minutes
Cooking time: 1 hour 30 minutes
Servings: 2–4
Ingredients:
- 1 turkey carcass
- 16 cups cold water
- 2 large celery ribs, sliced
- 2 large carrots, scraped and sliced
- 2 red onions, quartered

Directions:

6. Remove all meat from a turkey carcass and set it aside in a container.

7. Place the bones from the turkey carcass in a large pot and break them up. Add any leftover turkey skin or other non-meat "bits."

8. When the stock reaches a boil, add the remaining ingredients and reduce the heat until the bubbles barely break the surface. Allow cooking for 3–4 hours, stirring occasionally.

9. When the stock is ready, strain it through a fine-meshed sieve into a large bowl; if your sieve is not fine, line it first with cheesecloth.

10. Refrigerate stock, covered, for several hours or preferably overnight. You can either make soup the then day or freeze the stock.

Nutrition: Calories: 956 | Total Fat: 47 g. | Saturated Fat: 13 g. | Total Carbs: 1 g. | Net Carbs: 1 g. | Protein: 124 g. | Sugars: 0 g. | Fiber: 0 g. | Sodium: 1750 mg.

178.   Turkey by Rob's Cooks

Preparation time: 20 minutes
Cooking time: 5 hours
Servings: 2–4
Ingredients:
• 2 cups Kosher salt
• 2 cups sugar
• 2 water gallons (1/2 gal is iced)
• 1 (12-14 lb) turkey, fresh or thawed
• (3 sticks) unsalted butter
• Rub:
• 1/2 cup Kosher salt
• 1/2 cup coarse ground black pepper
Directions:
1. 1. Because this method requires bringing overnight, gather all your ingredients the day before your meal. Prepare your brine the day before by combining the kosher salt and sugar in a medium saucepan. Bring to a boil with a liter of water. Add salt and sugar to dissolve.
2. Fill a bucket halfway with ice and water (up to 2 gallons), then stir until cooled.
3. Remove the neck, gizzards, and truss, if pre-trussed, from your turkey (reserve gizzards for gravy or stock). Excess skin and fat in the cavity and around the neck should be removed.
4. Place the turkey in the brine bucket. Cover the turkey with a couple of plates to keep it submerged. Refrigerate bucket until ready to cook the next afternoon.
5. Take your turkey out of the brine. Remember that there is a cavity full of water, so do this over the sink, or you'll have brine all over the place.
6. Using cold water, rinse and pat dry the turkey. Place on a dry, clean surface.
7. In a shaker, combine kosher salt and pepper; sprinkle the rub on all parts of the turkey, but not inside the cavity! This method eliminates the need to bind the legs and wings. During the cooking process, the Traeger fan circulates air around the turkey.
8. Set the temperature to 180°F and preheat for 15 minutes with the lid closed. If available, use Super Smoke for the best flavor.
9. Place the turkey on the grill grate, legs and thighs facing the hotter side of the smoker and breast facing the cooler side. Cook for 2 hours at 180°F.
10. For the next hour, raise the grill temperature to 225°F.
11. Finally, raise the grill temperature to 325°F to complete the process.
12. After a few hours, check the color of the turkey. It should be a light golden brown.
13. Place the turkey in the foil pan once it has reached the desired color. Cut the butter into squares and place them on top of the turkey. Wrap in heavy-duty foil and return to the smoker.
14. Cook until the temperature in the breast reaches 165°F and the temperature in the thigh reaches 180°F.

15. Remove from the smoker and set aside for 30 minutes before carving.
Nutrition: Calories: 956 | Total Fat: 47 g. | Saturated Fat: 13 g. | Total Carbs: 1 g. | Net Carbs: 1 g. | Protein: 124 g. | Sugars: 0 g. | Fiber: 0 g. | Sodium: 1750 mg.

179.   Hellfire Chicken Wings

Preparation time: 15 minutes
Cooking time: 40 minutes
Servings: 6
Ingredients:
• 3 lb. chicken wings, tips removed
• 2 tbsp. olive oil
• For the rub:
• 1 tsp. onion powder
• 1 tsp. salt
• 1 tsp. garlic powder
• 1 tsp. paprika
• 1 tsp. ground black pepper
• 1 tsp. celery seed
• 1 tsp. cayenne pepper
• 2 tsp. brown sugar
• For the sauce:
• 4 Jalapeño peppers, sliced crosswise
• 8 tbsp. butter, unsalted
• ½ cup hot sauce
• ½ cup cilantro leaves
Directions:
1. Turn on the Traeger grill, fill the grill hopper with hickory-flavored wood pellets, turn on the grill using the control panel, select 'smoke' on the temperature dial, or set the temperature to 350°F and allow it to preheat for at least 15 minutes.
2. Remove the tips from the chicken wings, cut each wing through the joint into two pieces and place them in a large mixing bowl.
3. To make the rub, combine all ingredients in a small bowl and stir until well combined.
4. Toss the chicken wings in the prepared rub until well coated.
5. Meanwhile, when the grill is hot, open the lid, place the chicken wings on the grill grate, close the lid, and smoke for 40 minutes, turning halfway, until golden brown and the skin is crisp.
6. Meanwhile, make the sauce by heating a small saucepan over medium-low heat, adding butter, and when it melts, add the jalapeno and cook for 4 minutes.
7. After that, remove the pan from the heat and stir in the hot sauce and cilantro.
8. Transfer the chicken wings to a serving dish, top with the prepared sauce, toss until coated, and serve.
Nutrition: Calories: 250 | Fat: 15 g. | Carbs: 11 g. | Protein: 19 g. | Fiber: 1 g.

180. BBQ Half Chickens

Preparation time: 15 minutes
Cooking time: 75 minutes
Servings: 4
Ingredients:
• 3.5 lb. whole chicken, cleaned, halved
• Summer rub as needed
• Apricot BBQ sauce as needed
Directions:
1. Switch on the Traeger grill, fill the grill hopper with apple-flavored wood pellets, and power the grill on the control panel. Select 'smoke' on the temperature dial, or set the temperature to 375°F. Let the grill preheat for a minimum of 15 minutes.
2. In the meantime, cut chicken in half along with the backbone and then season using summer rub.
3. When the grill has preheated, open the lid, and put chicken halves on the grill grate skin-side up. Then, shut the grill, change the smoking temperature to 225°F, and smoke the chicken for 1 hour and 30 minutes until the internal temperature reaches 160°F.
4. Then brush chicken generously using apricot sauce and continue grilling for 10 minutes until glazed.
5. When done, put the chicken to cutting on a dish, let it rest for 5 minutes, and then serve.
Nutrition: Calories: 435 | Fat: 20 g. | Carbs: 20 g. | Protein: 42 g. | Fiber: 1 g.

181. Grilled Wild Turkey Orange Cashew Salad

Preparation time: 30 minutes
Cooking time: 1 hour 30 minutes
Servings: 2–4
Ingredients:
Turkey breast:
• 2 wild turkey breast halves without skin
• ¼ cup teriyaki sauce
• 1 tsp. fresh ginger
• 1 (12 oz.) can blood orange kill cliff or similar citrus soda
• 2 tbsp. Traeger chicken rub
• Cashew salad:
• 4 cups romaine lettuce, chopped
• ½ head red or white cabbage, chopped
• ½ cup shredded carrots
• ½ cup edamame, shelled
• 1 smoked yellow bell pepper, sliced into circles
• 1 smoked red bell pepper, sliced into circles
• 3 chive tips, chopped
• ½ cup smoked cashews
• Blood orange vinaigrette:
• 1 tsp. orange zest
• Juice from ½ large orange
• 1 tsp. fresh ginger, finely grated
• 2 tbsp. rice vinegar, seasoned

• 1 tsp. honey
• Sea salt to taste
• ¼ cup light vegetable oil
Directions:
1. Combine teriyaki sauce, Kill Cliff soda, and fresh ginger for the marinade. Pour marinade over turkey breasts in a Ziplock bag or dish and seal.
2. When ready to cook, set temperature to 375°F and preheat, lid closed for 15 minutes.
3. Remove turkey from the refrigerator, drain the marinade, and pat turkey dry with paper towels.
4. Place the turkey into a shallow oven-proof dish and season with Traeger Chicken rub.
5. Place dish in the Traeger and cook for 30–45 minutes or until the breast reaches an internal temperature of 160°F.
6. Remove the breast from the grill and wrap it in Traeger Butcher Paper. Let the turkey rest for 10 minutes. While the turkey is resting, prepare the salad.
7. Assemble salad ingredients in a bowl and toss to mix. Combine all ingredients in the list for the vinaigrette.
8. After resting for 10 minutes, slice turkey and serve with cashew salad and blood orange vinaigrette. Enjoy!
Nutrition: Calories: 956 | Total Fat: 47 g. | Saturated Fat: 13 g. | Total Carbs: 1 g. | Net Carbs: 1 g. | Protein: 124 g. | Sugars: 0 g. | Fiber: 0 g. | Sodium: 1750 mg.

182. Lemon Chicken

Preparation time: 4 hours and 30 minutes
Cooking time: 10 minutes
Servings: 6
Ingredients:
• 2 tsp. honey
• 1 tbsp. lemon juice
• 1 tsp. lemon zest
• 1 clove garlic, coarsely chopped
• 2 sprigs thyme
• Salt and pepper to taste
• ½ cup olive oil
• Chicken breast fillets
Directions:
1. Mix the honey, lemon juice, lemon zest, garlic, thyme, salt, and pepper in a bowl.
2. Gradually add olive oil to the mixture.
3. Soak the chicken fillets in the mixture.
4. Cover and refrigerate for 4 hours.
5. Preheat the Traeger wood pellet grill to 400°F for 15 minutes while the lid is closed.
6. Grill the chicken for 5 minutes per side.
Nutrition: Calories: 140 | Fat: 5 g. | Carbs: 6 g. | Fiber: 2 g.

183. Honey Garlic Chicken Wings

Preparation time: 30 minutes
Cooking time: 1 hour and 15 minutes
Servings: 4
Ingredients:
• 2 ½ lb. chicken wings
• Poultry dry rub
• 4 tbsp. butter
• 3 garlic cloves, minced
• ½ cup hot sauce
• ¼ cup honey
Directions:
1. Sprinkle chicken wings with the dry rub. Place on a baking pan.
2. Set the Traeger wood pellet grill to 350°F. Preheat for 15 minutes while the lid is closed. Place the baking pan on the grill. Cook for 50 minutes. Add butter to a pan over medium heat. Sauté garlic for 3 minutes. Stir in hot sauce and honey.
3. Cook for 5 minutes while stirring. Coat the chicken wings with the mixture.
4. Grill for 10 more minutes.
Nutrition: Calories: 230 │ Fat: 7 g. │ Carbs: 1 g. │ Fiber: 2 g.

184. Cajun Chicken

Preparation time: 15 minutes
Cooking time: 30 minutes
Servings: 4
Ingredients:
• 2 lb. chicken wings
• Poultry dry rub
• Cajun seasoning
Directions:
1. Season the chicken wings using the dry rub and Cajun seasoning.
2. Preheat the Traeger to 350°F for 15 minutes while the lid is closed.
3. Grill for 30 minutes, flipping twice.
Nutrition: Calories: 290 │ Fat: 15 g. │ Carbs: 20 g. │ Fiber: 1 g.

185. Chili Barbecue Chicken

Preparation time: 5 hours and 30 minutes
Cooking time: 2 hours and 10 minutes
Servings: 4
Ingredients:
• 1 tbsp. brown sugar
• 1 tbsp. lime zest
• 1 tsp. chili powder
• ½ tsp. ground cumin
• ½ tbsp. ground espresso
• Salt to taste
• 2 tbsp. olive oil
• 8 chicken legs
• ½ cup barbecue sauce

Directions:
1. Combine sugar, lime zest, chili powder, cumin, ground espresso, and salt.
2. Drizzle the chicken legs with oil.
3. Sprinkle sugar mixture all over the chicken.
4. Cover with foil and refrigerate for 5 hours.
5. Set the Traeger wood pellet grill to 180°F.
6. Preheat it for 15 minutes while the lid is closed.
7. Smoke the chicken legs for 1 hour.
8. Increase temperature to 350°F.
9. Grill the chicken legs for another 1 hour, flipping once.
10. Brush the chicken with barbecue sauce and grill for another 10 minutes.
Nutrition: Calories: 140 │ Fat: 5 g. │ Carbs: 6 g. │ Fiber: 2 g.

186. Serrano Chicken Wings

Preparation time: 12 hours and 30 minutes
Cooking time: 40 minutes
Servings: 4
Ingredients:
• lb. chicken wings
• 2 cups beer
• 2 tsp. crushed red pepper
• Cajun seasoning powder
• 1 lb. Serrano chili peppers
• 1 tsp. fresh basil
• 1 tsp. dried oregano
• 4 garlic cloves
• 1 cup vinegar
• Salt and pepper to taste
Directions:
1. Soak the chicken wings in beer.
2. Sprinkle it with crushed red pepper.
3. Cover and refrigerate for 12 hours.
4. Remove chicken from the brine.
5. Season with Cajun seasoning.
6. Preheat your Traeger wood pellet grill to 325°F for 15 minutes while the lid is closed. Add the chicken wings and Serrano chili peppers to the grill. Grill for 5 minutes per side.
7. Remove chili peppers and place them in a food processor. Grill the chicken for another 20 minutes.
8. Add the rest of the ingredients to the food processor. Pulse until smooth.
9. Dip the chicken wings in the sauce.
10. Grill for 5 minutes and serve.
Nutrition: Calories: 140 │ Fat: 5 g. │ Carbs: 6 g. │ Fiber: 2 g.

187.   Smoked Fried Chicken

Preparation time: 1 hour and 30 minutes
Cooking time: 3 hours
Servings: 6
Ingredients:
• Chicken
• Vegetable oil
• Salt and pepper to taste
• 2 tbsp. hot sauce
• ¼ buttermilk
• 2 tbsp. brown sugar
• 1 tbsp. poultry dry rub
• 2 tbsp. onion powder
• 2 tbsp. garlic powder
• 2 ½ cups all-purpose flour
• Peanut oil
Directions:
1. Set the Traeger wood pellet grill to 200°F.
2. Preheat it for 15 minutes while the lid is closed.
3. Drizzle chicken with vegetable oil and sprinkle with salt and pepper.
4. Smoke chicken for 2 hours and 30 minutes.
5. In a bowl, mix the hot sauce, buttermilk, and sugar.
6. Soak the smoked chicken in the mixture.
7. Cover and refrigerate for 1 hour.
8. Mix the dry rub, onion powder, garlic powder, and flour in another bowl.
9. Coat the chicken with the mixture.
10. Heat the peanut oil in a pan over medium heat.
11. Fry the chicken until golden and crispy.
Nutrition: Calories: 230 | Fat: 7 g. | Carbs: 1 g. | Fiber: 2 g.

188.   Maple Turkey Breast

Preparation time: 4 hours and 30 minutes
Cooking time: 2 hours
Servings: 4
Ingredients:
• 3 tbsp. olive oil
• 3 tbsp. dark brown sugar
• 3 tbsp. garlic, minced
• 2 tbsp. Cajun seasoning
• 2 tbsp. Worcestershire sauce
• 1 lb. breast fillets
Directions:
1. In a bowl, combine olive oil, sugar, garlic, Cajun seasoning, and Worcestershire sauce.
2. Soak the turkey breast fillets in the marinade.
3. Cover and marinate for 4 hours.
4. Grill the turkey at 180°F for 2 hours.
Nutrition: Calories: 290 | Fat: 15 g. | Carbs: 20 g. | Fiber: 1 g.

189.   Chicken Tikka Masala

Preparation time: 12 hours and 40 minutes
Cooking time: 1 hour
Servings: 4
Ingredients:
• 2 tbsp. garam masala
• 2 tbsp. smoked paprika
• 2 tbsp. ground coriander
• 2 tbsp. ground cumin
• 1 tsp. ground cayenne pepper
• 1 tsp. turmeric
• 1 onion, sliced
• garlic cloves, minced
• ¼ cup olive oil
• 1 tbsp. ginger, chopped
• 1 tbsp. lemon juice
• 1 ½ cups Greek yogurt
• 1 tbsp. lime juice
• 1 tbsp. curry powder
• Salt to taste
• 1 tbsp. lime juice
• 12 chicken drumsticks
• Chopped cilantro
Directions:
1. Make the marinade by mixing all the spices, onion, garlic, olive oil, ginger, lemon juice, yogurt, lime juice, curry powder, and salt.
2. Transfer to a food processor. Pulse until smooth.
3. Divide the mixture into 2. Marinade the chicken in the first bowl.
4. Cover the bowl and refrigerate for 12 hours.
5. Set the Traeger wood pellet grill to high.
6. Preheat it for 15 minutes while the lid is closed.
7. Grill the chicken for 50 minutes. Garnish with chopped cilantro.
Nutrition: Calories: 140 | Fat: 5 g. | Carbs: 6 g. | Fiber: 2 g.

190.   Turkey With Apricot Barbecue Glaze

Preparation time: 30 minutes
Cooking time: 30 minutes
Servings: 4
Ingredients:
• 4 turkey breast fillets
• 4 tbsp. chicken rub
• 1 cup apricot barbecue sauce
Directions:
1. Preheat the Traeger wood pellet grill to 365°F for 15 minutes while the lid is closed.
2. Season the turkey fillets using the chicken rub.
3. Grill the turkey fillets for 5 minutes per side.
4. Brush both sides using the barbecue sauce. Then, grill for another 5 minutes per side.
Nutrition: Calories: 140 | Fat: 5 g. | Carbs: 6 g. | Fiber: 2 g.

191. Turkey Meatballs

Preparation time: 40 minutes
Cooking time: 40 minutes
Servings: 8
Ingredients:
- 1 whole KIKOK approx. 1.5 kg
- 400–500 g. potatoes
- 2–3 medium-sized onions
- 3–4 garlic cloves
- Rub garlic/Chili pepper from Traeger

Directions:
1. Peel and boil potatoes; in the recipe, there are triplets where the skin can be eaten. Cut the onions into rings and halve them; either leave the garlic cloves whole or divide them into 4–5 parts.
2. Spread the potatoes on a baking sheet and press gently until flat; spread the garlic and onions over the potatoes. Remove the back from the KIKOK and season the chicken from both sides. Place the KIKOK on the potatoes and Traeger smoke for about 30 minutes at about 100°C, then the temperature to 190°C and heat a barbecue to a core temperature of 80°C.
3. The potatoes catch the leaked fat and become wonderfully "choppy," making them crispy from below. If you have now used potatoes without their skins, you can process them into the puree and serve them gratinated with cheese to serve with the chicken

Nutrition: Calories: 230 | Fat: 7 g. | Carbs: 1 g. | Fiber: 2 g.

192. Herb Roasted Turkey

Preparation time: 15 minutes
Cooking time: 3 hours and 30 minutes
Servings: 12
Ingredients:
- 14 lb. turkey, cleaned
- 2 tbsp. mixed herbs, chopped
- Pork and poultry rub as needed
- ¼ tsp. ground black pepper
- 3 chopped butter, unsalted, melted
- 8 chopped butter, unsalted, softened
- 2 cups chicken broth

Directions:
1. Remove the giblets from the turkey, wash it inside and out, pat dry with paper towels, place it on a roasting pan and tuck the turkey wings with butcher's string.
2. Switch on the Traeger grill, fill the grill hopper with hickory-flavored wood pellets, power the grill on by using the control panel, select 'smoke' on the temperature dial, or set the temperature to 325°F and let it preheat for a minimum of 15 minutes.
3. Meanwhile, prepare herb butter and for this, take a small bowl, place the softened butter in it, add black pepper and mixed herbs and beat until fluffy.

4. Using the handle of a wooden spoon, massage some of the prepared herb butter underneath the turkey's skin to distribute the butter evenly.
5. Then, rub the turkey's skin with melted butter, season with pork and poultry rub, and pour the broth into the roasting pan.
6. Open the lid, place a roasting pan containing turkey on the grill grate, close the grill, and smoke for 3 hours and 30 minutes, or until the internal temperature reaches 165°F and the top has turned golden brown.
7. Transfer the turkey to a cutting board to rest for 30 minutes before carving into slices and serving.

Nutrition: Calories: 154.6 | Fat: 3.1 g. | Carbs: 8.4 g. | Protein: 28.8 g. | Fiber: 0.4 g.

193. Turkey Legs

Preparation time: 24 hours
Cooking time: 5 hours
Servings: 4
Ingredients:
- 4 turkey legs
- For the brine:
- ½ cup curing salt
- 1 tbsp. whole black peppercorns
- 1 cup BBQ rub
- ½ cup brown sugar
- 2 bay leaves
- 2 tsp. liquid smoke
- 16 cups warm water
- 4 cups ice
- 8 cups cold water

Directions:
1. Prepare the brine by filling a large stockpot halfway with warm water, adding peppercorn, bay leaves, and liquid smoke, stirring in salt, sugar, and BBQ rub, and bringing it to a boil.
2. Remove the pot from the heat, bring it to room temperature, add cold water and ice cubes, and chill the brine in the refrigerator. Then add the turkey legs and completely submerge them in it. Refrigerate for 24 hours.
3. After 24 hours, remove turkey legs from the brine, rinse well and pat dry with paper towels. When ready to cook, switch on the Traeger grill, fill the grill hopper with hickory-flavored wood pellets, power the grill on by using the control panel, select 'smoke' on the temperature dial, or set the temperature to 250°F and let it preheat for a minimum of 15 minutes.
4. Open the lid, place the turkey legs on the grill grate, close the grill, and smoke for 5 hours, or until nicely browned and the internal temperature reaches 165°F.
5. Serve immediately.

Nutrition: Calories: 416 | Fat: 13.3 g. | Carbs: 0 g. | Protein: 69.8 g. | Fiber: 0 g.

194.   Turkey Breast

Preparation time: 12 hours
Cooking time: 8 hours
Servings: 6
Ingredients:
For the brine:
• 2 lb. turkey breast, deboned
• 2 tbsp. ground black pepper
• ¼ cup salt
• 1 cup brown sugar
• 4 cups cold water
• For the BBQ rub:
• 2 tbsp. onions, dried
• 2 tbsp. garlic powder
• ¼ cup paprika
• 2 tbsp. ground black pepper
• 1 tbsp. salt
• 2 tbsp. brown sugar
• 2 tbsp. red chili powder
• 2 tbsp. sugar
• 2 tbsp. ground cumin
Directions:
1. Prepare the brine by combining salt, black pepper, and sugar in a large mixing bowl, then adding water and stirring until the sugar has dissolved.
2. Place the turkey breast in it, submerge it completely, and refrigerate it for at least 12 hours.
3. Meanwhile, make the BBQ rub by combining all ingredients in a small bowl and stirring until combined. Set aside until needed.
4. After that, remove the turkey breast from the brine and season it generously with the prepared BBQ rub.
5. When ready to cook, switch on the Traeger grill, fill the grill hopper with apple-flavored wood pellets, power the grill on by using the control panel, select 'smoke' on the temperature dial, or set the temperature to 180°F and let it preheat for a minimum of 15 minutes.
6. Open the lid, place the turkey breast on the grill grate, close the grill, raise the smoking temperature to 225°F, and smoke for 8 hours, or until the internal temperature reaches 160°F.
7. Transfer the turkey to a cutting board to rest for 10 minutes before slicing and serving.
Nutrition: Calories: 250 | Fat: 5 g. | Carbs: 31 g. | Protein: 18 g. | Fiber: 5 g.

195.   Spicy BBQ Chicken

Preparation time: 8 hours and 10 minutes
Cooking time: 3 hours
Servings: 6
Ingredients:
• 1 whole chicken, cleaned
• For the marinade:
• 1 medium white onion, peeled
• Thai chilies
• 5 garlic cloves, peeled
• 1 scotch bonnet
• 3 tbsp. salt
• 2 tbsp. sugar
• 2 tbsp. sweet paprika
• 4 cups grapeseed oil
Directions:
1. Prepare the marinade; place all its ingredients in a food processor and pulse for 2 minutes until smooth.
2. Smoother whole chicken with the prepared marinade and let it marinate in the refrigerator for a minimum of 8 hours.
3. When ready to cook, switch on the Traeger grill, fill the grill hopper with apple-flavored wood pellets, power the grill on by using the control panel, select 'smoke' on the temperature dial, or set the temperature to 300°F and let it preheat for a minimum of 15 minutes.
4. When the grill has preheated, open the lid, place the chicken on the grill grate breast-side up, shut the grill, and smoke for 3 hours until the internal temperature of the chicken reaches 165°F.
5. Transfer chicken to a cutting board, let it rest for 15 minutes, then cut into slices and serve.
Nutrition: Calories: 100 | Fat: 2.8 g. | Carbs: 13 g. | Protein: 3.5 g. | Fiber: 2 g.

196.   Teriyaki Wings

Preparation time: 8 hours
Cooking time: 50 minutes
Servings: 8
Ingredients:
• 2 ½ lb. large chicken wings
• 1 tbsp. toasted sesame seeds
• For the marinade:
• 2 scallions, sliced
• 2 tbsp. grated ginger
• ½ tsp. garlic, minced
• ¼ cup brown sugar
• ½ cup soy sauce
• 2 tbsp. rice wine vinegar
• 2 tbsp. sesame oil
• ¼ cup water
Directions:
1. Remove the tips from the chicken wings, cut each chicken wing through the joint into three pieces, and place them in a large plastic bag.
2. Prepare the sauce by placing a small saucepan over medium-high heat, adding all the ingredients, stirring until combined, and bringing to a boil.
3. Then, reduce the heat to medium and set aside for 10 minutes before serving.
4. Pour the sauce over the chicken wings, seal the bag, turn it upside down to coat the chicken wings with the sauce and let it marinate for a minimum of 8 hours in the refrigerator.
5. When ready to cook, switch on the Traeger grill, fill the grill hopper with maple-flavored wood pellets, power the

grill on by using the control panel, select 'smoke' on the temperature dial, or set the temperature to 350°F and let it preheat for a minimum of 15 minutes.

6. Meanwhile, when the grill is hot, open the lid, place the chicken wings on the grill grate, close the lid, and smoke for 50 minutes, turning halfway, until crispy and the meat is no longer pink.

7. Transfer the chicken wings to a serving dish, sprinkle with sesame seeds, and serve.

Nutrition: Calories: 150 | Fat: 7.5 g. | Carbs: 6 g. | Protein: 12 g.

197. Louisiana Hot Apple-Smoked Turkey

Preparation time: 10 minutes
Cooking time: 3 hours, 45 minutes
Servings: 8–10
Ingredients:
- 1 whole turkey, rinsed, patted dry (14-lb, 6.3-kgs)
- The spice injection:
- 1 bottle beer, room temperature (12-oz, 230-MLS)
- ½ cup butter, melted
- Garlic cloves, peeled
- 2 tbsp. Worcestershire sauce
- 2 tbsp. creole seasoning
- 1 tbsp. liquid crab boil
- 1 tbsp. Louisiana hot sauce
- 1 tbsp. sea salt
- ½ tsp. cayenne pepper
- For the rub:
- ½ tsp. onion powder
- ½ tsp. garlic powder
- 1 tsp. paprika
- ¼ tsp. cumin
- ½ tsp. dried thyme
- ¼ tsp. dried oregano –tsp.
- ¼ tsp. sea salt
- ¼ tsp. freshly ground black pepper
- ⅛ tsp. cayenne pepper
- 1 tbsp. vegetable oil

Directions:
1. Fire up your grill or smoker to 325°F (165°C). When the temperature is reached, add Applewood pellets.

2. First, prepare the injection. To a food blender, add allspice injection ingredients and blend until smooth.

3. Using a meat syringe, inject the spicy mixture into the meat all over. Space the injections approximately 1-ins (5-cms) apart.

4. Next, prepare the rub. In a bowl, combine all rubbed ingredients, excluding the oil.

5. Season the turkey all over and in its cavity with the prepared rub.

Nutrition: Calories: 321 | Total Carbohydrates: 15.5 g. 6% | Dietary Fiber: 0.3 g. 1% | Total Sugars: 13.5 g. | Protein:

42.2 g. Vitamin D: 0mcg 0% | Calcium: 25 mg. 2% | Iron: 4 mg. 24% | Potassium: 454 mg. 10%

198. Whole Maple-Smoked Turkey

Preparation time: 15 minutes
Cooking time: 5 hours 35 minutes
Servings: 15–20
Ingredients:
- 1 whole turkey (16 –lb., 7.2-kgs)
- Olive oil
- 1 cup maple syrup, 100% pure
- ¼ cup butter
- Seasoning salt
- Freshly ground black pepper

Directions:
1. Load your grill with maple pellets and preheat to 350°F (177°C).

2. Rub the whole turkey with a light coating of olive oil.

3. Place the turkey on the preheated grill, the breast side facing upward, and increase the bird's internal temperature by 100°F (39°C). It is best to use a meat thermometer to do this.

4. Reduce the grill heat down to 225°F (107°C) until the turkey achieves an internal temperature of 170°F (80°C); this will take between 4–5 hours, depending on the outside temperature and variety of wood pellets.

5. To make the glaze. In a pan, combine the maple syrup with butter, salt, and a dash of black pepper. Brush the glaze all over the bird. Continue to brush the turkey with the glaze every 60 minutes or so.

6. Remove it from the grill when the turkey reaches an internal temperature of 170°F (74°C). Cover it with aluminum foil and allow it to rest for 15–30 minutes before serving.

Nutrition: Calories: 321 Total Carbohydrate 15.5 g. 6% | Dietary Fiber: 0.3 g. 1% | Total Sugars 13.5 g. | Protein: 42.2 g. | Vitamin D: 0mcg 0% | Calcium: 25 mg. 2% | Iron: 4 mg. 24% | Potassium: 454 mg. 10%

199. Smoked Whole Chicken

Preparation time: 10 minutes
Cooking time: 1 hour 55 minutes
Servings: 4–6
Ingredients:
- 1 Whole roasting chicken (3–4 lb.)
- For the mixture:
- Garlic cloves
- ½ red onion, chopped
- ½ lemon.
- For the dry rub:
- 1 cup. brown sugar
- ½ cup Kosher salt
- tbsp. smoked paprika
- 2 tbsp. coarse black pepper
- ½ tbsp. cumin
- ½ tbsp. onion powder
- ½ tbsp. garlic powder
- 1 tsp. cayenne pepper

Directions:
1. Combine all the ingredients to make the dry rub. We only need a ¼ cup for the recipe. You can keep the rest for later use.
2. Preheat the wood pellet smoker to 225°F.
3. Ensure the chicken's cavity is clean and remove any remaining residue. Clean the chicken thoroughly and cover it with a dry rub.
4. Stuff the chicken's cavity with red onion, lemon, and garlic.
5. Tie the legs and wings of the chicken closer to the body. It is done to make sure that they do not overcook.
6. Put the chicken inside the smoker. Let it smoke for an hour. After an hour, get the temperature high up to 350°F. Until the internal temperature reaches 160°F, do not take the chicken out. The time it reaches that temperature depends on the size of the bird.
7. After taking out the chicken, let it rest for 10 minutes before serving it.

Nutrition: Calories: 501 | Protein: 44 g. | Vitamin D: 5mcg 26% | Calcium: 122 mg. 9% | Iron: 16 mg: 90% | Potassium: 625 mg.

200. Smoked Whole Chicken With Carolina Glaze

Preparation time: 10 minutes
Cooking time: 2 hours
Servings: 4
Ingredients:
- (4–5 lb.) Fryer chicken (halved)
- 2 tbsp. salt
- 2 tbsp. freshly cracked pepper
- Glaze
- For the glaze:
- 2 cups Carolina BBQ sauce
- ⅔ cup honey
- 2 tbsp. Dijon mustard

Directions:
1. First, rinse your chicken thoroughly and pat it dry.
2. Take a cookie sheet and place the chicken pieces on it.
3. Season it well with salt and pepper. Put the chicken in the refrigerator in an isolated spot. This step should be almost 6 hours before you want to start cooking.
4. Now preheat the smoker up to 225°F.
5. Take the chicken out of the refrigerator. The color of the chicken may be darker, but it is normal after dehydration and salting.
6. Now, put the chicken on the smoker. Wait until the internal temperature is 150–155°F. When it reaches that temperature, put the glaze on the chicken with a brush.
7. Continue cooking until the temperature reaches 165°F, then take the chicken out of the smoker. Glaze it once more. Cover the chicken with a foil sheet so that the juices redistribute. Leave it like that for 15 minutes.
8. Serve and enjoy.

Nutrition: Calories: 641 | Protein: 0.7 g. | Vitamin D: 0mcg | Calcium: 19 mg. | Iron: 1 mg. | Potassium: 223 mg.

201. Cajun Smoked Chicken Wings

Preparation time: 8 minutes
Cooking time: 1 hour 30 minutes
Servings: 6–8
Ingredients:
- 3 lb. chicken wings (cut into drumettes and flats)
- For the rub:
- ¼ tsp. Kosher salt
- 1 tbsp. baking powder
- 1 tsp. paprika
- ½ tsp. garlic powder
- ½ tsp. onion powder
- ½ tsp. dry thyme
- ¼ tsp. oregano, dried
- ¼ tsp. cumin
- ¼ tsp. black pepper
- ⅛ tsp. cayenne pepper
- For the sauce:
- ¼ cup butter
- ¼ cup Louisiana-style hot sauce
- 1 tbsp. Worcestershire sauce

Directions:
1. Firstly, mix garlic powder, paprika, onion powder, cumin, oregano, cayenne, baking powder, thyme, salt, and pepper to prepare the rub.
2. Rinse your chicken wings carefully and pat them with dry towels. Take a large bowl to fit all of the wings. Sprinkle the rub on top of it. Make sure the wings are evenly coated.
3. Put the wire rack on the baking and line with aluminum foil; arrange wings closely in a single layer, and place it in the refrigerator overnight.

4. Just keep the lid open until the fire is established in the smoker. Preheat for 10–15 minutes with the lid closed.

5. Smoke the chicken wings for about 30 minutes. Crank up the temperature after 30 minutes to about 350°F. Let it smoke for about 45 minutes.

6. Now take out the wings in a bowl and add the sauce to coat all the wings.

7. Transfer to a platter, and the dish is ready to serve.

Nutrition: Calories: 501 | Protein: 44 g. | Vitamin D: 5mcg 26% | Calcium: 122 mg. 9% | Iron: 16 mg: 90% | Potassium: 625 mg.

202. Smoked Chicken

Preparation time: 10 minutes
Cooking time: 4 hours
Servings: 6
Ingredients:
- 1-gallon water
- ½ cup Kosher salt
- 1 cup brown sugar
- For the rub:
- Traeger big game rub
- 1 lemon, halved
- 1 tbsp. garlic, minced
- 3 garlic cloves, whole
- 1 yellow onion, medium, quartered
- 4–5 thyme sprigs
- 3–3½ lbs. whole chicken

Directions:
1. Dissolve the brown sugar and kosher salt in a gallon of water. Place the chicken in this brine, soaking it completely. Refrigerate the chicken overnight.

2. Preheat the smoker to 225°F for about 15 minutes with the lid closed.

3. Take the chicken out from the brine and dry it.

4. Rub the chicken with the Traeger big game rub and minced garlic.

5. Now, stuff the cavity with garlic, lemon, onion, and thyme. Tie the chicken legs.

6. Place the chicken on the grill grate and smoke it for about 3 hours or until the internal temperature reaches 160°F.

7. Remove the chicken and rest it for about 30 minutes.

8. Slice and serve!

Nutrition: Carbohydrates: 0 g. | Protein: 26 g. | Fat: 16 g.

203. Chicken, Applewood Smoked

Preparation time: 15 minutes
Cooking time: 5 hours
Servings: 6
Method of Preparation: Smoking
Ingredients:
- 2 tbsp. chili powder
- ¼ cup dark brown sugar, packed
- 1 tbsp. smoked paprika
- 1 tbsp. garlic powder
- 1 tbsp. onion powder
- 1 tsp. salt
- 1 tbsp. oregano
- 4–5 lbs. whole chicken

Directions:
1. Clean the chicken and rinse it with cold water. Dry it with a paper towel.

2. Cut the chicken at the center. Put it in a glass dish.

3. Mix all the dry ingredients in a small bowl. Rub the chicken in the dish well.

4. Wrap the bowl with plastic and put it in the refrigerator for about 12 hours.

5. Preheat, the smoker to 225°F. Put the chicken in the smoker with the breast side up and close the lid.

6. Cook it for about 4–5 hours or until the chicken reaches an internal temperature of 165°F.

7. Remove the chicken and rest it for about 10 minutes.

8. Slice and serve!

Nutrition: Carbohydrates: 8 g. | Protein: 28.9 g. | Fat: 23 g.

Chapter 11. Fish and Seafood Recipes

204.   Traeger Salmon With Togarashi

Preparation time: 5 minutes
Cooking time: 20 minutes
Servings: 3
Ingredients:
• 1 salmon fillet
• ¼ cup olive oil
• ½ tbsp. Kosher salt
• 1 tbsp. Togarashi seasoning
Directions:
1. Preheat your Traeger to 400°F.
2. Place the salmon on a sheet lined with non-stick foil with the skin side down.
3. Rub the oil into the meat, then sprinkle salt and Togarashi.
4. Place the salmon on the grill and cook for 20 minutes or until the internal temperature reaches 145°F with the lid closed.
5. Remove from the Traeger and serve when hot.
Nutrition: Calories 119 | Total Fat: 10 g. | Saturated Fat: 2 g. | Sodium: 720 mg.

205.   Trager Rockfish

Preparation time: 10 minutes
Cooking time: 20 minutes
Servings: 6
Ingredients:
• 6 rockfish fillets
• 1 lemon, sliced
• ¾ tbsp. salt
• 2 tbsp. fresh dill, chopped
• ½ tbsp. garlic powder
• ½ tbsp. onion powder
• 6 tbsp. butter
Directions:
1. Preheat your Traeger to 400°F.
2. Season the fish with salt, dill, garlic, and onion powder on both sides, then place it in a baking dish.
3. Place a pat of butter and a lemon slice on each fillet. Place the baking dish in the Traeger and close the lid.
4. Cook for 20 minutes or until the fish is no longer translucent and is flaky.
5. Remove from Traeger and let rest before serving.
Nutrition: Calories: 270 | Total Fat: 17 g. | Saturated Fat: 9 g. | Total Carbs: 2 g. | Net Carbs: 2 g. | Protein: 28 g. | Sodium: 381 mg.

206.   Traeger Grilled Lingcod

Preparation time: 10 minutes
Cooking time: 15 minutes
Servings: 6
Ingredients:
• 2 lb. lingcod fillets
• ½ tbsp. salt
• ½ tbsp. white pepper
• ¼ tbsp. cayenne pepper
• Lemon wedges
Directions:
1. Preheat your Traeger to 375°F.
2. Place the lingcod on parchment paper or a grill mat
3. Season the fish with salt, pepper, and top with lemon wedges.
4. Cook the fish for 15 minutes or until the internal temperature reaches 145°F.
Nutrition: Calories 245 | Total Fat: 2 g. | Total Carbs: 2 g. | Protein: 52 g. | Sugars: 1 g. | Fiber: 1 g. | Sodium: 442 mg.

207.   Crab Stuffed Lingcod

Preparation time: 20 minutes
Cooking time: 30 minutes
Servings: 6
Ingredients:
Lemon cream sauce:
• 4 garlic cloves
• 1 shallot
• 1 leek
• 2 tbsp. olive oil
• 1 tbsp. salt
• ¼ tbsp. black pepper
• 3 tbsp. butter
• ¼ cup white wine
• 1 cup whipping cream
• 2 tbsp. lemon juice
• 1 tbsp. lemon zest
• Crab mix:
• 1 lb. crab meat
• ⅓ cup mayo
• ⅓ cup sour cream
• ⅓ cup lemon cream sauce
• ¼ green onion, chopped
• ¼ tbsp. black pepper
• ½ tbsp. old bay seasoning
Fish:
• 2 lb. lingcod
• 1 tbsp. olive oil
• 1 tbsp. salt
• 1 tbsp. paprika
• 1 tbsp. green onion, chopped
• 1 tbsp. Italian parsley

Directions:

Lemon cream sauce:

1. Chop garlic, shallot, and leeks, then add oil, salt, pepper, and butter to a saucepan.
2. Sauté over medium heat until the shallot is translucent.
3. Deglaze with white wine, then add whipping cream. Bring the sauce to boil, reduce heat, and simmer for 3 minutes.
4. Remove from heat and add lemon juice and lemon zest. Transfer the sauce to a blender and blend until smooth.
5. Set aside ⅓ cup for the crab mix
6. Crab Mix:
7. Add all the ingredients to a mixing bowl and mix thoroughly until well combined.
8. Set aside
9. Fish
10. Fire up your Traeger to high heat, then slice the fish into 6 oz. portions.
11. Lay the fish on its side on a cutting board and slice it ¾ way through the middle, leaving a ½ inch on each end to have a nice pouch.
12. Rub the oil into the fish, then place them on a baking sheet. Sprinkle with salt.
13. Stuff crab mix into each fish, sprinkle paprika, and place it on the grill.
14. Cook for 15 minutes or more if the fillets are more than 2 inches thick.
15. Remove the fish and transfer them to serving platters. Pour the remaining lemon cream sauce on each fish and garnish with onions and parsley.

Nutrition: Calories: 476 | Total Fat: 33 g. | Saturated Fat: 14 g. | Total Carbs: 6 g. | Net Carbs: 5 g. | Protein: 38 g. | Sugars: 3 g. | Fiber: 1 g. | Sodium: 1032 mg.

208.   Traeger Smoked Shrimp

Preparation time: 10 minutes
Cooking time: 10 minutes
Servings: 6
Ingredients:
• 1 lb. tail-on shrimp, uncooked
• ½ tbsp. onion powder
• ½ tbsp. garlic powder
• ½ tbsp. salt
• 4 tbsp. teriyaki sauce
• 2 tbsp. green onion, minced
• 4 tbsp. sriracha mayo

Directions:
1. Peel the shrimp shells leaving the tail on, then wash well and rise.
2. Drain well and pat dry with a paper towel.
3. Preheat your Traeger to 450°F.
4. Season the shrimp with onion powder, garlic powder, and salt. Place the shrimp in the Traeger and cook for 6 minutes on each side.
5. Remove the shrimp from the Traeger and toss with teriyaki sauce, then garnish with onions and mayo.

Nutrition: Calories 87 | Total Carbs: 2 g. | Net Carbs: 2 g. | Protein: 16 g. | Sodium: 1241 mg.

209.   Grilled Shrimp Kabobs

Preparation time: 5 minutes
Cooking time: 10 minutes
Servings: 4
Ingredients:
• 1 lb. colossal shrimp, peeled and deveined
• 2 tbsp. oil
• ½ tbsp. garlic salt
• ½ tbsp. salt
• ⅛ tbsp. pepper
• 6 skewers
Directions:
1. Preheat your Traeger to 375°F.
2. Pat the shrimp dry with a paper towel.
3. In a mixing bowl, mix oil, garlic salt, salt, and pepper
4. Toss the shrimp in the mixture until well coated.
5. Skewer the shrimp and cook in the Traeger with the lid closed for 4 minutes.
6. Open the lid, flip the skewers, cook for another 4 minutes, or wait until the shrimp is pink and the flesh is opaque.
7. Serve.

Nutrition: Calories: 325 | Protein: 20 g. | Sodium: 120 mg.

210.   Bacon-Wrapped Shrimp

Preparation time: 20 minutes
Cooking time: 10 minutes
Servings: 12
Ingredients:
• 1 lb. raw shrimp
• ½ tbsp. salt
• ¼ tbsp. garlic powder
• 1 lb. bacon, cut into halves
Directions:
1. Preheat your Traeger to 350°F.
2. Remove the shrimp's shells and tails, then dry them with paper towels.
3. Season the shrimp with salt and garlic, then wrap in bacon and secure with a toothpick.
4. Place the shrimp on a baking rack sprayed with cooking spray.
5. Cook for 10 minutes on one side, flip and cook for another 10 minutes on the other, or until the bacon is crisp enough.
6. Serve immediately after removing from the Traeger.

Nutrition: Calories: 204 | Total Fat: 14 g. | Saturated Fat: 5 g. | Total Carbs: 1 g. | Net Carbs: 1 g. | Protein: 18 g. | Sodium: 939 mg.

211. Traeger Spot Prawn Skewers

Preparation time: 10 minutes
Cooking time: 10 minutes
Servings: 6
Ingredients:
• 2 lb. spot prawns
• 2 tbsp. oil
• Salt and pepper to taste
• **Directions:**
• Preheat your Traeger to 400°F.
• Skewer your prawns with soaked skewers, then generously sprinkle with oil, salt, and pepper.
• Place the skewers on the grill, then cook with the lid closed for 5 minutes on each side.
• Remove the skewers and serve when hot.
Nutrition: Calories: 221 | Total Fat: 7 g. | Saturated Fat: 1 g. | Total Carbs: 2 g. | Net Carbs: 2 g. | Protein: 34 g. | Sodium: 1481 mg.

212. Traeger Bacon-Wrapped Scallops

Preparation time: 15 minutes
Cooking time: 20 minutes
Servings: 8
Ingredients:
• 1 lb. sea scallops
• ½ lb. bacon
• Sea salt
Directions:
1. Preheat your Traeger to 375°F.
2. Pat dries the scallops with a towel, then wrap them with a piece of bacon and secure them with a toothpick.
3. Lay the scallops on the grill with the bacon side down. Close the lid and cook for 5 minutes on each side.
4. Keep the scallops on the bacon side so that you will not get grill marks on the scallops.
5. Serve and enjoy.
Nutrition: Calories: 261 | Total Fat: 14 g. | Saturated Fat: 5 g. | Total Carbs: 5 g. | Net Carbs: 5 g. | Protein: 28 g. | Sodium: 1238 mg.

213. Traeger Lobster Tail

Preparation time: 10 minutes
Cooking time: 15 minutes
Servings: 2
Ingredients:
• 10 oz. lobster tail
• ¼ tbsp. old bay seasoning
• ¼ tbsp. Himalayan salt
• 2 tbsp. butter, melted
• 1 tbsp. fresh parsley, chopped
Directions:
1. Preheat your Traeger to 450°F.
2. Slice the tail down the middle and season with salt and bay seasoning.

3. Place the tails directly on the grill, meat side up. Grill for 15 minutes until the internal temperature reaches 140 degrees Fahrenheit.
4. Remove from Traeger and brush with butter.
5. Serve when hot, garnished with parsley.
Nutrition: Calories: 305 | Total Fat: 14 g. | Saturated Fat: 8 g. | Total Carbs: 5 g. | Net Carbs: 5 g. | Protein: 38 g. | Sodium: 684 mg.

214. Salmon Cakes

Preparation time: 5 minutes
Cooking time: 25 minutes
Servings: 4
Ingredients:
• 1 cup cooked salmon, flaked
• ½ red bell pepper, chopped
• 2 eggs, beaten
• ¼ cup mayonnaise
• ½ tbsp. dry sweet rub
• 1 ½ cups breadcrumbs
• 1 tbsp. mustard
• Olive oil
Directions:
1. Combine all the ingredients except the olive oil in a bowl.
2. Form patties from this mixture. Let sit for 15 minutes.
3. Turn on your wood pellet grill.
4. Set it to 350°F. Add a baking pan to the grill.
5. Drizzle a little olive oil on top of the pan.
6. Add the salmon cakes to the pan.
7. Grill each side for 3–4 minutes.
Nutrition: Calories: 119 | Total Fat: 10 g. | Saturated Fat: 2 g. | Sodium: 720 mg.

215. Swordfish Steaks With Corn Salsa

Preparation time: 10 minutes
Cooking time: 30 minutes
Servings: 4
Ingredients:
• 4 whole ears corn, husked
• Olive oil, as needed
• Salt and black pepper to taste
• 1-pint cherry tomatoes
• 1 whole Serrano chili, chopped
• 1 whole red onion, diced
• 1 whole lime, juiced
• 4 whole swordfish fillets
Directions:
1. When ready to cook, put the Traeger to High and preheat for 15 minutes.
2. Brush the corn with olive oil and season with salt and pepper. Place the corn on the grill grate and grill for 12–15 minutes, or until cooked through and lightly browned. Set aside to cool.
3. Once the corn has cooled, cut the kernels from the corn and transfer them to a medium bowl. Stir in the tomatoes, serrano, red onion, and lime juice.

4. Brush the swordfish fillets with olive oil and season with salt and pepper.

5. Arrange the fillets on the grill grate and grill for about 18 minutes, or until the fish is opaque and flakes easily when pressed with a fork.

6. Serve the grilled swordfish topped with corn salsa.

Nutrition: Calories: 270 | Total Fat: 17 g. | Saturated Fat: 9 g. | Total Carbs: 2 g. | Net Carbs: 2 g. | Protein: 28 g. | Sodium: 381 mg.

216.   Grilled Oysters With Veggie Sauce

Preparation time: 20 minutes
Cooking time: 25 minutes
Servings: 4
Ingredients:
• 5 tbsp. extra-virgin olive oil
• 2 ½ onions, chopped
• 1 ½ red bell pepper, chopped
• 2 lemons, juiced
• 3 bay leaves, dried
• 5 tbsp. garlic, minced
• 3 tbsp. Traeger Chicken rub
• 3 tsp. thyme, dried
• ¼ cup white wine
• 5 tbsp. hot pepper sauce
• 3 tbsp. Worcestershire sauce
• 4 butter sticks
• 12 whole oysters, cleaned and shucked
• Italian cheese blend, as needed
Directions:
1. When ready to cook, put the Traeger to High and preheat, lid closed for 15 minutes.

2. Heat the olive oil in a cast-iron pan over medium heat. Add the onions, bell peppers, lemon juice, bay leaves, garlic, Traeger Chicken rub, and thyme to the pan. Sauté the vegetable mixture for 5–7 minutes, until the onions are translucent and the peppers are tender.

3. Add the white wine, hot pepper sauce, Worcestershire sauce, and butter to the pan. Sauté for another 15 minutes.

4. Place the oysters and top with the sauce—Cook for 5 minutes.

5. Top with Italian cheese and serve hot.

Nutrition: Calories: 261 | Total Fat: 14 g. | Saturated Fat: 5 g. | Total Carbs: 5 g. | Net Carbs: 5 g. | Protein: 28 g. | Sodium: 1238 mg.

217.   Crispy Fried Halibut Fish Sticks

Preparation time: 10 minutes
Cooking time: 3–4 minutes
Servings: 4
Ingredients:
• Extra-virgin olive oil, as needed
• 1 ½ lb. (680 g.) halibut, rinsed, patted dry, and cut into 1-inch strips
• ½ cup all-purpose flour
• 1 ½ tp. salt

• 1 tsp. ground black pepper
• 2 large eggs
• 1½ cups panko bread crumbs
• 2 tbsp. parsley, dried
• 1 tsp. dill weed, dried
Directions:
1. When ready to cook, put Traeger temperature to 500°F (260°C) and preheat, lid closed for 15 minutes.

2. Place a Dutch oven inside the grill to preheat for about 10 minutes, with enough olive oil to fry the fish.

3. In a bowl, stir together the all-purpose flour, salt, and pepper. In a separate bowl, beat the eggs. In a third bowl, combine the panko, parsley, and dill.

4. Dredge the fish fillets in the flour mixture, the eggs, and the panko mixture.

5. Place the coated fish fillets in the oil and fry for about 3–4 minutes, or until they reach an internal temperature of 130°F (54°C).

6. Serve warm.

Nutrition: Calories: 245 | Total Fat: 2 g. | Total Carbs: 2 g. | Protein: 52 g. | Sugars: 1 g. | Fiber: 1 g. | Sodium: 442 mg.

218.   White Fish Steaks With Orange Basil Pesto

Preparation time: 10 minutes
Cooking time: 15 minutes
Servings: 4
Ingredients:
• 1 orange, juiced
• 2 cups fresh basil
• 1 cup flat-leaf parsley, chopped
• ½ cup toasted walnuts
• 2 tsp. orange zest
• ½ cup olive oil
• 1 cup grated Parmesan cheese
• 4 white fish steaks, rinsed and patted dry
• ½ tsp. coarse sea salt
• ½ tsp. black pepper
Directions:
1. Make the pesto: In a food processor, combine the orange juice, basil, parsley, walnuts, and orange zest and pulse until finely chopped. With the machine running, slowly drizzle in the olive oil until the mixture is emulsified.

2. Scrape the pesto into a bowl and stir in the Parmesan cheese.

3. Brush the fish steaks with olive oil and season with salt and pepper.

4. Arrange the fish steaks on the grill grate. Grill for 12–15 minutes, turning once with a thin-bladed metal spatula, or until the fish is opaque and breaks into chunks when pressed with a fork.

5. Transfer the steaks to a platter. Drizzle with the prepared pesto and serve immediately.

Nutrition: Calories: 245 | Total Fat: 2 g. | Total Carbs: 2 g. | Protein: 52 g. | Sugars: 1 g. | Fiber: 1 g. | Sodium: 442 mg.

219. Grilled Salmon Teriyaki Sauce

Preparation time: 10 minutes
Cooking time: 15 minutes
Servings: 2
Ingredients:
• 1 cup soy sauce
• 6 tbsp. brown sugar
• 1 tbsp. ginger, minced
• 4 garlic cloves
• Juice and zest of 2 whole oranges
• 4 (6 oz./170-g) pieces salmon fillets
• 1 tbsp. sesame seeds
• Toasted sesame seeds, as needed
• Chopped scallions as needed
Directions:
1. Place the soy sauce, brown sugar, ginger, garlic, orange juice, and zest in a saucepan. Bring to a boil and slowly boil for 1o minutes, or until a syrupy consistency is achieved, about a 50 percent reduction. Let cool completely. Add the salmon and sesame seeds and marinate for 1 hour.
2. Remove the salmon from the marinade and bring the sauce to a boil.
3. Place the salmon fillets straight on the grill grate, skin-side up. Cook for about 3–5 minutes per side until they are done until you're liking and occasionally, brush the salmon with the sauce.
4. Remove the salmon from the grill and serve topped with the toasted sesame seeds and chopped scallions.
Nutrition: Calories: 119 | Total Fat: 10 g. | Saturated Fat: 2 g. | Sodium: 720 mg.

220. Roasted Stuffed Rainbow Trout

Preparation time: 10 minutes
Cooking time: 15 minutes
Servings: 1
Ingredients:
• 4 tbsp. butter
• Lemon juice, as needed
• 1 whole rainbow trout, rinsed
• 1 tbsp. salt
• 1 tsp. chipotle pepper
• 2 whole oranges, sliced
• 4 sprigs thyme sprigs
• 3 whole bay leaves
• 1 garlic clove, chopped
Directions:
1. When ready to cook, custom Traeger temperature to 400°F (204°C) and preheat, lid closed for 15 minutes.
2. Melt the butter in a pot over medium-high heat. After the butter melts completely, it will begin to foam, and the milk

solids will begin to brown. After all foam subsides and the butter looks golden brown, remove the pan from the heat and drizzle in a bit of lemon juice to stop the browning process. Set aside.
3. Lay out a piece of foil 3 inches longer on each end than the fish. Drizzle the fish's exterior and cavity with brown butter and season with salt and chipotle powder. Stuff the cavity with the remaining ingredients and fold the foil into a packet.
4. Place the packet directly on the grill grate and cook for about 15 minutes, until the internal temperature reaches 145°F (63°C).
5. Remove from the grill and serve hot.
Nutrition: Calories 305 | Total Fat: 14 g. | Saturated Fat: 8 g. | Total Carbs: 5 g. | Net Carbs: 5 g. | Protein: 38 g. | Sodium: 684 mg.

221. Buttery Crab Legs

Preparation time: 10 minutes
Cooking time: 30 minutes
Servings: 4
Ingredients:
• 3 lb. (1.4 kg.) crab legs, thawed and halved
• 1 cup butter, melted
• 2 tbsp. fresh lemon juice
• 2 garlic cloves, minced
• 1 tbsp. Traeger Fin & Feather rub
• Chopped Italian parsley for garnish
Directions:
1. When ready to cook, custom Traeger temperature to 350°F (177°C) and preheat, lid closed for 15 minutes.
2. Split the crab shells open lengthwise. Transfer to the roasting pan.
3. Stick the butter, lemon juice, and garlic in a small bowl.
4. Spread the butter mixture over the crab legs, turning the legs to coat. Sprinkle the Traeger Fin & Feather rub over the legs.
5. Place the pan on the grill grate. Cook for 20–30 minutes, or until warmed through, basting once or twice with the butter sauce from the pan's bottom.
6. Transfer the crab legs to a large platter and divide the sauce and accumulated juices between 4 dipping bowls. Serve topped with parsley.
Nutrition: Calories 305 | Total Fat: 14 g. | Saturated Fat: 8 g. | Total Carbs: 5 g. | Net Carbs: 5 g. | Protein: 38 g. | Sodium: 684 mg.

222. Grilled Buttery BBQ Oysters

Preparation time: 10 minutes
Cooking time: 6 minutes
Servings: 4
Ingredients:
- 1 lb. (454 g.) unsalted butter, softened
- 1 bunch green onions, chopped, plus more for garnish
- 2 garlic cloves, minced
- 1 tbsp. Meat Church Holy Gospel BBQ rub
- 12 oysters, shucked, juice reserved
- ¼ cup seasoned bread crumbs
- 8 oz. (227 g.) shredded Pepper Jack cheese
- Traeger Sweet & Heat BBQ sauce, as needed

Directions:
1. Make the compound butter: Stir the butter, green onions, garlic, and Meat Church Holy Gospel BBQ rub in a medium bowl.
2. Lay the butter on parchment paper. Roll it up to form a log and tie each end with cooking twine. Place in the freezer for an hour to solidify.
3. Sprinkle the bread crumbs over the oysters and place them directly on the grill. Cook for 5 minutes, or until the edge of the oyster starts to curl slightly.
4. After 5 minutes, place a spoonful of compound butter in the oysters. After the butter melts, add a pinch of Pepper Jack cheese. Cook for 1 more minute.
5. Remove the oysters from the grill; top the oysters with a squirt of Traeger Sweet & Heat BBQ sauce and a few chopped onions, and then let cool for 5 minutes before serving.

Nutrition: Calories: 261 | Total Fat: 14 g. | Saturated Fat: 5 g. | Total Carbs: 5 g. | Net Carbs: 5 g. | Protein: 28 g. | Sodium: 1238 mg.

223. Smoked Vodka Salmon

Preparation time: 5 minutes
Cooking time: 1 hour
Servings: 4
Ingredients:
- 1 cup brown sugar
- 1 cup vodka
- ½ cup coarse salt
- 1 tbsp. black pepper
- 1 wild-caught salmon (1½ to 2 lbs. / 680–907 g.)
- 1 lemon, wedged, for serving
- Capers, for serving

Directions:
1. Whisk together the brown sugar, vodka, salt, and pepper in a small bowl.
2. Place the salmon in a large resealable bag. Pour in the marinade and massage into the salmon. Refrigerate for 2–4 hours.
3. Remove the salmon from the bag, rinse, and dry with paper towels.

4. Set Traeger temperature to 180°F (82°C) and preheat, lid closed for 15 minutes.
5. Place the salmon on the grill, skin-side down, and smoke for 30 minutes.
6. Increase the temperature to 225°F (107°C) and cook the salmon for an additional 45–60 minutes, or until the fish flakes easily when pressed with a fork.
7. Serve with the lemons and capers.

Nutrition: Calories: 119 | Total Fat: 10 g. | Saturated Fat: 2 g. | Sodium: 720 mg.

224. Jerk Shrimp

Preparation time: 15 minutes
Cooking time: 6 minutes
Servings: 12
Ingredients:
- 2 lb. shrimp, peeled, deveined
- 3 tbsp. olive oil
- For the spice mix:
- 1 tsp. garlic powder
- 1 tsp. sea salt
- ¼ tsp. ground cayenne
- 1 tbsp. brown sugar
- ⅛ tsp. smoked paprika
- 1 tbsp. smoked paprika
- ¼ tbsp. ground thyme
- 1 lime, zested

Directions:
1. Switch on the Traeger grill, occupy the grill hopper with flavored wood pellets, power the grill onion the Traeger grill, close the grill hopper with flavored wood pellets, power the grill on by the control panel, select 'smoke' on the temperature set the temperature to 450°F and leave it to warm for at least 5 minutes
2. Meanwhile, mix the spice by placing the ingredients in a small dish and stirring until well combined.
3. Put season the shrimp in a large mixing bowl with the spice mixture, then drizzle with oil and toss to coat completely.
4. Open the cover when the grill is hot, place the shrimp on the grill grate, close the top, and smoke for 3 minutes per side until firm and cooked through.
5. Transfer the shrimp to a serving dish and serve.

Nutrition: Calories: 131 | Fat: 4.3 g. | Carbs: 0 g. | Protein: 22 g. | Fiber: 0 g.

225.   Grilled Fish With Salsa Verde

Preparation time: 15 minutes
Cooking time: 30 minutes
Servings: 4
Ingredients:
• 2 garlic cloves
• 3 tbsp. fresh orange juice
• 1 tsp. oregano, dried
• 2 cups white onion, chopped
• ¾ cup cilantro, chopped
• 1/4 cup extra virgin olive oil plus additional for grilling
• 5 tbsp. fresh lime juice
• 1 lb. tilapia, striped bass, or sturgeon fillets
• Kosher salt and grounded pepper
• 1 cup mayonnaise
• 1 tbsp. milk
• 4 corn tortillas
• 2 avocados, peeled and sliced
• ½ small head of cabbage, cored and thinly sliced
• Salsa Verde
• Lime wedges
Intolerances:
• Gluten-Free
• Egg-Free
Directions:
1. Mix the garlic, orange juice, oregano, 1 cup onion, ¼ cup cilantro, ¼ cup oil, and 1 tbsp of lime juice in a medium bowl.
2. Add season the fish with salt and pepper to taste. Spoon the 12 onion mixture into a glass baking dish, then top with the fish.
3. Chill the leftover onion mixture over the fish for 30 minutes. Cover and refrigerate the fish for another 30 minutes.
4. Combine the mayonnaise, milk, and the remaining 2 tablespoons of lime juice in a small bowl.
5. Preheat the grill over medium-high heat and brush the grill grate with olive oil.
6. Grill the salmon in the marinade for 3–5 minutes per side or until opaque in the center.
7. Grill the tortillas till slightly burned, about 10 seconds per side. Coarsely chop the fish and put it onto a platter.
8. Serve with lime mayonnaise, tortillas, avocados, cabbage, Salsa Verde, lime wedges, and the remaining cup of sliced onion and ½ cup of cilantro.
Nutrition: Calories: 270 | Fat: 22 g. | Cholesterol: 11 mg. | Carbs: 2 g. | Protein: 20 g.

226.   Grilled Salmon Steaks With Cilantro Yogurt Sauce

Preparation time: 10 minutes
Cooking time: 20 minutes
Servings: 4
Ingredients:
• Vegetable oil (for the grill)
• 2 Serrano chilis
• 2 garlic cloves
• 1 cup cilantro leaves
• ½ cup plain whole-milk Greek yogurt
• 1 tbsp. extra virgin olive oil
• 1 tsp. honey
• Kosher salt
• 2 12-oz. bone-in salmon steaks
• Intolerances:
• Gluten-Free
• Egg-Free
Directions:
1. Preheat the grill to medium-high heat before oiling the grate.
2. Remove and discard the seeds from one chili. In a blender, combine the 2 chilis, garlic, cilantro, yogurt, oil, nectar, and 1/4 cup of water until smooth, then season with salt.
3. Half of the sauce should be kept aside in a small bowl. Season the salmon steaks with salt and pepper.
4. Grill it, turning it several times, until it darkens, about 4 minutes.
5. Continue grilling for at least 4 more, turning frequently and seasoning with residual sauce.
Nutrition: Calories: 290 | Fat: 14 g. | Cholesterol: 80 g. | Carbs: 1 g. | Protein: 38 g.

227.   Grilled Scallops With Lemony Salsa Verde

Preparation time: 15 minutes
Cooking time: 15 minutes
Servings: 2
Ingredients:
• 2 tbsp. vegetable oil and more for the grill
• 12 large sea scallops, side muscle removed
• Kosher salt and ground black pepper
• Lemony Salsa Verde
• Intolerances:
• Gluten-Free
• Egg-Free
• Lactose-Free
Directions:
1. Preheat the grill to medium-high heat before oiling the grate. Toss the scallops with 2 tablespoons of the sauce. a rimmed baking sheet with oil and season with salt and pepper
2. Place the scallops on the grill with a fish spatula or your hands.
3. Grill them occasionally until lightly charred and cooked, about 2 minutes per side.
4. Serve the scallops alongside a lemony salsa verde.
Nutrition: Calories: 30 | Fat: 1 g. | Cholesterol: 17 mg. | Carbs: 1 g. | Protein: 6 g.

228. Grilled Shrimp With Shrimp Butter

Preparation time: 15 minutes
Cooking time: 15 minutes
Servings: 4
Ingredients:
- 6 tbsp. unsalted butter
- ½ cup finely chopped red onion
- 1 ½ tsp. crushed red pepper
- 1 tsp. Malaysian shrimp paste
- 1 ½ tsp. lime juice
- Salt
- Grounded black pepper
- 24 shelled and deveined large shrimp
- 6 skewers made of wood (better if soaked in water for 30 minutes)
- Torn mint leaves and assorted sprouts
- Intolerances:
- Gluten-Free
- Egg-Free

Directions:
1. 3 tbsp. liquefied in a small skillet with a stick of butter. After adding the onion, cook for about 3 minutes over medium heat.
2. Cook until the smashed red pepper and shrimp paste are aromatic, about 2 minutes.
3. Combine the lime juice and the remaining 3 tablespoons of the season with salt and butter. Warm the shrimp sauce.
4. Prepare the grill. Add seasoning the shrimp with salt and pepper before loosely threading them onto the skewers.
5. Grill over high heat for 4 minutes, rotating once until nicely charred and cooked.
6. Place on a dish and drizzle with shrimp sauce. Serve with the mint leaves and sprouts on top.

Nutrition: Calories: 224 | Fat: 10 g. | Cholesterol: 260 mg. | Carbs: 1 g. | Protein: 30 g.

229. Grilled Sea Scallops With Corn Salad

Preparation time: 25 minutes
Cooking time: 30 minutes
Servings: 6
Ingredients:
- 6 shucked ears of corn
- 1-pint grape tomatoes halved
- 3 sliced scallions, only the white and light green sections
- ⅓ cup basil leaves, finely shredded
- Salt and grounded pepper
- 1 small shallot, minced
- 2 tbsp. balsamic vinegar
- 2 tbsp. hot water
- 1 tsp. Dijon mustard
- 3 tbsp. sunflower oil
- 1 ½ lb. sea scallops
Intolerances:
- Gluten-Free
- Egg-Free
- Lactose-Free

Directions:
1. Cook the corn for 5 minutes or more in a pot of salted water.
2. Drain and allow to cool.
3. Put the corn in a large dish and remove the kernels. Season with salt and ground pepper after adding the tomatoes, scallions, and basil.
4. Combine the shallot, vinegar, hot water, and mustard in a blender. While the blender is running, gradually add 6 tbsp. from sunflower oil
5. Season the vinaigrette with salt and pepper, then pour it over the corn salad.
6. Toss the remaining 1 tablespoon in a large mixing bowl. a drizzle of oil over the scallops, then season with salt and freshly ground pepper
7. Preheat the grill pan. Grill half the scallops on high heat, flipping once until toasted, about 4 minutes.
8. Repeat with the remaining scallops.
9. Serve the corn salad on plates, topped with the scallops.

Nutrition: Calories: 230 | Fat: 5 g. | Cholesterol: 60 mg. | Carbs: 13 g. | Protein: 33 g.

230. Grilled Oysters With Tequila Butter

Preparation time: 20 minutes
Cooking time: 25 minutes
Servings: 6
Ingredients:
- ½ tsp. fennel seeds
- ¼ tsp. crushed red pepper
- 7 tbsp. unsalted butter
- 1/4 cup sage leaves, plus 36 small sage leaves for garnish
- 1 tsp. oregano, dried
- 2 tbsp. lemon juice
- 2 tbsp. tequila
- Kosher salt
- Rock salt for the serving
- 3 dozen scrubbed medium oysters
- Intolerances:
- Gluten-Free
- Egg-Free
- Lactose-Free

Directions:
1. Toast the fennel seeds and smashed red pepper in a pan over medium heat for 1 minute or until aromatic.
2. Allow it to cool on a mortar. Pound the spices into a coarse powder with a pestle, then transfer to a basin.
3. Cook 3 1/2 tbsp n the same skillet. Heat the butter over medium heat for about 2 minutes or until it turns dark brown.
4. Cook, stirring periodically, for about 2 minutes after adding 1/4 cup of sage. Place the sage on a dish.
5. Combine the butter and spices in a mixing dish. Rep with the rest of the butter and sage leaves. Set aside some for decoration.

6. Squeeze the pestle over the cooked sage leaves in the mortar. Season with salt after adding the smashed sage, oregano, lemon juice, and tequila to the butter. Stay warm.

7. Prepare the grill. Rock salt should be used to line a dish. Grill the oysters over high heat for 1–2 minutes or until they open.

8. Remove the top shell and place the oysters on the rock salt, careful not to spill the juice.

9. Serve the oysters with the warm tequila sauce, garnished with a fresh sage leaf.

Nutrition: Calories: 68 | Fat: 3 g. | Carbs: 4 g. | Protein: 10 g.

231. Grilled Tilapia

Preparation time: 10 minutes
Cooking time: 2o minutes
Servings: 6
Ingredients:
• 2 tsp. parsley, dried
• ½ tsp. garlic powder
• 1 tsp. cayenne pepper
• ½ tsp. ground black pepper
• ½ tsp. thyme
• ½ tsp. basil, dried
• ½ tsp. oregano
• 3 tbsp. olive oil
• ½ tsp. lemon pepper
• 1 tsp. Kosher salt
• 1 lemon (juiced)
• 6 tilapia fillets
• 1 ½ tsp. Creole seafood seasoning

Directions:
1. In a mixing bowl, combine spices
2. Brush the fillets with oil and lemon juice.
3. Liberally, season all sides of the tilapia fillets with the seasoning mix.
4. Preheat your grill to 325°F. Try a non-stick BBQ grilling on the grill and arrange the tilapia fillets onto it.
5. Grill for 15–20 minutes. Remove fillets and cool down

Nutrition: Calories: 176 Kcal | Fat: 9.6 g. | Carbohydrates: 1.5 g. | Protein: 22.3 g. | Fiber: 0.5 g.

232. Citrus Soy Squid

Preparation time: 15 minutes
Cooking time: 45 minutes
Servings: 4
Ingredients:
• 1 cup mirin
• 1 cup soy sauce
• ⅓ cup yuzu juice or fresh lemon juice
• 2 cups water
• 2 lb. squid tentacles left whole; bodies cut crosswise 1 inch thick
• Intolerances:
• Gluten-Free
• Egg-Free

• Lactose-Free
Directions:
1. Combine the mirin, soy sauce, yuzu juice, and water in a mixing bowl.
2. Put some of the marinade in a container and store it in the refrigerator for later use.
3. Set aside for 30 minutes, or refrigerate the squid in the bowl with the leftover marinade for 4 hours.
4. Prepare the grill. Remove the squid.
5. Grill over medium-high heat, flipping once, for 3 minutes, or until completely white.
6. Serve immediately.

Nutrition: Calories: 110 | Fat: 6 g. | Carbs: 6 g. | Protein: 8 g.

233. Spiced Salmon Kebabs

Preparation time: 20 minutes
Cooking time: 25 minutes
Servings: 4
Ingredients:
• 2 tbsp. fresh oregano, chopped
• 2 tsp. sesame seeds
• 1 tsp. ground cumin
• 1 tsp. Kosher salt
• ¼ tsp. crushed red pepper flakes
• 1 ½ lb. skinless salmon fillets, cut into 1" pieces
• 2 lemons, thinly sliced into rounds
• 2 tbsp. olive oil
• 1 hour soak in water for 16 bamboo skewers
Intolerances:
• Gluten-Free
• Egg-Free
• Lactose-Free
Directions:
1. Preheat the grill to medium. In a small bowl, combine the oregano, sesame seeds, cumin, salt, and red pepper flakes. Set aside the spice mixture.
2. String the fish and lemon slices onto eight parallel skewers to produce eight kebabs.
3. Season with the spice combination and drizzle with oil.
4. Grill, occasionally turning, until the salmon is done.

Nutrition: Calories: 230 | Fat: 10 g. | Carbs: 1 g. | Protein: 30 g.

234. Grilled Onion Butter Cod

Preparation time: 10 minutes
Cooking time: 15 minutes
Servings: 4
Ingredients:
- ¼ cup butter
- 1 finely chopped small onion
- ¼ cup white wine
- 4 (6 oz.) cod fillets
- 1 tbsp. extra-virgin olive oil
- ½ tsp. salt (or to taste)
- ½ tsp. black pepper
- Lemon wedges

Intolerances:
- Gluten-Free
- Egg-Free

Directions:
1. Set up the grill for medium-high heat.
2. In a small skillet, liquefy the butter. Add the onion and cook for 1 or 2 minutes.
3. Add the white wine and let stew for an extra 3 minutes. Take it away and let it cool for 5 minutes.
4. Spoon the fillets with extra virgin olive oil and sprinkle with salt and pepper. Put the fish on a well-oiled rack and cook for 8 minutes.
5. Season it with sauce and cautiously flip it over. Cook for 6–7 minutes more, turning more times or until the fish arrives at an inside temperature of 145°F.
6. Take away from the grill, top with lemon wedges, and serve.

Nutrition: Calories: 140 | Fat: 5 g. | Cholesterol: 46 mg. | Carbs: 4 g. | Protein: 20 g.

235. Grilled Calamari With Mustard Oregano and Parsley Sauce

Preparation time: 10 minutes
Cooking time: 35 minutes
Servings: 6
Ingredients:
- 8 Calamari, cleaned
- 2 cups milk

Sauce:
- 4 tsp. sweet mustard
- Juice from 2 lemons
- ½ cup olive oil
- 2 tbsp. fresh oregano, finely chopped
- Pepper, ground
- ½ bunch of parsley, finely chopped

Intolerances:
- Gluten-Free
- Egg-Free
- Lactose-Free

Directions:
1. Calamari should be well cleaned and sliced into slices.
2. Cover and marinate the calamari in milk overnight in a big metal bow.
3. Remove the calamari from the milk and pat dry with a paper towel. Lightly coat the fish in olive oil.
4. Combine mustard and the juice of two lemons in a mixing basin.
5. Beat lightly and slowly drizzle in the olive oil, constantly stirring until all ingredients are well blended.
6. Stir in the oregano and pepper until well combined.
7. Start the pellet grill and adjust the temperature to medium; warm for 10–15 minutes with the lid covered.
8. Place the calamari on the grill for 2–3 minutes per side, or until charred, then remove from the grill.
9. Place the calamari on a serving plate and top with the mustard sauce and chopped parsley.

Nutrition: Calories: 212 | Fat: 19 g. | Cholesterol: 651 mg. | Carbs: 7 g. | Protein: 3 g.

236. Salad of Grilled Cuttlefish with Spinach and Pine Nuts

Preparation time: 15 minutes
Cooking time: 30 minutes
Servings: 6
Ingredients:
- ½ cup olive oil
- 1 tbsp. lemon juice
- 1 tsp. oregano
- Pinch salt
- 8 large cuttlefish, cleaned
- Serve with spinach, pine nuts, olive oil, and vinegar.
- Intolerances:
- Gluten-Free
- Egg-Free
- Lactose-Free

Directions:
- Make a marinade using olive oil, lemon juice, oregano, and salt & pepper to taste (be careful, cuttlefish do not need too much salt).
- Toss the cuttlefish in the marinade to coat evenly. Cover and set aside for 1 hour to marinate.
- Take the cuttlefish out of the marinade and dry them with a paper towel.
- Start the pellet grill, set the temperature to high, and preheat for 10–15 minutes with the lid closed.
- Grill the cuttlefish for 3 to 4 minutes per side.
- Serve with spinach, pine nuts, olive oil, and vinegar on the side.

Nutrition: Calories: 299 | Fat: 19 g. | Cholesterol: 186 mg. | Carbs: 3 g. | Protein: 28 g.

Chapter 12. Vegetables and Vegetarian Recipes

237.   Traeger Smoked Mushrooms

Preparation time: 15 minutes
Cooking time: 45 minutes
Servings: 2
Ingredients:
• cups whole baby Portobello, cleaned
• 1 tbsp. canola oil
• 1 tbsp. onion powder
• 1 tbsp. garlic, granulated
• 1 tbsp. salt
• 1 tbsp. pepper
Directions:
1. In a mixing bowl, combine all of the ingredients.
2. Set your Traeger to 180°F.
3. Place the mushrooms on the grill directly and smoke for about 30 minutes.
4. Increase heat to high and cook the mushroom for another 15 minutes.
5. Serve warm, and enjoy!
Nutrition: Calories: 118 │ Total Fat: 7.6 g. │ Saturated Fat: 0.6 g. │ Total Carbs: 10.8 g. │ Net Carbs: 8.3 g. │ Protein: 5.4 g. │ Sugars: 3.7 g. │ Fiber: 2.5 g. │ Sodium: 3500 mg. │ Potassium: 536 mg.

238.   Grilled Zucchini Squash Spears

Preparation time: 5 minutes
Cooking time: 10 minutes
Servings: 4
Ingredients:
6. zucchinis, medium
7. 2 tbsp. olive oil
8. 1 tbsp. sherry vinegar
9. 2 thymes, leaves pulled
10. Salt to taste
11. Pepper to taste
Directions:
1. Remove the ends of the zucchini, then cut each half lengthwise into thirds.
2. In a medium zip lock bag, combine all the other ingredients, then add the spears.
3. To coat the zucchini, toss and mix thoroughly.
4. Preheat Traeger to 350°F for about 15 minutes with the lid closed.
5. Remove the spears from the zip lock bag and place them on the grill grate.
6. Cook for 3–4 minutes until zucchini is tender and grill marks appear.
7. Remove them from the grill and enjoy.

Nutrition: Calories: 93 │ Total Fat: 7.4 g. │ Saturated Fat: 1.1 g. │ Total Carbs: 7.1 g. │ Net Carbs: 4.9 g. │ Protein: 2.4 g. │ Sugars: 3.4 g. │ Fiber: 2.2 g. │ Sodium: 59 mg. │ Potassium: 515 mg.

239.   Grilled Asparagus & Honey-Glazed Carrots

Preparation time: 15 minutes
Cooking time: 35 minutes
Servings: 4
Ingredients:
• 1 bunch asparagus, woody ends removed
• 2 tbsp. olive oil
• 1 lb. peeled carrots
• 2 tbsp. honey
• Sea salt to taste
• Lemon zest to taste
Directions:
1. Cold water should be used to rinse the vegetables.
2. Brush the asparagus with oil and season it generously with salt.
3. Drizzle honey over carrots and season lightly with salt.
4. Preheat your Traeger to 350°F for about 15 minutes with the lid closed.
5. First, place the carrots on the grill and cook for 10–15 minutes.
6. Place the asparagus on the grill for about 15–20 minutes, or until done to your liking.
7. Garnish with lemon zest and serve.
Nutrition: Calories: 245 │ Total Fat: 7.3 g. │ Saturated Fat: 1.1 g. │ Total Carbs: 28.6 g. │ Net Carbs: 21 g. │ Protein: 6 g. │ Sugars: 185 g. │ Fiber: 7.6 g. │ Sodium: 142 mg. │ Potassium: 826 mg.

240.   Traeger Grilled Vegetables

Preparation time: 5 minutes
Cooking time: 15 minutes
Servings: 12
Ingredients:
• 1 veggie tray
• ¼ cup vegetable oil
• 1–2 tbsp. Traeger veggie seasoning
Directions:
1. Preheat your Traeger to 375°F.
2. Meanwhile, toss the veggies in oil on a sheet pan, then splash with the seasoning.
3. Place on the Traeger and grill for about 10–15 minutes.
4. Remove, serve, and enjoy.
Nutrition: Calories 44 │ Total Fat: 5 g. │ Saturated Fat: 0 g. │ Total Carbs: 1 g. │ Net Carbs: 1 g. │ Protein: 0 g. │ Sugars: 0 g. │ Fiber: 0 g. │ Sodium: 36 mg. │ Potassium: 116 mg.

241. Smoked Acorn Squash

Preparation time: 10 minutes
Cooking time: 2 hours
Servings: 6
Method of Preparation: Smoking
Ingredients:
- 3 acorn squashes, seeded and halved
- 3 tbsp. olive oil
- ¼ cup butter, unsalted
- 1 tbsp. cinnamon, ground
- 1 tbsp. chili powder
- 1 tbsp. nutmeg, ground
- ¼ cup brown sugar

Directions:
1. Brush olive oil on the cut sides of your squash, then cover with foil, poking holes in the foil to allow smoke and steam to escape.
2. Preheat the Traeger to 225°F.
3. Place the squash halves on the grill, cut the side down, and smoke for 112- 2 hours. Take out of the Traeger.
4. Set aside while you make the spiced butter. In a saucepan, melt the butter, then stir in the spices and sugar.
5. Peel the foil off the squash halves.
6. Place 1 tbsp. of the butter mixture onto each half.
7. Serve and enjoy!
Nutrition: Calories 149, Total 10 g. | Saturated Fat: 5 g. | Total Carbs: 14 g. | Net Carbs: 12 g. | Protein: 2 g. | Sugars: 2 g. | Fiber: 2 g. | Sodium: 19 mg. | Potassium: 101m

242. Vegan Smoked Carrot Dogs

Preparation time: 10 minutes
Cooking time: 35 minutes
Servings: 2
Method of Preparation: Smoking
Ingredients:
- 2 carrots, thick
- 2 tbsp. avocado oil
- ½ tbsp. garlic powder
- 1 tbsp. liquid smoke
- Pepper to taste
- Kosher salt to taste

Directions:
1. Preheat your Traeger to 425°F, and line a parchment paper on a baking sheet.
2. Peel the carrots to resemble a hot dog around the edges when peeling.
3. Whisk together oil, garlic powder, liquid smoke, pepper, and salt in a bowl, small.
4. Now place carrots on the baking sheet and pour the mixture over. Roll your carrots in the mixture to massage seasoning and oil into them. Use fingertips.
5. Roast the carrots in the Traeger until fork tender for about 35 minutes. Brush the carrots using the marinade mixture every 5 minutes.

6. Remove and place into hot dog buns, then top with hot dog toppings of your choice.
7. Serve and enjoy!
Nutrition: Calories 76 | Total Fat: 1.8 g., Saturated 0.4 g., Total 14.4 g. | Net Carbs: 10.6 g. | Protein: 1.5 g. | Sugar: 6.6 g. | Fiber: 3.8 g. | Sodium: 163 mg. | Potassium: 458 mg.

243. Stuffed Grilled Zucchini

Preparation time: 25 minutes
Cooking time: 10 minutes
Servings: 4
Ingredients:
- 4 zucchinis, medium
- 5 tbsp. olive oil, divided
- 2 tbsp. red onion, finely chopped
- ¼ tbsp. garlic, minced
- ½ cup breadcrumbs, dry
- ½ cup shredded Mozzarella cheese, part-skim
- ½ tbsp. salt
- 1 tbsp. fresh mint, minced
- 3 tbsp. Parmesan cheese, grated

Directions:
1. Halve zucchini lengthwise and scoop the pulp out. Leave a ¼ -inch shell. Now brush using 2 tbsp. oil set aside, and chop the pulp.
2. In a large skillet, sauté the onion and pulp for 1 minute before adding the garlic.
3. Cook for about 2 minutes, stirring constantly, or until the breadcrumbs are golden brown.
4. Take the pan off the heat and add the mozzarella cheese, salt, and mint.
5. Top the zucchini shells with the mixture and parmesan cheese.
6. Preheat your Traeger to 375 degrees Fahrenheit.
7. Place stuffed zucchini on the Traeger grill and grill while covered for about 8–10 minutes until tender.
8. Serve warm and enjoy.
Nutrition: Calories 186 | Total Fat: 10 g. | Saturated Fat: 3 g. | Total Carbs: 17 g. | Net Carbs: 14 g. | Protein: 9 g. | Sugars: 4 g. | Fiber: 3 g. | Sodium: 553 mg. | Potassium: 237 mg.

244. Smoked Stuffed Mushrooms

Preparation time: 15 minutes
Cooking time: 1 hour 15 minutes
Servings: 12
Ingredients:
- 12–16 white mushrooms, large, cleaned, and stems removed
- ½ cup parmesan cheese
- ½ cup breadcrumbs, Italian
- 2 garlic cloves, minced
- 2 tbsp. fresh parsley, chopped
- ¼–⅓ cup olive oil
- Salt and pepper to taste

Directions:

1. Preheat your Traeger 375°F.

2. Remove the mushroom's bottom stem, then dice the rest into small pieces.

3. Combine the mushroom stems, parmesan cheese, breadcrumbs, garlic, parsley, and 3 tablespoons of olive oil. Mix the oil, pepper, and salt in a large mixing bowl. Mix until everything is moist.

4. Layer the mushrooms in a disposable pan, then fill them to the brim with the mixture. Drizzle with additional oil. Place the grill pan on the Traeger.

5. Smoke for 1 hour and 20 minutes, or until the filling browns and the mushrooms become tender.

6. Remove from Traeger and serve.

Nutrition: Calories: 74 | Total Fat: 6.1 g. | Saturated Fat: 1 g. | Total Carbs: 4.1 g. | Net Carbs: 3.7 g. | Protein: 1.6 g. | Sugars: 0.6 g. | Fiber: 0.4 g. | Sodium: 57 mg. | Potassium: 72 mg.

245.   Roasted Tomatoes With Hot Pepper Sauce

Preparation time: 20 minutes

Cooking time: 90 minutes

Servings: 4–6

Ingredients:

• Pellet: hardwood, alder

• 2 lbs. roman fresh tomatoes

• 3 tbsps. parsley, chopped

• 2 tbsps. garlic, chopped

• Black pepper, to taste

• ½ cup olive oil

• Hot pepper, to taste

• 1 lb. spaghetti or other pasta

Directions:

1. Prepare and ready to cook, set the temperature to 400°F and preheat, lid closed for 15 minutes

2. Rinse with water the tomatoes and cut them in half, length and width, then place them in a baking dish cut side up.

3. Sprinkle with chopped parsley and garlic, add salt and black pepper, and pour ¼ cup of olive oil over them.

4. Place on preheated and bake for 1 ½ hour, the tomatoes will shrink, and the skins will be partly blackened.

5. Take the tomatoes from the baking dish and place them in a food processor, leaving the cooking oil and puree them.

6. Put the pasta into boiling salted water and cook until tender. Then drain and mix immediately with the pureed tomatoes.

7. Add the remaining ¼ cup of raw olive oil and crumbled hot red pepper to taste. Toss and serve. Enjoy!

Nutrition: Calories: 111 | Carbs: 5 g. | Fat: 11 g. | Protein: 1 g.

246.   Grilled Fingerling Potato Salad

Preparation time: 15 minutes

Cooking time: 15 minutes

Servings: 6–8

Ingredients:

• 10 whole scallions

• 2/3 cup extra-virgin olive oil, divided

• 1 1/2 lb. fingerling potatoes, cut in half lengthwise

• Pepper to taste

• 2 tsp Kosher salt, divided, plus more as needed

• 2 tbsp rice vinegar

• 2 tsp lemon juice

• 1 small Jalapeño, sliced

Directions:

1. When ready to cook, set Traeger temperature to 450°F and preheat, lid closed for 15 minutes.

2. Brush the scallions with oil and place them on the grill.

3. Cook until lightly charred, about 2 to 3 minutes. Remove and let cool.

4. Once the scallions have cooled, slice and set aside.

5. Brush the fingerling potatoes with oil (reserving 1/3 cup for later use), then salt and pepper. Place cut-side down on the grill until cooked through, about 4 to 5 minutes.

6. Whisk the remaining 1/3 cup olive oil, 1 teaspoon salt, rice vinegar, and lemon juice in a bowl. Next, mix in the scallions, potatoes, and sliced Jalapeño.

7. Season with salt and pepper, and serve. Enjoy!

Nutrition: Calories: 270 | Carbs: 18 g. | Fat: 18 g. | Protein: 3 g.

247.   Smoked Jalapeño Poppers

Preparation time: 15 minutes

Cooking time: 60 minutes

Servings: 4–6

Ingredients:

• Pellet: hardwood, mesquite

• 12 medium Jalapeños

• 6 slices bacon, cut in half

• 8 oz. cream cheese, softened

• 1 cup cheese, grated

• 2 tbsps. pork & poultry rub

Directions:

1. Prepare and ready to cook, turn the temperature up to 180°F and preheat, lid closed for 15 minutes.

2. Cut Jalapeños in half lengthwise. Remove the seeds and ribs.

3. Combine softened cream cheese with pork & poultry rub and grated cheese.

4. Divide the mixture over each jalapeño in half. Wrap in bacon and secure with a toothpick.

5. Put the jalapeños on a rimmed baking sheet. Place on the grill and smoke for 30 minutes.

6. Increase the grill's temperature to 375°F and cook for another 30 minutes or until the bacon is cooked to the desired level. Serve hot, enjoy!

91

Nutrition: Calories: 280 | Carbs: 24 g. | Fat: 19 g. | Protein: 4 g.

248. Bacon-Wrapped Jalapeño Poppers

Preparation time: 10 minutes
Cooking time: 20 minutes
Servings: 6
Ingredients:
- 6 Jalapeños, Fresh
- ½ cup shredded cheddar cheese
- 4 oz. soft cream cheese
- 1½ tbsp. Traeger veggie rub
- 12 bacon slices, thin cut

Directions:
1. Preheat your Traeger grill to 375°F.
2. Cut the Jalapeños lengthwise, then scrape the membrane and seeds with a spoon. Set them aside after rinsing them.
3. Meanwhile, in a mixing bowl, combine the cheddar cheese, cream cheese, and veggie rub and stir on medium until completely combined.
4. Fill the jalapenos with the cheese mixture, then wrap each half in bacon.
5. Grill for 15–20 minutes until the bacon is crispy and the peppers are soft.
6. Serve immediately and enjoy.

Nutrition: Calories: 329 | Total Fat: 25.7 g. | Saturated Fat: 11.4 g. | Total Carbs: 5 g. | Net Carbs: 4.6 g. | Protein: 18.1 g. | Sugars: 0.6 g. | Fiber: 0.4 g. | Sodium: 1667 mg. | Potassium: 277 mg.

249. Roasted Green Beans With Bacon

Preparation time: 15 minutes
Cooking time: 20 minutes
Servings: 6
Method of Preparation: Grilling
Ingredients:
- 1 lb. green beans
- 4 strips bacon, cut into small pieces
- 4 tbsp. extra virgin olive oil
- 2 garlic cloves, minced
- 1 tsp. salt

Directions:
1. Fire the Traeger Grill to 400°F. Use desired wood pellets when cooking. Keep the lid unopened and let it preheat for at most 15 minutes
2. Toss all ingredients on a sheet tray and spread out evenly.
3. Place the tray on the grill grate and roast for 20 minutes.

Nutrition: Calories: 65 | Fat: 5.3 g. | Carbohydrates: 3 g. | Protein: 1.3 g. | Fiber: 0 g.

250. Smoked Watermelon

Preparation time: 15 minutes
Cooking time: 45–90 minutes
Servings: 5
Ingredients:
- 1 small seedless watermelon
- Balsamic vinegar
- Wooden skewers

Directions:
1. Slice ends of small seedless watermelons
2. Slice the watermelon into 1-inch cubes. Put the cubes in a container and drizzle vinegar on the watermelon cubes.
3. Preheat the smoker to 225°F. Add wood chips and water to the smoker before starting preheating.
4. Place the cubes on the skewers.
5. Place the skewers on the smoker rack for 50 minutes.
6. Cook.
7. Remove the skewers.
8. Serve!

Nutrition: Calories: 20 | Fat: 0 g. | Carbohydrates: 4 g. | Protein: 1 g. | Fiber: 0.2 g.

251. Grilled Corn With Honey Butter

Preparation time: 15 minutes
Cooking time: 10 minutes
Servings: 6
Ingredients:
- 6 pieces corn, husked
- 2 tbsp. olive oil
- Salt and pepper to taste
- ½ cup butter, room temperature
- ½ cup honey

Directions:
1. Fire the Traeger Grill to 350°F. Use desired wood pellets when cooking. Keep lid unopened to preheat until 15 minutes.
2. Coat corn with oil and add salt and pepper.
3. Place the corn on the grill grate and cook for 10 minutes. Make sure to flip the corn halfway through the cooking time for even cooking.
4. Meanwhile, mix the butter and honey in a small bowl. Set aside.
5. Remove corn from the grill and coat with honey butter sauce.

Nutrition: Calories: 387 | Fat: 21.6 g. | Carbohydrates: 51.2 g. | Protein: 5 g. | Fiber: 0 g.

252. Smoked Mushrooms

Preparation time: 20 minutes
Cooking time: 2 hours
Servings: 6
Ingredients:
- 6–12 large Portobello mushrooms
- Sea salt
- Black pepper
- Extra-virgin olive oil
- Herbs de Provence

Directions:
1. Preheat the smoker to 200°F while adding water and wood chips to the smoker bowl and tray.
2. Wash and dry mushrooms.
3. Rub the mushrooms with olive oil, salt, and pepper, seasoning with herbs in a bowl.
4. Place the mushrooms with the cap side down on the smoker rack. Smoke the mushrooms for 2 hours while adding water and wood chips to the smoker every 60 minutes.
5. Remove the mushrooms and serve.

Nutrition: Calories: 106 | Fat: 6 g. | Carbohydrates: 5 g. | Protein: 8 g. | Fiber: 0.9 g.

253. Smoked Cherry Tomatoes

Preparation time: 20 minutes
Cooking time: 1 ½ hour
Servings: 8–10
Ingredients:
- 2 pints tomatoes

Directions:
1. Preheat the electric smoker to 225°F while filling it with wood chips and water.
2. Clean the tomatoes with clean water and thoroughly dry them.
3. Put the tomatoes on the pan and put them in the smoker.
4. While adding water and wood chips to the smoker, smoke for 90 minutes.

Nutrition: Calories: 16 | Fat: 0 g. | Carbohydrates: 3 g. | Protein: 1 g. | Fiber: 1 g.

254. Smoked Tomato and Mozzarella Dip

Preparation time: 5 minutes
Cooking time: 1 hour
Servings: 4
Ingredients:
- Pellet: mesquite
- 8 oz. Colby cheese, shredded
- 8 oz. smoked Mozzarella cheese, shredded
- ½ cup Parmesan cheese, grated
- 1 cup sour cream
- 1 cup sun-dried tomatoes
- 1 and ½ tsp. salt
- 1 tsp. fresh ground pepper
- 1 tsp. basil, dried
- 1 tsp. oregano, dried
- 1 tsp. red pepper flakes
- 1 garlic clove, minced
- ½ tsp. onion powder
- French toast, serving

Directions:
1. Pre-heat your smoker to 275°F using your preferred wood.
2. Mix well in a large bowl and stir the cheeses, tomatoes, pepper, salt, basil, oregano, red pepper flakes, garlic, and onion powder.
3. Transfer the mix to a small metal pan and transfer to a smoker.
4. Smoke for 1 hour.
5. Serve with toasted French bread Enjoy!

Nutrition: Calories: 174 | Fat: 11 g. | Carbs: 15 g. | Fiber: 2 g.

255. Feisty Roasted Cauliflower

Preparation time: 15 minutes
Cooking time: 10 minutes
Servings: 4
Ingredients:
- Pellet: maple
- 1 cauliflower head, cut into florets
- 1 tbsp. oil
- 1 cup Parmesan cheese, grated
- 2 garlic cloves, crushed
- ½ tsp. pepper
- ½ tsp. salt
- ¼ tsp. paprika

Directions:
1. Pre-heat your Smoker to 180°F.
2. Transfer florets to smoker and smoke for 1 hour.
3. Take a bowl and add all ingredients except cheese.
4. Once smoking is done, remove florets.
5. Increase temperature to 450°F, brush florets with the brush and transfer to grill.
6. Smoke for 10 minutes more.
7. Sprinkle cheese on top and let them sit (Lid closed) until cheese melts.
8. Serve and enjoy!

Nutrition: Calories: 45 | Fat: 2 g. | Carbs: 7 g. | Fiber: 1 g.

256. Savory Applesauce on the Grill

Preparation time: 0 minutes
Cooking time: 45 minutes
Servings: 2
Ingredients:
• 1 ½ lb. whole apples
• Salt
Directions:
1. Start the coals or turn a gas grill for medium direct cooking. Just make sure the grates are clean.
2. Put the apples on the grill directly over the fire.
3. Close the lid and cook until the fruit feels soft when gently squeezed with tongs, 10–20 minutes total, depending on their size.
4. Move to a cutting board and sit until cool enough to touch.
5. Cut the flesh from around the core of each apple; discard the cores.
6. Put the chunks in a blender or food processor and process until smooth, or put them in a bowl and purée with an immersion blender until as chunky or smooth as you like.
7. Add some salt, and then taste and adjusts the seasoning.
8. Serve or refrigerate in a container for up to 3 days.
Nutrition: Calories: 15 | Fat: 0 g. | Cholesterol: 0 mg. | Carbohydrates: 3 g. | Fiber: 0 g. | Sugars: 3 g. | Proteins: 0

257. Avocado With Lemon

Preparation time: 5 minutes
Cooking time: 20 minutes
Servings: 4
Ingredients:
• 2 ripe avocados
• Good-quality olive oil for brushing
• 1 halved lemon
• Salt and pepper
Directions:
1. Start the coals or turn a gas grill for medium direct cooking. Just make sure the grates are clean.
2. Cut the avocados in half lengthwise. Carefully strike a chef's knife into the pit, then wiggle it a bit to lift and remove it. Insert a spoon underneath the flesh against the skin and run it around to separate the entire half of the avocado.
3. Repeat with the other avocado. Brush with oil, then thoroughly squeeze one of the lemon halves over them on both sides, so they don't discolor.
4. Cut the other lemon half into four wedges.
5. Put the avocados directly over the fire on the grill, and cut the side down. Cover with lid and cook, turning once, until browned in places, 5–10 minutes total.
6. Serve the halved avocados as is, or slice and fan them for a prettier presentation. Sprinkle with salt and pepper and garnish with lemon wedges.
Nutrition: Calories: 50.3 | Fat: 4.6 g. | Cholesterol: 0 mg. | Fiber: 1.7 g. | Carbohydrates: 2.8 g. | Sugars: 0.2 g. | Protein: 0.6 g.

258. Smoked and Smashed New Potatoes

Preparation time: 5 minutes
Cooking time: 8 hours
Servings: 4
Method of Preparation: Smoking
Ingredients:
• 1-½ lb. small new red potatoes or fingerlings
• Extra-virgin olive oil
• Sea salt and black pepper
• 2 tbsp. softened butter
Directions:
1. Let the potatoes dry. Once dried, put in a pan and coat with salt, pepper, and extra virgin olive oil.
2. Place the potatoes on the top rack of the smoker.
3. Smoke for 60 minutes.
4. Once done, take them out and smash each one.
5. Mix with butter and season.
Nutrition: Calories: 258 | Fat: 2.0 g. | Carbohydrates: 15.5 g. | Protein: 4.1 g. | Fiber: 1.5 g.

259. Smoked Brussels Sprouts

Preparation time: 15 minutes
Cooking time: 45 minutes
Servings: 6
Ingredients:
• 1 ½ lb. Brussels sprouts
• 2 garlic cloves, minced
• 2 tbsp. extra-virgin olive oil
• Sea salt and cracked black pepper
Directions:
1. Rinse sprouts.
2. Remove the outer leaves and brown bottoms off the sprouts.
3. Put sprouts in a large bowl and coat them using olive oil.
4. Add a coat of garlic, salt, and pepper and transfer them to the pan.
5. Add to the top rack of the smoker with water and woodchips.
6. Smoke for 45 minutes or until it reaches 250°F temperature.
7. Serve.
Nutrition: Calories: 84 | Fat: 4.9 g. | Carbohydrates: 7.2 g. | Protein: 2.6 g. | Fiber: 2.9 g.

260. Grilled Veggie Sandwich

Preparation time: 30 minutes
Cooking time: 30 minutes
Servings: 4–6
Ingredients:
- Pellet: hardwood, pecan
- Smoked hummus
- 1 ½ cups chickpeas
- ⅓ cup tahini
- 1 tbsp. minced garlic
- 2 tbsps. olive oil
- 1 tsp. Kosher salt
- 4 tbsps. lemon juice
Grilled Veggie Sandwich:
- 1 small eggplant, sliced into strips
- 1 small zucchini, cut into strips
- 1 small yellow squash, sliced into strips
- 2 large Portobello mushrooms
- Olive oil
- Salt and pepper to taste
- 2 heirloom tomatoes, sliced
- 1 bunch of basil leaves pulled
- 4 ciabatta buns
- ½ cup ricotta
- Juice 1 lemon
- 1 garlic clove minced; salt and pepper to taste

Directions:
1. Ready to cook, turn temperature to 180°F and preheat, lid closed for 15 minutes.
2. In a prepared food processor bowl, combine the smoked chickpeas, tahini, garlic, olive oil, salt, and lemon juice and blend until smooth but not completely smooth. Transfer to a bowl and reserve.
3. Increase grill temp to high (400–500°F).
4. While the vegetables are cooking, mix the ricotta, lemon juice, garlic, salt, and some pepper.
5. Cut the ciabatta buns in half and then open them up—spread the hummus on one side and ricotta on the other. Stack the grilled veggies and top with tomatoes and basil.
6. Enjoy!
Nutrition: Calories: 376 | Carbs: 57 g. | Fat: 16 g. | Protein: 10 g.

261. Smoked Healthy Cabbage

Preparation time: 10 minutes
Cooking time: 2 hours
Servings: 5
Ingredients:
- Pellet: maple
- 1 head cabbage, cored
- 4 tbsp. butter
- 2 tbsp. rendered bacon fat
- 1 chicken bouillon cube
- 1 tsp. fresh ground black pepper
- 1 garlic clove, minced

Directions:
1. Pre-heat your smoker to 240°F using your preferred wood.
2. Fill the hole of your cored cabbage with butter, bouillon cube, bacon fat, pepper, and garlic.
3. Wrap the cabbage in foil about ⅔ of the way up.
4. Make sure to leave the top open.
5. Transfer to your smoker rack and smoke for 2 hours.
6. Unwrap and enjoy!
Nutrition: Calories: 231 | Fat: 10 g. | Carbs: 26 g. | Fiber: 1 g.

262. Garlic and Rosemary Potato Wedges

Preparation time: 15 minutes
Cooking time: 1 hour 30 minutes
Servings: 4
Ingredients:
- Pellet: maple
- 4–6 large russet potatoes, cut into wedges
- ¼ cup olive oil
- 2 tsp. salt
- 2 garlic cloves, minced
- 2 tbsp. rosemary leaves, chopped
- 1 tsp. fresh ground black pepper
- 1 tsp. sugar
- 1 tsp. onion powder
Directions:
1. Pre-heat your smoker to 250°F using maple wood.
2. Take a large bowl and add potatoes and olive oil. Toss well.
3. Take another small bowl and stir garlic, salt, rosemary, pepper, sugar, and onion powder.
4. Sprinkle the mix on all sides of the potato wedge.
5. Transfer the seasoned wedge to your smoker rack and smoke for one and a ½ hours. Serve and enjoy!
Nutrition: Calories: 291 | Fat: 10 g. | Carbs: 46 g. | Fiber: 2 g.

263. Apple Veggie Burger

Preparation time: 10 minutes
Cooking time: 35 minutes
Servings: 6
Ingredients:
- 3 tbsp. ground flax or ground chia
- ⅓ cup warm water
- ½ cup rolled oats
- 1 cup chickpeas, drained and rinsed
- 1 tsp. cumin
- ½ cup onion
- 1 tsp. dried basil
- 2 granny smith apples
- ⅓ cup parsley or cilantro, chopped
- 2 tbsp. soy sauce
- 2 tsp. liquid smoke
- 2 cloves garlic, minced
- 1 tsp. chili powder

• ¼ tsp. black pepper

Directions:

1. Preheat the smoker to 225°F while adding wood chips and water to it.

2. In a separate bowl, add chickpeas and mash. Mix the remaining ingredients along with the dipped flax seeds.

3. Form patties from this mixture.

4. Put the patties on the rack of the smoker and smoke them for 20 minutes on each side.

5. When brown, take them out and serve.

Nutrition: Calories: 241 │ Fat: 5 g. │ Carbohydrates: 40 g. │ Protein: 9 g. │ Fiber: 10.3 g.

264.   Smoked Tofu

Preparation time: 10 minutes
Cooking time: 2 hours and 30 minutes
Servings: 4
Ingredients:

6. 400 g. plain tofu
7. Sesame oil

Directions:

1. Preheat the smoker to 225°F while adding wood chips and water to it.

2. In the meantime, take the tofu out of the packet and let it rest.

3. Slice the tofu into one-inch-thick pieces and apply sesame oil.

4. Put the tofu inside the smoker for 45 minutes, adding water and wood chips after one hour.

5. Once cooked, take it out and serve!

Nutrition: Calories: 201 │ Fat: 13 g. │ Carbohydrates: 1 g. │ Protein: 20 g. │ Fiber: 0 g.

265.   Smoked Cauliflower

Preparation time: 15 minutes
Cooking time: 10 minutes
Servings: 3–4
Ingredients:

• 1 cauliflower head
• 1 cup Parmesan cheese
• 1 tbsp. olive oil
• 2 garlic cloves, crushed
• ¼ tsp. paprika
• ½ tsp. salt
• ½ tsp. pepper

Directions:

1. Start your Wood Pellet smoker grill with the lid open for about 4–5 minutes

2. Set the temperature to about 180°F and preheat with the lid closed for about 10–15 minutes

3. Cut the cauliflower into florets medium-sized; then place the cauliflower right on top of the grate and mix all the ingredients except for the cheese

4. After about 1 hour, remove the cauliflower; then turn the smoker grill on high for about 10–15 minutes

5. Brush the cauliflower with the mixture of the ingredients and place it on a sheet tray

6. Place the cauliflower back on the grate for about 10 minutes

7. Sprinkle with the parmesan cheese

8. Serve and enjoy your smoked cauliflower!

Nutrition: Calories: 60 │ Fat: 3.6 g. │ Carbohydrates: 3.1 g. │ Dietary Fiber: 1 g. │ Protein: 4 g.

266.   Smoked Peppers

Preparation time: 5 minutes
Cooking time: 20 Minutes
Servings: 4
Ingredients:

• 1 pearl onion bag, about 14.4 oz.
• 1 small sweet pepper bag, 1lb.
• Cooking sprays, like butter or olive oil
• 1 pinch garlic salt
• 1 pinch black pepper
• ¼ tsp. steak seasoning

Directions:

1. Preheat your wood pellet smoker grill to a temperature of about 350°F.

2. Spray the rack of your wood pellet smoker grill with cooking spray and cut the tops of the peppers into half; then remove the seeds.

3. Spray the peppers with cooking spray and cover with the garlic salt, the black pepper, and the seasoning; then place on top of the rack.

4. Smoke the peppers for about 15–20 minutes.

5. Serve and enjoy!

Nutrition: Calories: 62 │ Fat: 3.6 g. │ Carbohydrates: 0 g. │ Dietary Fiber: 1.4 g. │ Protein: 1 g.

267.   Smoked Aubergine

Preparation time: 10 minutes
Cooking time: 30 minutes
Servings: 3
Ingredients:

• 2 ½ whole aubergine
• 2 ½ spring onions
• 2 tsp. toasted sesame seeds
• 4 tsp. miso paste
• 2 tsp. soy sauce
• 1 tsp. sesame oil
• 1 garlic clove
• 1-inch fresh ginger, cube

Directions:

1. Add the miso, the soy, and the sesame oil to a bowl; then crush a garlic clove

2. Grate the ginger and stir with the help of a teaspoon until you get a paste

3. Slice the aubergine into half; then score the flesh to create a pattern of a diamond shape

4. Add the miso paste on top of the aubergine

5. Brush to add the miso concoction to the aubergine flesh

6. through diagonal scoring of the aubergine

7. Let the paste rest for about 30 minutes

8. Place the aubergine with the side up over indirect heat at a temperature of about 320°F

9. Smoke for about 30 minutes

10. Add a few cherry wood pellets to the coals for any extra flavor.

11. Turn the aubergine over onto direct heat and cook for about 60 seconds

12. Serve and enjoy your dish!

Nutrition: Calories: 112 | Fat: 6 g. | Carbohydrates: 8 g. | Dietary Fiber: 4 g. | Protein: 5 g.

268.   Smoked Mackerel

Preparation time: 15 minutes

Cooking time: 30 minutes

Servings: 9

Ingredients:

• ½ tsp. Garam Masala

• 1 pinch dried red chili flakes

• 1 tbsp. softened butter

• 3 ½ oz. smoked mackerel fillets

• To prepare the raita:

• 2 tbsp. Greek-style plain yogurt

• 1 tbsp. roughly chopped fresh mint

• Half a lime; only use the juice

• ½ thinly sliced halved cucumber

• Roughly chopped radishes

• 1 pinch salt

Directions:

1. Start by making the raita and to do that, combine the yogurt with the mint and 1 squeeze of lime juice in a medium bowl and season it with 1 pinch of salt.

2. Add in the cucumber and the radishes.

3. Then, cover and put in the refrigerator until you are ready to use it.

4. Preheat the charcoal grill to high heat and line a baking pan with kitchen foil.

5. In a medium bowl, combine the Garam Masala with the chili and the butter

6. Then, spread the butter over the mackerel.

7. Place the fillets over the baking tray and place them on the smoker and close the smoker with a lid.

8. Smoke the mackerel for about 30 minutes.

9. Remove the mackerel from the smoker; then set it aside for about 5 minutes.

10. Serve and enjoy your mackerel with the raita!

Nutrition: Calories: 283 | Fat: 23.4 g. | Carbohydrates: 2 g. | Protein: 20 g. | Dietary Fiber: 0.1 g.

269.   Easy Smoked Vegetables

Preparation time: 15 minutes

Cooking time: 1 ½ hour

Servings: 6

Ingredients:

• 1 cup pecan wood chips

• 1 fresh ear corn, silk strands removed, and husks, cut corn into 1-inch pieces

• 1 ½ yellow squash, ½-inch slices

• 1 small red onion, thin wedges

• 1 small green bell pepper, 1-inch strips

• 1 small red bell pepper, 1-inch strips

• 1 small yellow bell pepper, 1-inch strips

• 1 cup mushrooms, halved

• 2 tbsp. vegetable oil

• Vegetable seasonings

Directions:

1. In a large mixing bowl, combine all of the vegetables. Season it generously and coat all of the vegetables in it.

2. In the smoker, place the wood chips and a bowl of water.

3. Preheat the smoker for 10 minutes at 100°F.

4. Place the vegetables in a pan on the electric smoker's middle rack.

5. Cook for 30 minutes or until the vegetable is tender.

6. When done, serve, and enjoy.

Nutrition: Calories: 97 | Fat: 5 g. | Carbohydrates: 11 g. | Protein: 2 g.

270.   Zucchini With Red Potatoes

Preparation time: 15 minutes

Cooking time: 4 hours

Servings: 4

Ingredients:

• 2 zucchinis, sliced in ¾-inch-thick disks

• 1 red pepper, cut into strips

• 2 yellow squashes, sliced in ¾-inch-thick disks

• 1 medium red onion, cut into wedges

• small red potatoes, cut into chunks

• Balsamic vinaigrette:

• ⅓ cup extra virgin olive oil

• ¼ tsp. salt

• ¼ cup balsamic vinegar

• 2 tsp. Dijon mustard

• ⅛ tsp. pepper

Directions:

1. For Vinaigrette: Take a medium-sized bowl and blend olive oil, Dijon mustard, salt, pepper, and balsamic vinegar.

2. Place all the veggies into a large bowl, pour the vinaigrette mixture over it, and evenly toss.

3. Put the vegetable in a pan and then smoke for 4 hours at a temperature of 225°F.

4. Serve and enjoy the food.

Nutrition: Calories: 381 | Fat: 17.6 g. | Carbohydrates: 49 g. | Protein: 6.7 g. | Fiber: 6.5 g.

271. Shiitake Smoked Mushrooms

Preparation time: 15 minutes
Cooking time: 45 minutes
Servings: 4–6
Ingredients:
• Cup Shiitake mushrooms
• 1 tbsp. canola oil
• 1 tsp. onion powder
• 1 tsp. granulated garlic
• 1 tsp. salt
• 1 tsp. pepper
Directions:
1. 1. Combine all of the ingredients.
2. 2. Apply the mixture liberally to the mushrooms.
3. 3. Set the smoker to 180°F. Fill the side tray halfway with wood chips and half a water bowl.
4. 4. Place it in the smoker for 45 minutes to smoke.
5. Serve warm and enjoy.
Nutrition: Calories: 301 | Fat: 9 g. | Carbohydrates: 47.8 g. | Protein: 7.1 g. | Fiber: 4.8 g.

272. Coconut Bacon

Preparation time: 10 minutes
Cooking time: 30 minutes
Servings: 2
Ingredients:
• 3 ½ cups flaked coconut
• 1 tbsp. pure maple syrup
• 1 tbsp. water
• 2 tbsp. liquid smoke
• 1 tbsp. soy sauce
• 1 tsp. smoked paprika (optional)
Directions:
1. Preheat the smoker to 325°F.
2. A large mixing bowl combines liquid smoke, maple syrup, soy sauce, and water.
3. Pour flaked coconut over the mixture. Add it to a cooking sheet.
4. Place in the middle rack of the smoker.
5. Smoke it for 30 minutes, and flip the sides every 7–8 minutes.
6. Serve and enjoy.
Nutrition: Calories: 1244 | Fat: 100 g. | Carbohydrates: 70 g. | Protein: 16 g. | Fiber: 2 g.

Chapter 13. Vegan Recipes

273.   Toasted-Baked Tofu Cubes

Preparation time: 5 minutes
Cooking time: 30 minutes
Servings: 2
Ingredients:
- ½ tofu block, cubed
- 1 tbsp. olive oil
- 1 tbsp. nutritional yeast
- 1 tbsp. flour
- ¼ tsp. black pepper
- 1 tsp. sea salt
- ½ tsp. garlic powder

Directions:
1. Combine all the ingredients with tofu
2. Preheat the Grill to 230°C or 400°F.
3. Bake tofu on a lined baking tray for 15–30 minutes, and turn it around every 10 minutes.
Nutrition: Calories: 100 | Carbs: 5 g. | Protein: 8 g., Fat 6 g.

274.   Eggplant Pizza

Preparation time: 5 minutes
Cooking time: 35 minutes
Servings: 2
Ingredients:
- Eggplant (sliced ¼ -inch)
- Gluten-free pizza dough
- 1 cup pizza sauce
- Fresh rosemary and basil
- Cheese to taste
- Garlic cloves, chopped
- Red pepper, salt, and pepper
- Olive oil

Directions:
1. Rub eggplant slices with olive oil, rosemary, salt, and pepper, and bake for 25 minutes at 218°C or 425°F on the Grill.
2. Roll the dough round and spread the remaining ingredients on top.
3. Preheat the Grill to 230°C or 450°F at the pizza setting and bake the pizza for 10 minutes.
Nutrition: Calories: 260 | Carbs: 24 g. | Protein: 9 g., Fat 14 g.

275.   Sriracha Roasted Potatoes

Preparation time: 5 minutes
Cooking time: 30 minutes
Servings: 3
Ingredients:
- 3 potatoes, diced
- 2–3 tsp. sriracha
- ¼ garlic powder

- Salt & pepper
- Olive oil
- Fresh parsley, chopped

Directions:
1. Combine the potatoes with the remaining ingredients.
2. Preheat the Grill to 230°C or 450°F.
3. Line the pan with olive oil and spread the coated potatoes. Sprinkle parsley.
4. Bake for 30 minutes.
Nutrition: Calories: 147 | Carbs: 24.4 | Protein: 3 g. | Fat: 4.7 g.

276.   Brussel Sprouts, Mango, Avocado Salsa Tacos

Preparation time: 10 minutes
Cooking time: 30 minutes
Servings: 4
Ingredients:
- 4 taco shells
- 8 oz. Brussels sprouts, diced
- ½ mango, diced
- ½ avocado, diced
- ½ cup black beans, cooked
- 2 tbsp. onions, chopped
- ¼ cup cilantro, chopped
- 1 tbsp. Jalapeño, chopped
- Lime juice
- Olive oil
- 1 tbsp. taco seasoning
- Salt & pepper

Directions:
1. Preheat the Grill to 230°C or 400°F.
2. Mix the sprouts with taco seasoning, olive oil, salt, and pepper on the pan.
3. Roast for 15 minutes. Turn every 5 minutes.
4. To make the salsa, combine the mango, avocado, black beans, lime juice, cilantro, onion, jalapeno, salt, and pepper.
5. Cook taco shells and fill them with sprouts and salsa.
Nutrition: Calories: 407 | Carbs: 63.20 g. | Protein: 11.4 g. | Fat: 13.9 g.

277.   Garlic and Herb Smoke Potato

Preparation time: 5 minutes
Cooking time: 2 hours
Servings: 6
Ingredients:
- 1.5 lb. bag of Gemstone potatoes
- ¼ cup Parmesan cheese, fresh grated
- For the marinade:
- 2 tbsp. olive oil
- 6 garlic cloves, freshly chopped
- ½ tsp. oregano, dried
- ½ tsp. basil, dried
- ½ tsp. dill, dried
- ½ tsp. salt

- ½ tsp. Italian seasoning, dried
- ¼ tsp. ground pepper

Directions:

1. Preheat the smoker to 225°F.
2. Wash the potatoes thoroughly and add them to a sealable plastic bag.
3. Add garlic cloves, basil, salt, Italian seasoning, dill, oregano, and olive oil to the zip lock bag. Shake.
4. Place in the fridge for 2 hours to marinate.
5. Next, take an Aluminum foil and put 2 tbsp. of water along with the coated potatoes. Fold the foil so that the potatoes are sealed in.
6. Place in the preheated smoker. Smoke for 2 hours
7. Remove the foil and pour the potatoes into a bowl.
8. Serve with grated Parmesan cheese.

Nutrition: Calories: 146 | Fat: 6 g. | Fiber: 2.1 g. | Carbohydrates: 19 g. | Protein: 4 g.

278. Smoked Baked Beans

Preparation time: 15 minutes
Cooking time: 3 hours
Servings: 12
Ingredients:

- 1 ½ yellow onion, diced
- 3 Jalapeños
- 2 tbsp. molasses
- 56 oz. pork and beans
- ¾ cup barbeque sauce
- ½ cup dark brown sugar
- ¼ cup apple cider vinegar
- 2 tbsp. Dijon mustard

Directions:

1. Preheat the smoker to 250°F.
2. Pour the beans along with all the liquid into a pan. Add diced onion, Jalapeño, brown sugar, barbeque sauce, Dijon mustard, apple cider vinegar, and molasses.
3. Stir. Place the pan on one of the racks.
4. Smoke for 3 hours until thickened
5. Remove after 3 hours.
6. Serve.

Nutrition: Calories: 214 | Fat: 2 g. | Carbohydrates: 42 g. | Protein: 7 g. | Fiber: 7 g.

279. Corn & Cheese Chili Rellenos

Preparation time: 30 minutes
Cooking time: 65 minutes
Servings: 8–12
Ingredients:

- Pellet: hardwood, maple
- 2 lbs. ripe tomatoes, chopped
- 4 garlic cloves, chopped
- ½ cup sweet onion, chopped
- 1 Jalapeño stemmed, seeded, and chopped
- 8 large green New Mexican or poblano chiles
- 3 ears sweet corn, husked
- ½ tsp. dry oregano, Mexican, crumbled

- 1 tsp. ground cumin
- 1 tsp. mild chili powder
- ⅛ tsp. ground cinnamon
- Salt and freshly ground pepper
- 3 cups grated Monterey Jack cheese
- ½ cup Mexican crema
- 1 cup queso fresco, crumbled
- Fresh cilantro leaves

Directions:

1. Before starting, place the tomatoes, garlic, onions, and Jalapeño in a shallow baking dish on the grill grate. This vegetable will expose more wood smoke.
2. When prepared to cook, start the grill on Smoke, with the lid open until the fire is established (4–5 minutes).
3. Mix the cooled tomato mixture in a blender and liquefy. Put in a pot.
4. To taste, stir in the cumin, oregano, chili powder, cinnamon, salt, and pepper.
5. Carefully peel the New Mexican chiles' blistered outer skin: Leave the stem ends intact and try not to tear the flesh.
6. Cut the corn off the cobs and put it in a large mixing bowl.
7. Bake or cook the Rellenos for 25–30 minutes or until the filling is bubbling and the cheese has melted.
8. Sprinkle with queso fresco and garnish it with fresh cilantro leaves, if desired.
9. Enjoy!

Nutrition: Calories: 206 | Carbs: 5 g. | Fat: 14 g. | Protein: 9 g.

280. Pumpkin Quesadillas

Preparation time: 5 minutes
Cooking time: 10 minutes
Servings: 3
Ingredients:

- ½ canned pumpkin (pure)
- 2 gluten-free tortillas
- ½ cup refried beans
- 1–2 tbsp. nutritional yeast
- 1 tsp. onion powder
- 1 tsp. garlic powder
- Pinch cayenne
- Salt & pepper

Directions:

1. Mix the pumpkin with nutritional yeast, onion powder, garlic powder, cayenne, salt, and pepper.
2. Spread the pumpkin paste mixture in one tortilla and the refried beans in another.
3. Sandwich them together and toast on the grill for 5 minutes.

Nutrition: Calories: 282 kcal | Carbs: 37 g. | Protein: 13 g. | Fat: 10 g.

281. Sweet Potato Toast

Preparation time: 5 minutes
Cooking time: 25 minutes
Servings: 2
Ingredients:
- 1 large sweet potato, cut
- Avocado/guacamole
- Hummus
- Radish/Tomato (optional)
- Salt & pepper
- Lemon slice

Directions:

1. Toast the potatoes on the grill for 10 minutes on each side.

2. Spread mashed avocado, add seasoning, top it with radish slices and squeeze a lime over it, or spread hummus, seasoning, and your choice of greens.

Nutrition: Calories: 114 kcal | Carbs: 13 g. | Protein: 2 g. | Fat: 7 g.

Chapter 14. Bread and Pizza Recipes

282. Cheesy Ham and Pineapple Sandwich

Preparation time: 10 minutes
Cooking time: 20 minutes
Servings: 4
Ingredients:
- 1 (10 oz.) package deli sliced ham
- 4 pineapple rings
- 4 slices of Swiss cheese
- 4 buns, like potato
- Butter softened
- Poppy seeds

Directions:
1. Cut a large piece of aluminum foil into 4 squares, large enough to wrap sandwiches in, and place on a flat work surface.
2. On top of each foil piece, stack a bottom bun, ¼ of the ham, a pineapple ring, and 1 slice of cheese.
3. Place the top bun on top and brush with melted butter; when all sandwiches are built, sprinkle poppy seeds on top.
4. Wrap the sandwiches with foil and leave the top slightly loose.
5. Preheat to medium-high and grill for 20 minutes.
6. Let cool slightly, unwrap, and enjoy it!

Nutrition: Energy (calories): 429 | Protein: 10.06 g. | Fat: 24.82 g. | Carbohydrates: 42.15 g. | Calcium: 317 mg. | Fiber: 1.2 g. | Magnesium: 27 mg. | Phosphorus: 407 mg. | Iron: 1.23 mg.

283. Garlic Parmesan Grilled Cheese Sandwiches

Preparation time: 2 minutes
Cooking time: 7 minutes
Servings: 1
Ingredients:
- 2 slices Italian bread, sliced thin
- 2 slices provolone cheese
- 2 tbsp. butter, softened
- Garlic powder, for dusting
- Dried parsley, for dusting
- Parmesan cheese, shredded, for dusting

Directions:
1. Spread batter evenly across 2 slices of bread and sprinkle each buttered side with garlic and parsley.
2. Sprinkle a few tbsp. Parmesan cheese over each buttered side of bread and gently press the cheese into the bread.
3. Preheat the grill to medium heat and place one slice of bread, buttered side down, into the skillet.
4. Top with provolone slices and the second slice of bread with the butter side up.
5. Cook for 3 minutes and flip to cook for 3 minutes on the other side; cook until bread is golden and parmesan cheese is crispy.
6. Serve warm with your favorite sides!

Nutrition: Energy (calories): 507 | Protein: 14.94 g. | Fat: 38.8 g. | Carbohydrates: 25.72 g. | Calcium: 447 mg. | Magnesium: 29 mg. | Phosphorus: 641 mg. | Iron: 1.67 m | Potassium: 222 mg.

284. Grilled Pizza Cheese

Preparation time: 10 minutes
Cooking time: 20 minutes
Servings: 4
Ingredients:
- 8 French bread slices
- 3 tbsp. butter, softened
- ½ cup pizza sauce
- ¼ cup Mozzarella cheese
- ½ cup pepperoni diced
- Garlic powder, for dusting
- Oregano, for dusting

Directions:
1. Cut bread slices into squares and spread with butter on both sides.
2. Place ¼ cup pizza sauce, 1 tbsp. Mozzarella cheese and 1 tbsp. diced pepperoni on each square.
3. Sprinkle cheese and pepperoni with garlic powder and oregano as desired.
4. Grill in a pan over medium heat for 5 minutes on each side to melt the cheese.
5. Enjoy it!

Nutrition: Energy (calories): 210 | Protein: 6.56 g. | Fat: 10.33 g. | Carbohydrates: 22.75 g. | Calcium: 145 mg. | Magnesium: 18 mg. | Phosphorus: 104 mg. | Iron: 1.75 mg.

285. Sun-Dried Tomato and Chicken Flatbreads

Preparation time: 5 minutes
Cooking time: 7 minutes
Servings: 4
Ingredients:
• 4 flatbreads or thin pita bread
• Topping:
• 1 ½ cups sliced grilled chicken
• ½ cup sun-dried tomatoes
• 6 fresh basil leaves, coarsely chopped
• 3 cups Mozzarella cheese, shredded
• 1 tsp. salt
• 1 tsp. ground black pepper
• 1 tsp. red pepper flakes
• Chili oil, for serving
Directions:
1. Smoke the grill to low heat.
2. Stir all the topping ingredients together with a rubber spatula.
3. Top with some topping mixture; spreading to the edges of each.
4. Tent the flatbreads with foil for 5 minutes each, or until cheese is just melted.
5. Cut each with a pizza cutter or kitchen scissors.
6. With chili oil to serve!
Nutrition: Energy (calories): 414 | Protein: 39.39 g. | Fat: 17.67 g. | Carbohydrates: 24.47 g. | Calcium: 858 mg. | Magnesium: 61 mg. | Phosphorus: 670 mg. | Iron: 2.54 mg. | Fiber: 3.3 g.

286. Veggie Pesto Flatbread

Preparation time: 30 minutes
Cooking time: 30 minutes
Servings: 4
Ingredients:
• 1 lb. frozen pizza dough
• 3 tbsp. olive oil
• 2 garlic cloves, chopped
• 1/2 onion, chopped
• 1/4 red bell pepper, diced
• 1/2 tomatoes, sliced
• 2 leaves dried oregano
• A pinch black pepper
Directions:
1. Thaw the dough according to the package directions. Coat the cake pan with nonstick spray, then press the dough into the pan to form a crust. 2 tablespoons of olive oil drizzled on the dough
2. Spread the garlic, onion, and red pepper on the dough, leaving the crust uncovered.
3. Arrange the tomatoes on the crust and drizzle with the remaining olive oil. Finish with oregano and pepper to taste.

4. When you're ready to cook, set the Traeger grill to Smoke and leave the lid open until the fire starts (4 to 5 minutes). Preheat the oven to 450°F and leave the lid closed for 10 to 15 minutes.
5. Cook for 30 minutes. The crust should be golden and firm to the touch. Enjoy!
Nutrition: Energy (calories): 110 | Protein: 12.63 g. | Fat: 3.85 g. | Carbohydrates: 7.9 g. | Calcium: 404 mg. | Magnesium: 39 mg. | Phosphorus: 251 mg. | Iron: 1.09 mg. | Fiber: 2.4 g.

287. Grilled Vegetable Pizza

Preparation time: 30 minutes
Cooking time: 10 minutes
Servings: 6
Ingredients:
• 8 small fresh mushrooms, halved
• 1 small zucchini
• 1 small yellow pepper, sliced
• 1 small red pepper, sliced
• 1 small red onion, sliced
• 1 tbsp. white wine vinegar
• 1 tbsp. water
• 4 tsp. olive oil, divided
• ½ tsp. dried basil
• ¼ tsp. sea salt
• ¼ tsp. pepper
• 1 prebaked 12-inch thin whole wheat pizza crust
• 1 can (8 oz.) pizza sauce
• 2 small tomatoes, chopped
• 2 cups shredded part-skim mozzarella cheese
Directions:
1. Heat the wood pellet to medium-high heat.
2. Combine all the seasoning ingredients in a large mixing bowl.
3. Transfer to grill and cook over medium heat for 10 minutes or until tender, stirring often.
4. Brush crust with remaining oil and spread with pizza sauce.
5. Top evenly with grilled vegetables, tomatoes, and cheese.
6. Tent with aluminum foil and grill over medium heat for 5–7 minutes or until edges are lightly browned, and cheese is melted.
7. Serve warm!
Nutrition: Energy (calories): 168 | Protein: 10.76 g. | Fat: 9.77 g. | Carbohydrates: 9.95 g. | Calcium: 238 mg. | Magnesium: 25 mg. | Phosphorus: 187 mg. | Iron: 0.85 mg. | Fiber: 1.3 g.

288. Decadent Chocolate Cheesecake

Preparation time: 20 minutes
Cooking time: 1 hour
Servings: 8
Ingredients:
• 1 cup chocolate wafer crumbs
• 2 tbsp. butter, melted
• 4 oz. unsweetened baking chocolate, chopped
• 16 oz. cream cheese softened
• ¾ cup white sugar
• 2 eggs
• 1 tsp. vanilla extract
• ¼ cup heavy cream
• 2 oz. unsweetened baking chocolate, chopped finely
• ¼ cup white sugar
• 1 tbsp. unsalted butter
Directions:
1. Preheat the grill to 350°F (175°C). Grease a 9-inch springform pan. Sprinkle the chocolate cookie crumbs on the bottom of the pan.
2. Melt the 2 oz. of unsweetened baking chocolate and 4 tbsp. of butter till smooth.
3. Stir till.
4. Mix the cream cheese, ½ cup of sugar, and 1 tsp. of vanilla.
5. Add eggs and beat till smooth.
6. Add the melted chocolate mixture into the cream cheese mixture. Beat till.
7. Pour the batter into a greased springform pan. Bake for 1 hour. Cool.
8. For the filling: In another bowl, beat the cream cheese, 2 oz. of unsweetened chocolate, ¼ C. of sugar, and 1 tbsp. of butter.
9. Beat until smooth. Add the whipped cream and beat till.
10. Pour the filling onto the cooled crust and refrigerate the cake.
Nutrition: Energy (calories): 625 | Protein: 10.5 g. | Fat: 39.57 g. | Carbohydrates: 58.12 g. | Calcium: 90 mg. | Magnesium: 102 mg. | Phosphorus: 234 mg. | Iron: 5.85 mg. | Potassium: 377 mg.

289. Pork Tenderloin Sandwiches

Preparation time: 10 minutes
Cooking time: 25 minutes
Servings: 6
Ingredients:
• 2 (¾-lb.) pork tenderloins
• 1 tsp. garlic powder
• 1 tsp. sea salt
• 1 tsp. dry mustard
• ½ tsp. coarsely ground pepper
• Olive oil, for brushing
• 6 whole-wheat hamburger buns
• 6 tbsp. barbecue sauce
Directions:
1. Mix the garlic, salt, pepper, and mustard in a small bowl.
2. Rub pork tenderloins evenly with olive oil, then seasoning mix.
3. Preheat the grill to medium-high heat, and cook 10–12 minutes on each side or until a meat thermometer inserted into the thickest portion registers 155°F.
4. Slice thin and evenly pile onto hamburger buns.
5. Drizzle each sandwich with barbecue sauce and serve.
Nutrition: Energy (calories): 250 | Protein: 39.97 g. | Fat: 5.54 g. | Carbohydrates: 7.57 g. | Calcium: 18 mg. | Magnesium: 47 mg. | Phosphorus: 412 mg. | Iron: 1.92 mg. | Potassium: 686 mg.

290. Amazing Irish Soda Bread

Preparation time: 15 minutes
Cooking time: 1 hour and 15 minutes
Servings: 10
Ingredients:
• 4 cups flour
• 1 cup raisins
• ¼ cup sugar
• 1 tbsp. caraway seeds
• 2 tsp. baking powder
• 1 tsp. baking soda
• ¾ tsp. salt
• 1 ¼ cup buttermilk
• 1 cup sour cream
• 2 eggs
Directions:
1. Preheat the Traeger grill to 375°F. Mix the dry ingredients in a large bowl. Be sure to measure and combine well.
2. Add the sour cream, eggs, and buttermilk to the dry ingredients. Mix until all of the ingredients are wet. Remove the dough from the bowl and form it into a rectangular loaf.
3. Bake for 60 minutes at 375 °F. After 45 minutes, remove the baking sheet from the oven and spread the remaining dough into a wider loaf. Return to the oven for the last 15 minutes or so.
4. Allow cooling for 30 minutes.
5. Serve.
Nutrition: Energy (calories): 286 | Protein: 9.71 g. | Fat: 6.25 | Carbohydrates: 47.1 g. | Calcium: 132 mg. | Magnesium: 21 mg. | Phosphorus: 197 mg. | Iron: 3.08 mg. | Potassium: 288 mg.

291. Grilled Pizza

Preparation time: 15 minutes
Cooking time: 10 minutes
Servings: 4
Ingredients:
• 2 tbsp. all-purpose flour, plus more as needed
• 6–8 oz. pizza dough
• 1 tbsp. oil, divided
• ½ cup Alfredo sauce
• 1 cup mozzarella cheese, shredded
• ½ cup ricotta cheese, pieces
• 14 pepperoni slices
• ½ tsp. dried oregano for serving, optional
Directions:
1. Place the grill grate inside the grill and close the hood. Set the temperature to 400°F and preheat for 8 minutes.
2. Meanwhile, roll the dough onto a floured surface with a rolling pin.
3. Roll the dough and then cut it in a rod shape that fits inside the grill grate.
4. Brush the dough with oil and flip to coat the dough on both sides.
5. Poke the dough with the fork.
6. Place it on the grill grate and close the hood.
7. Cook for 4 minutes, then flip and cook for 4 minutes more.
8. Now open the lid and spread sauce, cheeses, and pepperoni.
9. Close the grill and cook for 3 minutes. Serve with a sprinkle of oregano.
Nutrition: Calories: 465 | Fat: 31.6 g. | Carbs: 30.1 g. | Protein: 15 g.

292. Almond Flour Bread

Preparation time: 10 minutes
Cooking time: 1 hour 15 minutes
Servings: 24 slices
Ingredients:
• 1 tsp. sea salt or to taste
• 1 tbsp. apple cider vinegar
• ½ cup warm water
• ¼ cup coconut oil
• 4 eggs (beaten)
• 1 tbsp. gluten-free baking powder
• 2 cups blanched almond flour
• ¼ cup Psyllium husk powder
• 1 tsp. ginger
Directions:
1. Preheat the grill to 350°F with the lid closed for 15 minutes.
2. Line a loaf pan with parchment paper. Set aside.
3. Combine the ginger, psyllium husk powder, almond flour, salt, and baking powder in a large bowl.
4. Mix the oil, apple cider vinegar, eggs, and warm water in another bowl. Mix well.

5. Gradually pour the flour mixture into the egg mixture, stirring as you pour. Stir until it forms a smooth batter.
6. Fill the lined loaf pan with the batter and cover the batter with foil.
7. Place the loaf pan on the grill and bake for 1 hour or until a toothpick inserted in the middle comes out clean.
Nutrition: Calories: 93 | Fat: 7.5 g. | Carbs: 3.6 g. | Protein: 3.1 g.

293. Donut Bread Pudding

Preparation time: 15 minutes
Cooking time: 40 minutes
Servings: 8
Ingredients:
• 5 eggs
• ¾ cup sugar
• 2 cups heavy cream
• 1 tsp. ground cinnamon
• 16 cake donuts
• ½ cup raisins, seedless
• 2 tsp. vanilla extract
• ¾ cup butter, melted, cooled slightly
• Ice cream
Directions:
1. Grease a baking pan with butter and place the donuts in an even layer.
2. Sprinkle with raisins and drizzle with butter.
3. To make the custard: in a bowl, whisk together the cinnamon, vanilla, cream, eggs, and sugar.
4. Pour this mixture over the donuts and set aside for 15 minutes. Cover with foil.
5. Set the grill temperature to 350°F and preheat for 15 minutes with the lid closed.
6. Bake in the grill for 30–40 minutes or until the pudding is set.
7. Remove the foil and bake for 10 minutes more.
8. Cool and drizzle with ice cream. Serve.
Nutrition: Calories: 615 | Fat: 41.3 | Carbs: 55.3 g. | Protein: 7.7 g.

294. Mango Bread

Preparation time: 15 minutes
Cooking time: 1 hour
Servings: 4
Ingredients:
• 2½ cup cubed ripe mangoes
• 2 cups all-purpose flour
• 1 tsp. baking powder
• 1 tsp. baking soda
• 2 eggs (beaten)
• 1 tsp. cinnamon
• 1 tsp. vanilla extract
• ½ tsp. nutmeg
• ¾ cup olive oil
• ¾ cup sugar
• 1 tbsp. lemon juice

- ½ tsp. salt
- ½ cup chopped dates

Directions:

1. Preheat the grill to 350°F for 15 minutes with the lid closed.
2. Grease a loaf pan.
3. Combine flour, baking powder, soda, cinnamon, salt, and sugar in a bowl.
4. Whisk together the egg, lemon juice, oil, and vanilla in another bowl.
5. Pour the egg mixture into the flour mixture and mix well.
6. Fold in the mangoes and dates.
7. Pour the mixture into the loaf pan and place the pan on the grill.
8. Place the loaf pan on the grill and bake for 50–60 minutes or until a toothpick inserted in the middle comes out clean.
9. Cool, slice, and serve.

Nutrition: Calories: 856 | Fat: 41.2 g. | Carbs: 118.9 g. | Protein: 10.7 g.

295. Pellet-Grill Flatbread Pizza

Preparation time: 10 minutes
Cooking time: 20 minutes
Servings: 3
Ingredients:

Dough:
- 2 cups flour
- 1 tbsp. salt
- 1 tbsp. sugar
- 2 tbsp. yeast
- 6 oz. warm water
- Toppings:
- Green/red bell pepper
- ½ garlic
- Zucchini
- ½ onion
- Olive oil
- 5 bacon strips
- 1 cup halved yellow cherry tomatoes
- Jalapeños, sliced
- Green olives, sliced
- Kalamata olives, sliced
- Goat cheese
- For drizzling: Balsamic vinegar

Directions:

1. Combine all dough ingredients in a stand mixer bowl. Mix until the dough is smooth and elastic. Divide into 3 equal balls.
2. Roll each dough ball with a rolling pin into a thin round to fit a 12-inch skillet.
3. Grease the skillet using olive oil.
4. Meanwhile, turn your pellet grill on and smoke for about 4–5 minutes with the lid open. Turn to high and preheat for about 10–15 minutes with the lid closed.

5. Once ready, arrange peppers, garlic, zucchini, and onion on the grill grate, then drizzle with oil and salt. Check at 10 minutes.
6. Now remove zucchini from the grill and add bacon. Continue to cook for another 10 minutes until the bacon is done.
7. Transfer the toppings to a chopping board to cool. Chop tomatoes, jalapenos, and olive.
8. Brush your crust with oil and smash garlic with a fork over the crust. Smear carefully not to tear the crust.
9. Add toppings to the crust in the skillet.
10. Place the skillet on the grill and cook for about 20 minutes until brown edges.
11. Repeat for the other crusts.
12. Now drizzle each with vinegar and slice.
13. Serve and enjoy.

Nutrition: Calories 342 | Total Fat: 1.2 g. | Saturated Fat: 0.2 g. | Total Carbs: 70.7 g. | Net Carbs: 66.8 g. | Protein: 11.7 g. | Sugars: 4.2 g. | Fiber: 3.9 g. | Sodium: 2333 mg. | Potassium: 250 mg.

296. Grilled Homemade Croutons

Preparation time: 10 minutes
Cooking time: 30 minutes
Servings: 6
Ingredients:
- 2 tbsp. Mediterranean Blend Seasoning
- ¼ cup olive oil
- 6 cups cubed bread

Directions:

1. Preheat your wood pellet grill to 250°F.
2. Combine seasoning and oil in a bowl, then drizzle the mixture over the bread cubes. Toss to coat evenly.
3. Layer the bread cubes on a cookie sheet, large, and place on the grill.
4. Bake for about 30 minutes. Stir at intervals of 5 minutes for browning evenly.
5. Once dried out and golden brown, remove it from the grill.
6. Serve and enjoy!

Nutrition: Calories 188 | Total Fat: 10 g. | Saturated Fat: 2 g. | Total Carbs: 20 g. | Net Carbs: 19 g. | Protein: 4 g. | Sugars: 2 g. | Fiber: 1 g. | Sodium: 1716 mg. | Potassium: 875 mg.

Chapter 15. Dessert Recipes

297. Grilled Pound Cake With Fruit Dressing

Preparation time: 20 minutes
Cooking time: 50 minutes
Servings: 12
Ingredients:
- 1 buttermilk pound cake, sliced into ¾-inch slices
- ⅛ cup butter, melted
- 1 ½ cup whipped cream
- ½ cup blueberries
- ½ cup raspberries
- ½ cup strawberries, sliced

Directions:
1. Preheat the grill to 400°F.
2. Brush both sides of each pound cake slice with melted butter.
3. Place directly on the grill grate and cook for 5 minutes per side. Turn 90°F halfway through cooking each side of the cake for checkered grill marks.
4. Remove and cool.
5. Top slices with whipped cream, blueberries, raspberries, and sliced strawberries.
6. Serve.
Nutrition: Calories: 222.1 | Fat: 8.7 g. | Carbs: 33.1 g. | Protein: 3.4 g.

298. Grilled Pineapple With Chocolate Sauce

Preparation time: 10 minutes
Cooking time: 25 minutes
Servings: 6
Ingredients:
- 1 pineapple
- 8 oz. bittersweet chocolate chips
- ½ cup spiced rum
- ½ cup whipping cream
- 2 tbsp. light brown sugar

Directions:
1. Preheat the grill to 400°F.
2. De-skin the pineapple and slice the pineapple into 1-inch cubes.
3. In a saucepan, combine the chocolate chips and start to melt.
4. Add the rum when the chips start to melt. Stir to mix well. Add a splash of pineapple juice.
5. Add in whipping cream and continue to mix. Lower heat to simmer to keep warm.
6. Thread pineapple cubes onto skewers. Sprinkle skewers with brown sugar.

7. Place skewers on the grill grate. Grill for 5 minutes per side.
8. Remove skewers from the grill and rest for 5 minutes.
9. Serve with chocolate sauce.
Nutrition: Calories: 112.6 | Fat: 0.5 g. | Carbs: 28.8 g. | Protein: 0.4 g.

299. Nectarine and Nutella Sundae

Preparation time: 10 minutes
Cooking time: 25 minutes
Servings: 4
Ingredients:
- 2 nectarines, halved and pitted
- 2 tsp. honey
- 4 tbsp. Nutella
- 4 scoops vanilla ice cream
- ¼ cup pecans, chopped
- Whipped cream to top
- 4 cherries to top

Directions:
1. Preheat the grill to 400°F.
2. Slice the nectarines in half and remove the pits.
3. Brush the cut side of each nectarine half with honey.
4. Place nectarines directly on the grill grate, and cut side down. Cook for 5–6 minutes or until grill marks develop.
5. Flip nectarines and cook on the other side for 2 minutes.
6. Remove nectarines and cool.
7. Fill the pit cavity on each nectarine half with 1 tbsp. Nutella.
8. Place 1 scoop of ice cream on top of Nutella. Top with whipped cream and cherries, and sprinkle chopped pecans.
9. Serve.
Nutrition: Calories: 90 | Fat: 3 g. | Carbs: 15 g. | Protein: 2 g.

300. Cinnamon Sugar Donut Holes

Preparation time: 10 minutes
Cooking time: 35 minutes
Servings: 4
Ingredients:
- ½ cup flour
- 1 tbsp. cornstarch
- ½ tsp. baking powder
- ⅛ tsp. baking soda
- ⅛ tsp. ground cinnamon
- ½ tsp. Kosher salt
- ¼ cup buttermilk
- ¼ cup sugar
- 1½ tbsp. butter, melted
- 1 egg
- ½ tsp. vanilla
Topping:
- 2 tbsp. sugar
- 1 tbsp. sugar
- 1 tsp. ground cinnamon

Directions:
1. Preheat the grill to 350°F.
2. In a bowl, combine the flour, cornstarch, baking powder, baking soda, ground cinnamon, and salt. Mix well.
3. Combine the buttermilk, sugar, melted butter, egg, and vanilla in another bowl. Whisk to mix.
4. Pour the wet mixture into the flour mixture and mix. Stir just until combined. Careful not to overmix.
5. Spray mini muffin tin with cooking spray.
6. Spoon 1 tbsp. of donut mixture into each mini muffin hole.
7. Place the tin on the grill grate and bake for 18 minutes or until a toothpick comes out clean.
8. Remove muffin tin from the grill and cool for 5 minutes.
9. In a small bowl, combine 1 tbsp. sugar and 1 tsp. ground cinnamon.
10. Melt 2 tbsp. butter in a glass dish. Dip each donut hole in the melted butter, then mix and toss with cinnamon sugar.
11. Serve.
Nutrition: Calories: 190 | Fat: 17 g. | Carbs: 21 g. | Protein: 3 g.

301.   Grill Chocolate Chip Cookies

Preparation time: 20 minutes
Cooking time: 45 minutes
Servings: 12
Ingredients:
• 1 cup salted butter, softened
• 1 cup sugar
• 1 cup light brown sugar
• 2 tsp. vanilla extract
• 2 eggs
• 3 cups all-purpose flour
• 1 tsp. baking soda
• ½ tsp. baking powder
• 1 tsp. natural sea salt
• 2 cups semi-sweet chocolate chips or chunks
Directions:
1. Preheat the grill to 375°F.
2. Line a baking sheet with parchment paper and set it aside.
3. Mix flour, baking soda, and salt in a bowl. Mix and set aside.
4. Mix butter, white, and brown sugar in a bowl until mixed. Beat in eggs and vanilla. Beat until fluffy.
5. Mix in dry ingredients; continue to stir until combined.
6. Add chocolate chips and mix well.
7. Roll 3 tbsp. of dough at a time into balls and place them on the cookie sheet. Evenly space then apart, with about 2 inches in between each ball.
8. Place cookie sheet directly on the grill grate and bake for 20–25 minutes, or until slightly browned.
9. Cool and serve.
Nutrition: Calories: 120 | Fat: 4 g. | Carbs: 22.8 g. | Protein: 1.4 g.

302.   Pellet Grill Chocolate Chip Cookies

Preparation time: 20 minutes
Cooking time: 45 minutes
Servings: 12
Ingredients:
• 1 cup salted butter softened
• 1 cup sugar
• 1 cup light brown sugar
• 2 tsp. vanilla extract
• 2 large eggs
• 3 cups all-purpose flour
• 1 tsp. baking soda
• ½ tsp. baking powder
• 1 tsp. natural sea salt
• 2 cups semi-sweet chocolate chips or chunks
Directions:
1. Preheat the pellet grill to 375°F.
2. Line a large baking sheet with parchment paper and set it aside.
3. Mix flour, baking soda, salt, and baking powder in a medium bowl. Once combined, set aside.
4. In a stand mixer bowl, combine butter, white sugar, and brown sugar until combined. Beat in eggs and vanilla. Beat until fluffy.
5. Mix in dry ingredients, and continue to stir until combined.
6. Add chocolate chips and mix thoroughly.
7. Roll 3 tbsp. of dough at a time into balls and place them on your cookie sheet. Evenly space them apart, with about 2–3 inches between each ball.
8. Place cookie sheet directly on the grill grate and bake for 20–25 minutes until the cookies' outside is slightly browned.
9. Remove from grill and allow to rest for 10 minutes. Serve and enjoy!
Nutrition: Calories: 120 | Fat: 4 | Cholesterol: 7.8 mg. | Carbohydrate: 22.8 g. | Fiber: 0.3 g. | Sugar: 14.4 g. | Protein: 1.4 g.

303.   Delicious Donuts on a Grill

Preparation time: 5 minutes
Cooking time: 10 minutes
Servings: 6
Ingredients:
• 1 ½ cups sugar, powdered
• ⅓ cup whole milk
• ½ tsp. vanilla extract
• 16 oz. biscuit dough, prepared
• Oil spray for greasing
• 1cup chocolate sprinkles for sprinkling
Directions:
1. Take a medium bowl and mix sugar, milk, and vanilla extract.
2. Combine well to create a glaze. Set the glaze aside for further use.

3. Place the dough onto the flat, clean surface.

4. Flat the dough with a rolling pin. Use a ring mold, about an inch, and cut the hole in each round dough's center.

5. Place the dough on a plate and refrigerate for 10 minutes.

6. Open the grill and install the grill grate inside it. Close the hood.

7. Select the grill from the menu, and set the temperature to medium. Set the time to 6 minutes. Select start and begin preheating.

8. Remove the dough from the refrigerator and coat it with cooking spray from both sides.

9. When the unit beeps, the grill is preheated; place the adjustable amount of dough on the grill grate.

10. Close the hood, and cook for 3 minutes. Remove donuts and place the remaining dough inside. Cook for 3 minutes.

11. Once all the donuts are ready, sprinkle chocolate sprinkles on top.

Nutrition: Calories: 400 | Fat: 11 g. | Cholesterol: 1 mg. | Sodium: 787 mg. | Total Carbohydrate: 71.3 g. | Fiber: 0.9 g. | Total Sugars: 45.3 g. | Protein: 5.7 g.

304. Blueberry Cobbler

Preparation time: 15 minutes
Cooking time: 30 minutes
Servings: 6
Ingredients:
• 4 cups fresh blueberries
• 1 tsp. grated lemon zest
• 1 cup sugar, plus 2 tbsp.
• 1 cup all-purpose flour, plus 2 tbsp.
• Juice of 1 lemon
• 2 tsp. baking powder
• ¼ tsp. salt
• 6 tbsp. unsalted butter
• ¾ cup whole milk
• ⅛ tsp. ground cinnamon
Directions:
1. In a prepared medium bowl, combine the blueberries, lemon zest, and 2 tbsp. sugar, 2 tbsp. flour, and lemon juice.

2. In a prepared medium bowl, combine the remaining 1 cup of flour and 1 cup of sugar, baking powder, and salt. Cut the butter into the flour mixture until it forms an even crumb texture. Stir in the milk until a dough forms.

3. Select BAKE, set the temperature to 350°F, and set the time to 30 minutes. Select START/STOP to begin preheating.

4. Meanwhile, pour the blueberry mixture into the Multi-Purpose Pan, spreading it evenly across the pan. Gently pour the batter over the blueberry mixture, then sprinkle the cinnamon over the top.

5. If the unit beeps to signify it has preheated, place the pan directly in the pot. Close the hood and cook for 30 minutes, until lightly golden.

6. When cooking is complete, serve warm.

Nutrition: Calories: 408 | Saturated Fat: 8 g. | Carbohydrates: 72 g. | Protein: 5 g.

305. Rum-Soaked Grilled Pineapple Sundaes

Preparation time: 15 minutes
Cooking time: 8 minutes
Servings: 6
Ingredients:
• ½ cup dark rum
• ½ cup packed brown sugar
• 1 tsp. the ground cinnamon, plus more for garnish
• 1 pineapple, cored and sliced
• Vanilla ice cream for serving
Directions:
1. Combine the rum, sugar, and cinnamon in a large shallow bowl or storage container. Add the pineapple slices and arrange them in a single layer. Coat with the mixture, then let soak for at least 5 minutes per side.

2. Insert the Grill Grate and cover the hood. Select GRILL, set the temperature to MAX, and set the time to 8 minutes. Select START/STOP to begin preheating.

3. While the unit is heating up, strain the pineapple of any excess rum sauce.

4. When the unit beeps to indicate that it has preheated, arrange the fruit in a single layer on the Grill Grate (you may need to do this in multiple batches). To get the best grill marks, gently press the fruit down; close the grill hood, and cook for 6–8 minutes without flipping. Remove the pineapple and repeat with the remaining pineapple slices if working in batches.

5. Remove from the oven and top each pineapple ring with a scoop of ice cream. Serve immediately with a sprinkle of cinnamon.

Nutrition: Calories: 240 | Saturated Fat: 2 g. | Carbohydrates: 43 g. | Protein: 2 g.

306. Charred Peaches With Bourbon Butter Sauce

Preparation time: 10 minutes
Cooking time: 12 minutes
Servings: 4
Ingredients:
• 4 tbsp. salted butter
• ¼ cup bourbon
• ¼ cup candied pecans
• ½ cup brown sugar
• 4 ripe peaches halved and pitted
Directions:
1. Insert the Grill Grate and cover the hood. Select GRILL, set the temperature to MAX, and set the time to 12 minutes. Select START/STOP to begin preheating.

2. While the unit is preheating, in a saucepan over medium heat, melt the butter for about 5 minutes. Once the butter is

browned, remove the pan from the heat and carefully add the bourbon.

3. Return the saucepan to medium-high heat and add the brown sugar. Bring to a boil and let the sugar dissolve for 5 minutes, stirring occasionally.

4. Pour the bourbon butter sauce into a medium shallow bowl and arrange the peaches to cut side down to coat the sauce.

5. When the unit beeps a sign that it has preheated, place the fruit on the Grill Grate in a single layer (you may need to do this in multiple batches). Gently press the fruit down to maximize grill marks. Close the hood and grill for 10–12 minutes without flipping. If working in batches, repeat this step for all the peaches.

6. When cooking is complete, remove the peaches and top each with the pecans. Drizzle with the remaining bourbon butter sauce and serve immediately.

Nutrition: Calories: 309 | Saturated Fat: 8 g. | Carbohydrates: 34 g. | Protein: 2 g.

307. Chocolate-Hazelnut and Strawberry Grilled Dessert Pizza

Preparation time: 10 minutes
Total **Cooking time:** 6 minutes
Servings: 4
Ingredients:
• 2 tbsp. all-purpose flour, plus more as needed
• ½ store-bought pizza dough (about 8 ounces)
• 1 tbsp. canola oil
• 1 cup fresh strawberries, sliced
• 1 tbsp. sugar
• ½ cup chocolate-hazelnut spread
Directions:
1. Insert the Grill Grate and cover the hood. Select GRILL, set the temperature to MAX, and set the time to 6 minutes. Select START/STOP to begin preheating.

2. While the unit is preheating, dust a clean work surface with the flour, place the dough on the floured surface and roll it out to a 9-inch round of even thickness. Sprinkle the roller and work the surface with additional flour, as needed, to ensure the dough does not stick.

3. Brush the surface of the rolled-out dough evenly with half the oil. Flip the dough over, and brush with the remaining oil. Poke the dough with a fork 5 or 6 times across its surface to prevent air pockets from forming during cooking.

4. When the unit beeps to signify it has preheated, place the dough on the Grill Grate. Close the hood and cook for 3 minutes.

5. After 3 minutes, flip the dough. Close the hood and continue cooking for the remaining 3 minutes.

6. Meanwhile, in a medium mixing bowl, combine the strawberries and sugar.

7. Move the pizza to a cutting board and let it cool. Top with the chocolate-hazelnut spread and strawberries. Cut into pieces and serve.

Nutrition: Calories: 377 | Saturated Fat: 4 g. | Sodium: 258 mg. | Carbs: 53 g. | Protein: 7 g.

308. Smoked Pumpkin Pie

Preparation time: 10 minutes
Cooking time: 50 minutes
Servings: 8
Ingredients:
• 1 tbsp. cinnamon
• 1-½ tbsp. pumpkin pie spice
• 1 (5 oz.) pumpkin can
• 1 (4 oz.) can sweeten condensed milk
• 2 beaten eggs
• 1 unbaked pie shell
Topping:
• Whipped cream
Directions:
1. Preheat the grill to 325°F. Place a baking sheet on the grill.
2. Combine all your ingredients in a bowl, except the pie shell, then pour the mixture into a pie crust.
3. Place the pie on the baking sheet and smoke for 50–60 minutes or until a knife comes out clean when inserted.
4. Remove and cool for 2 hours. Serve with whipped cream topping.

Nutrition: Calories: 292 | Fat: 11 g. | Carbs: 42 g. | Protein: 7 g.

309. Smoked Nut Mix

Preparation time: 15 minutes
Cooking time: 20 minutes
Servings: 8
Ingredients:
• 3 cups mixed nuts (pecans, peanuts, almonds, etc.)
• ½ tbsp. brown sugar
• 1 tbsp. thyme, dried
• ¼ tbsp. mustard powder
• 1 tbsp. olive oil, extra-virgin
Directions:
1. Preheat the grill to 250°F with the lid closed for 15 minutes.
2. Combine all ingredients in a bowl, then transfer them to a cookie sheet lined with parchment paper.
3. Place the cookie sheet on a grill and grill for 20 minutes.
4. Cool and serve.

Nutrition: Calories: 249 | Fat: 21.5 g. | Carbs: 12.3 g. | Protein: 5.7 g.

310.   Grilled Peaches and Cream

Preparation time: 15 minutes
Cooking time: 8 minutes
Servings: 8
Ingredients:
• 4 halved and pitted peaches
• 1 tbsp. vegetable oil
• 2 tbsp. clover honey
• 1 cup cream cheese, soft with honey and nuts
Directions:
1. Preheat the grill to 300°F.
2. Coat the peaches lightly with oil and place on the grill pit side down.
3. Grill for 5 minutes or until nice grill marks on the surfaces.
4. Turn over the peaches, then drizzle with honey.
5. Spread a cream cheese dollop where the pit was and grill for 2–3 minutes.
6. Serve.
Nutrition: Calories: 139 | Fat: 10.2 g. | Carbs: 11.6 g. | Protein: 1.1 g.

311.   Berry Cobbler

Preparation time: 15 minutes
Cooking time: 35 minutes
Servings: 8
Ingredients:
For Fruit Filling:
• 3 cups frozen mixed berries
• 1 lemon juice
• 1 cup brown sugar
• 1 tbsp. vanilla extract
• 1 tbsp. lemon zest, finely grated
• A pinch salt
For Cobbler Topping:
• 1 ½ cups all-purpose flour
• 1 ½ tbsp. baking powder
• 3 tbsp. sugar, granulated
• ½ tbsp. salt
• 8 tbsp. cold butter
• ½ cup sour cream
• 2 tbsp. raw sugar
Directions:
1. Preheat the grill to 350°F for 15 minutes with the lid closed.
2. Meanwhile, combine frozen mixed berries, lemon juice, brown sugar, vanilla, lemon zest, and a pinch of salt. Transfer into a skillet and let the fruit sit and thaw.
3. Mix flour, baking powder, sugar, and salt in a bowl. Cut cold butter into peas using a pastry blender, then add to the mix. Mix everything.
4. Stir in the sour cream until the dough starts to come together.
5. Pinch small pieces of dough and place them over the fruit until fully covered. Splash the top with raw sugar.
6. Place the skillet directly on the grill grate, close the lid and cook for 35 minutes or until the juices bubble.
7. Remove the skillet from the grill and cool for a few minutes.
8. Scoop and serve.
Nutrition: Calories: 371 | Fat: 13 g. | Carbs: 60 g. | Protein: 3 g.

312.   Grill Apple Crisp

Preparation time: 20 minutes
Cooking time: 1 hour
Servings: 15
Ingredients:
Apples:
• 10 large apples
• ½ cup flour
• 1 cup sugar, dark brown
• ½ tbsp. cinnamon
• ½ cup butter slices
Crisp:
• 3 cups oatmeal, old-fashioned
• 1-½ cups softened butter, salted
• 1-½ tbsp. cinnamon
• 2 cups brown sugar
Directions:
1. Preheat the grill to 350°F.
2. Wash, peel, core, and dice the apples into cubes.
3. Mix flour, dark brown sugar, and cinnamon with apples.
4. Spray a baking pan with cooking spray and place apples inside. Top with butter slices.
5. Mix all crisp ingredients in a bowl until well combined. Place the mixture over the apples.
6. Place on the grill and cook for 1 hour, checking after every 15 minutes to ensure cooking is even. Do not place it on the hottest grill part.
7. Remove and cool a bit. Serve.
Nutrition: Calories: 528 | Fat: 26 g. | Carbs: 75 g. | Protein: 4 g.

313.   Smoked Peach Parfait

Preparation time: 20 minutes
Cooking time: 35–45 minutes
Servings: 4
Ingredients:
• 4 barely ripe peaches, halved and pitted
• 1 tbsp. firmly packed brown sugar
• 1-pint vanilla ice cream
• 3 tbsp. honey
Directions:
1. Preheat the grill to 200°F.
2. Sprinkle-cut peach halves with brown sugar.
3. Transfer them to the grill and smoke for 33–45 minutes.
4. Transfer the peach halves to dessert plates and top with vanilla ice cream.
5. Drizzle with honey and serve.

Nutrition: Calories: 309 | Fat: 27 g. | Carbs: 17 g. | Protein: 4 g.

314. Grilled Fruit and Cream

Preparation time: 15 minutes
Cooking time: 10 minutes
Servings: 4
Ingredients:
• 2 apricots, halved
• 1 nectarine, halved
• 2 peaches, halved
• ¼ cup blueberries
• ½ cup raspberries
• 2 tbsp. honey
• 1 orange, peel
• 2 cups cream
• ½ cup balsamic vinegar
Directions:
1. Preheat the grill to 400°F with the grill closed.
2. Grill peaches, nectarines, and apricots for 4 minutes on each side.
3. Place the pan on the stove and turn on medium heat.
4. Add 2 tbsp. honey, vinegar, and orange peel.
5. Simmer until medium-thick.
6. Add honey and cream to a bowl and whip until it reaches a soft form.
7. Place fruits on a serving plate, sprinkle berries and drizzle balsamic reduction.
8. Serve with cream.
Nutrition: Calories: 230 | Fat: 3 g. | Carbs: 35 g. | Protein: 2 g.

315. Apple Pie Grill

Preparation time: 20 minutes
Cooking time: 30 minutes
Servings: 4
Ingredients:
• ¼ cup sugar
• 4 apples, sliced
• 1 tbsp. cornstarch
• 1 tsp. cinnamon, ground
• 1 pie crust, refrigerator, soften according to the directions on the box
• ½ cup peach preserves
Directions:
1. Preheat the grill to 375°F with a closed lid.
2. Add cinnamon, cornstarch, sugar, and apples to a bowl, and keep it on the side.
3. Place pie crust in pie pan and spread preserves; place the apples.
4. Fold crust slightly.
5. Place pan on the grill (upside down) and smoke for 30–40 minutes.
6. Rest and serve.
Nutrition: Calories: 160 | Fat: 1 g. | Carbs: 35 g. | Protein: 3 g.

316. Grill Chicken Flatbread

Preparation time: 5 minutes
Cooking time: 30 minutes
Servings: 6
Ingredients:
• 6 mini bread pieces
• 1-½ cups divided buffalo sauce
• 4 cups cooked and cubed chicken breasts
• For drizzling:
• Mozzarella cheese
Directions:
1. Preheat the grill to 400°F.
2. Place the pieces of bread on a surface, flat, then evenly spread ½ cup of buffalo sauce on all pieces of bread.
3. Toss together chicken breasts and 1 cup of buffalo sauce, then top all the pieces of bread evenly.
4. Top each with mozzarella cheese.
5. Place the pieces of bread directly on the grill but over indirect heat. Close the lid.
6. Cook for 5–7 minutes or until slightly toasty edges and cheese is melted.
7. Remove and drizzle with cheese. Serve.
Nutrition: Calories: 346 | Fat: 7.6 g. | Carbs: 33.9 g. | Protein: 32.5 g.

317. Ice Cream Bread

Preparation time: 10 minutes
Cooking time: 1 hour
Servings: 12–16
Ingredients:
• 1 ½ quart full-fat butter pecan ice cream, softened
• 1 tsp. salt
• 2 cups semisweet chocolate chips
• 1 cup sugar
• 1 stick melted butter
• Butter, for greasing
• 4 cup self-rising flour
Directions:
1. Add wood pellets to your smoker and follow your cooker's startup program. Preheat your smoker with your lid closed until it reaches 350°F.
2. Set the cake on the grill, cover, and smoke for 50 minutes to an hour. A toothpick should come out clean.
3. Take the pan off of the grill for 10 minutes. Cool the bread.
Nutrition: Calories: 135 | Carbs: 0 g. | Fat: 0 g. | Protein: 0 g.

318. Apple Cake

Preparation time: 15 minutes
Cooking time: 45 minutes
Servings: 12
Ingredients:
Cake:
• ½ cup oil
• 1 ½ cup brown sugar
• 1 egg
• 1 cup sour cream
• 1 tbsp. baking soda
• ½ tbsp. baking soda
• ½ tbsp. baking powder
• 1 ½ tbsp. vanilla
• 2 ½ cups flour
• 2 apples, finely diced
Streusel:
• 1 stick butter
• ½ cup brown sugar
• ½ cup flour
• ½ cup oats
• ½ tbsp. cinnamon
Glaze:
• 2 cups powdered sugar
• 1 tbsp. apple cinnamon blend
• 3 tbsp. milk
Directions:
1. Preheat the grill to 325°F.
2. Add the cake ingredients except for the apples in a blender and pulse until mixed. Fold in the diced apples.
3. Spread the mixture on a baking pan.
4. Mix the streusel ingredients until crumbly, then pour the mixture over the cake mixture.
5. Place the baking pan on the top rack of your Traeger to create a space between the cake pan and the fire.
6. Bake for 45 minutes or until the tester comes out mostly crumbs only.
7. Rest and serve.
Nutrition: Calories: 452 | Fat: 21 g. | Carbs: 61 g. | Protein: 5 g.

319. Baked Caramel Pecan Brownie

Preparation time: 15 minutes
Cooking time: 50 minutes
Servings: 6
Ingredients:
• ½ cup cocoa powder
• ¾ tsp. baking soda
• ¾ cup pecans, halves
• ¼ cup butter
• ½ cup brown sugar
• ½ cup heavy cream
• 1 cup brown sugar
• 1 cup all-purpose flour
• ½ tsp. salt
• 6 tbsp. butter, melted
• 3 eggs
• ¼ cup heavy cream
• 6 oz. chocolate, chopped
Directions:
1. To make the caramel sauce: toast the pecans in a pan on the stovetop for 5 minutes. Stirring occasionally.
2. Add ½ cup brown sugar and ¼ cup butter to the pecans and mix. Cook until mixed well.
3. Remove the pan from the heat and add ½ cup of heavy cream. Return to heat and cook until mixed. Remove from heat and set aside.
4. For the brownies: In a bowl, combine the salt, baking soda, cocoa powder, flour, and brown sugar. Add the eggs, melted butter, and cream and mix well. Fold in the chocolate.
5. Pour the batter over the pecan-caramel mixture.
6. Set the grill temperature to 325°F and preheat for 15 minutes with the lid closed.
7. Cook the brownies on the grill for 35–40 minutes.
8. Remove from the heat and cool a bit. Serve with ice cream.
Nutrition: Calories: 844 | Fat:52.9 g. | Carbs: 90.5 g. | Protein: 11.7 g.

Chapter 16. Extra Recipes

320. Grilled Wild Boar Steaks with Blueberry Sauce

Preparation time: 40 minutes
Cooking time: 1 hour
Servings: 6
Ingredients:
- 4 wild boar large steaks
- For the marinade:
- 500 ml dry red wine
- Juice from 1 lemon, preferably organic
- 2 bay leaves
- 2 tbsp. sweet paprika powder
- 1 cup fresh celery, finely chopped
- Salt and black pepper, crushed
- 1 tsp. rosemary, fresh or dry
- For the sauce:
- ¾ lbs. blueberries
- 1 tsp. brown sugar
- Salt and white freshly ground pepper

Directions:
1. Combine the marinade ingredients in a small food processor and juice the lemon into it.
2. Place the meat into a suitable container and pour the marinade over it; cover and set it in the refrigerator to marinate for at least 3 hours
3. Brush the marinade off the meat and place it on a grill.
4. Cook it over medium or medium-high heat, turning it regularly and basting it with the marinade.
5. Transfer it to a serving plate. Meanwhile, boil a pan of water with a tsp. salt for the blueberries; cook these to the desired consistency.
6. Add the sugar and simmer the sauce for about 5 minutes, until it has thickened; season it before serving.

Nutrition: Energy (calories): 2447 | Protein: 99.16 g. | Fat: 7.78 g. | Carbohydrates: 515.74 g. | Calcium: 160 mg. | Magnesium: 1190 mg. | Phosphorus: 2906 mg. | Iron: 13.89 mg. | Fiber: 43.6 g. | Total Sugar: 30.21 g.

321. Grilled Wild Goose Breast in Beer Marinade

Preparation time: 2 hours
Cooking time: 50 minutes
Servings: 4
Ingredients:
- 4 goose breasts
- 2 cups beer, your choice
- 1 ½ tsp. Worcestershire sauce
- 1 tsp. garlic powder
- ½ tsp. paprika
- Salt and pepper

Directions:
1. Place the goose breasts in a Ziploc plastic bag.
2. Pour Worcestershire sauce, garlic powder, paprika, salt, and pepper into the beer. Close the bag and shake to combine all ingredients well.
3. Marinate in refrigerated for 2 hours.
4. Remove the goose meat from the marinade and pat dry on a kitchen towel (reserve the marinade).
5. Place the goose breasts on the grate. Brush occasionally with the marinade only for the first half an hour.
6. Continue to cook for 10–15 minutes longer.
7. Serve hot.

Nutrition: Energy (calories): 905 | Protein: 155.25 g. | Fat: 25.61 g. | Carbohydrates: 6.48 g. | Calcium: 35 mg. | Magnesium: 195 mg. | Phosphorus: 1651 mg. | Iron: 37.86 mg. | Fiber: 0.4 g. | Total Sugar: 1.07 g.

322. Grilled Wild Rabbit With Rosemary and Garlic

Preparation time: 15 minutes
Cooking time: 1 hour
Servings: 4
Ingredients:
- 1–2 wild rabbits (about 2 lbs.)
- 2 garlic cloves, melted
- 2 tbsp. rosemary dried, crushed
- Juice from 1 lemon
- ¼ cup olive oil
- Salt and freshly ground pepper

Directions:
1. If we use a whole rabbit, cut up a rabbit by removing the front legs, which are not attached to the body by bone.
2. Slide your knife up from underneath, along the ribs, and slice through. Cut the trunk into slices 4–5 cm thick.
3. In a bowl, mix the dry ingredients and lemon juice.
4. Brush the rabbit pieces with the garlic-rosemary mixtures.
5. Start the pellet grill to pre-heat to 300 °F.
6. Lay the rabbit pieces onto the grill rack.
7. Grill for about 12 - 15 minutes per side.
8. Serve.

Nutrition: Energy (calories): 733 | Protein: 25.22 g. | Fat: 15.42 g. | Carbohydrates: 128.9 g. | Calcium: 42 mg. | Magnesium: 303 mg. | Phosphorus: 740 mg. | Iron: 3.5 mg. | Fiber: 10.7 g. | Total Sugar: 4.57 g.

323. Stuffed Wild Duck on Pellet Grill

Preparation time: 2 hours
Cooking time: 2 hours
Servings: 6
Ingredients:
- 1 wild duck (about 4 lbs.), cleaned
- 1 mushroom cut into slices
- 1 tsp. fresh parsley, finely chopped
- ½ tsp. thyme
- ¼ cup fresh butter

• Salt and pepper

Directions:

1. Combine mushrooms, parsley, thyme, fresh butter, and salt and pepper.

2. Place the mushrooms mixture in the wild duck belly.

3. On the pellet grill on "Smoke" with the lid open until the fire is established (4–5 minutes).

4. Set the Smoke Temperature to 350°F and preheat, lid closed, for 10–15 minutes.

5. Place the duck directly on the grill grate.

6. Cover the grill and cook the duck for 1-½ hours.

7. After 1-½ hours, drain the juices and fat from the pan and flip the duck breast.

8. Let the duck cool down, pull the twigs, and serve.

Nutrition: Energy (calories): 261 | Protein: 15.91 g. | Fat: 21.39 g. | Carbohydrates: 0.81 g. | Calcium: 8 mg. | Magnesium: 20 mg. | Phosphorus: 157 mg. | Iron: 3.83 mg. | Fiber: 0.2 g. | Total Sugar: 0.56 g.

324. Smoked Peaches

Preparation time: 20 minutes
Cooking time: 20–30 minutes
Servings: 4
Ingredients:
• 6 fresh peaches

Directions:

1. Pre-heat your Traeger grill to 200°F

2. Transfer peaches directly onto your Kamado and smoke for 30 minutes; the first 20 minutes should be skin side down while the final 10 should be skin side up

3. Remove from Kamado and serve; enjoy it!

Nutrition: Energy (calories): 503 | Protein: 3.06 g. | Fat: 0.68 g. | Carbohydrates: 135.67 g. | Calcium: 20 mg. | Magnesium: 34 mg. | Phosphorus: 75 mg. | Iron: 1.84 mg. | Fiber: 8.8 g. | Total Sugar: 126.83 g.

325. Smoked Beet Pickled Eggs

Preparation time: 20 minutes
Cooking time: 30 minutes
Servings: 4
Ingredients:
• 6 eggs, hard-boiled
• 1 red beet, scrubbed and trimmed
• 1 cup apple cider vinegar
• 1 cup beet juice
• ¼ onion, sliced
• ⅓ cup granulated sugar
• 3 cardamoms
• 1-star anise

Directions:

1. Boil eggs, peel, and halve. Set aside.

2. Add the vinegar, beet and onion juice, sugar, cardamom, and star anise to a large saucepan. Bring to a boil. Reduce heat and cook until sauce is reduced to a quarter of its original volume, about 30 minutes.

3. Remove from heat and allow to cool.

Nutrition: Energy (calories): 313 | Protein: 14.36 g. | Fat: 14.55 g. | Carbohydrates: 28.84 g. | Calcium: 84 mg. | Magnesium: 38 mg. | Phosphorus: 255 mg. | Iron: 4.63 mg.

326. Stuffed Chorizo Peppers

Preparation time: 20 minutes
Cooking time: 120 minutes
Servings: 4
Ingredients:
• 3 cups shredded cheese
• 2 lb. ground chorizo sausage
• 4 Poblano peppers, halved lengthwise and seeded
• 8 bacon slices (uncooked)

Directions:

1. Take a large bowl and add 2 cups of cheddar with sausage

2. Divide the mix into 8 portions and press one portion into each pepper half

3. Sprinkle the rest of the cheddar on top

4. Wrap each pepper half with 1 bacon slice, making sure to tuck in the edges to secure it

5. Transfer peppers to your Kamado and smoke for 2 hours until the internal temperature of the sausage reaches 165°Fahrenheit

6. Enjoy it!

Nutrition: Energy (calories): 935 | Protein: 76.24 g. | Fat: 67.86 g. | Carbohydrates: 5.36 g. | Calcium: 792 mg. | Magnesium: 96 mg. | Phosphorus: 1007 mg. | Iron: 3.94 mg.

327. Delicious Bologna

Preparation time: 10 minutes
Cooking time: 60 minutes
Servings: 4
Ingredients:
• 2 tbsp. chili powder
• 2 tbsp. packed brown sugar
• 1 tsp. ground coriander
• 1 tsp. ground nutmeg
• 1 tsp. garlic powder
• 5 lbs. all-beef bologna chub
• ¼ cup prepped yellow mustard
• Salt as needed
• Freshly ground black pepper

Directions:

1. Preheat your new smoker to 250°F.

2. Take a small bowl and add chili powder, coriander, brown sugar, nutmeg, and garlic powder

3. Keep it on the side.

4. Cut the bologna into ½-inch slices and make a few small cuts all around the edges of the slices

5. Coat both sides with the mustard mix.

6. Season with salt, pepper, and spice mix.

7. Transfer the slices to the smoker and smoke for 60 minutes.

8. Enjoy it!

Nutrition: Energy (calories): 1761 | Protein: 54.2 g. | Fat: 129.86 g. | Carbohydrates: 98.38 g. | Calcium: 147 mg. | Magnesium: 65 mg. | Phosphorus: 402 mg. | Iron: 7.78 mg. | Total Sugar: 85.75 g.

328. Wild Boar

Preparation time: 20 minutes
Cooking time: 6 hours
Servings: 4
Ingredients:
• 1 (4 lb.) wild boar roast
• 2 cups BBQ sauce
Marinade:
• 1 tbsp. chopped fresh thyme
• ⅓ cup honey
• ¼ cup soy sauce
• ¼ tsp. cayenne pepper
• ½ tsp. oregano
• ¼ cup balsamic vinegar
• ½ tsp. garlic powder
• 1 cup apple juice
Directions:
1. Roast the wild boar at 350° of for approximately 20 minutes or until internal temperature reaches 145°Fahrenheit.
2. While the meat is cooking, combine all ingredients for the marinade in a bowl.
3. Marinate the meat for 6 hours in the refrigerator.
4. Drain the meat from the marinade.
5. Pour the marinade over the roast
6. Cover, and cook on low for 5–6 hours.
7. Serve with roasted potatoes.
Nutrition: Energy (calories): 388 | Protein: 40.35 g. | Fat: 5.5 g. | Carbohydrates: 44.5 g. | Calcium: 94 m | Magnesium: 105 mg. | Phosphorus: 320 mg. | Iron: 3.27 mg. | Fiber: 3.3 g.

329. Honey Apricot Smoked Lamb Shank

Preparation time: 1 hour
Cooking time: 3–4 Hours
Servings: 6 Servings
Ingredients:
• 3 lb. whole lamb shank
• 1 cup olive oil
Glaze:
• ½ cup honey
• ½ cup orange juice concentrate
• ½ cup soy sauce
• ½ cup apricot jams
• 1 tsp. ground nutmeg
• ½ tsp. ground cloves
Directions:
1. Take a large mixing bowl and combine all the glaze ingredients in it.
2. Brush the lamb shank generously with the glaze mixture.
3. Marinate the lamb shank a few hours before cooking.

4. Preheat the smoker grill at a high Temperature until the smoke form.
5. Put the lamb onto the electrical smoker grate and cook for 3–4 hours at 220°F or until the internal temperate reaches 150 °F.
6. After every 30 minutes, baste the lamb shank with the glaze.
7. Enjoy it!
Nutrition: Energy (calories): 833 | Protein: 48.58 g. | Fat: 50.28 g. | Carbohydrates: 48.31 g. | Calcium: 29 mg. | Magnesium: 77 mg. | Phosphorus: 470 mg. | Iron: 4.84 mg.

330. Braised Rabbit and Red Wine Stew

Preparation time: 30 minutes
Cooking time: 2 hours
Servings: 4–6 servings
Ingredients:
• 1 skinless rabbit, chopped into pieces (3 lb, 1.4-kgs)
• 1 tbsp. olive oil
• 2 tbsp. salted butter
• 1 yellow onion, peeled and chopped
• 1 celery stalk, peeled and chopped
• 1 carrot, peeled and chopped
• 2 garlic cloves, peeled and minced
• 2 tbsp. flour
• 4 cups chicken broth
• 1 cup dry red wine
• 1 thyme sprig
• 2 bay leaves
• Salt and black pepper to taste
• Crusty baguette to serve
Directions:
1. Warm the olive oil in a Dutch oven over moderately high heat. Add the rabbit pieces to the pot in batches and cook until browned and golden. Set the meat to one side.
2. Melt the butter in the same pot and add the onion, celery, and carrot. Sauté for10–12 minutes until soft. Add the garlic and sauté for another 60 seconds.
3. Sprinkle over the flour and stir well to combine; cook for 60 more seconds.
4. Next, pour in the chicken broth and red wine. Return the meat to the pot along with the thyme and bay leaves and bring to a simmer.
5. Cover the Traeger oven with a lid and place it on the grill. Cook for approximately 2 hours until the rabbit is cooked through and tender. Season with salt and pepper to taste.
6. Serve with crusty bread.
Nutrition: Energy (calories): 407 | Protein: 42.07 g. | Fat: 21.69 g. | Carbohydrates: 6.56 g. | Calcium: 40 mg. | Magnesium: 40 mg. | Phosphorus: 288 mg. | Iron: 2.48 mg. | Fiber: 0.8 g.

331.   Citrus Smoked Goose Breast

Preparation time: 45 minutes
Cooking time: 3 hours
Servings: 8 servings
Ingredients:
• 8 goose breast halves
• ½ cup freshly squeezed orange juice
• ⅓ cup olive oil
• ⅓ cup Dijon mustard
• ⅓ cup brown sugar
• ¼ cup Soy sauce
• ¼ cup runny honey
• 1 tbsp. dried onion, minced
• 1 tsp. garlic powder
Directions:
1. In a bowl, combine the marinade ingredients and whisk until combined. Coat the goose with the marinade. Cover the bowl and transfer to the fridge for between 3–6 hours.
2. Transfer the goose to the grill, occasionally brushing with the marinade for the first half an hour, before discarding any excess marinade.
3. Continue cooking until the bird's juices run clear and when using a meat thermometer, register an internal smoke temperature of 165°F (74°C), approximately 10–15 minutes.
Nutrition: Energy (calories): 1173 | Protein: 158.84 g. | Fat: 38.28 g. | Carbohydrates: 53.18 g. | Calcium: 60 mg. | Magnesium: 225 mg. | Phosphorus: 1723 mg. | Iron: 38.69 mg.

332.   Maple-Glazed Pheasants

Preparation time: 3 hours
Cooking time: 17 hours
Servings: 6 servings
Ingredients:
• 2 whole pheasants (2.5-lb, 1.1-kg each)
• ¼ cup brown sugar
• ¼ cup Kosher salt
• 4 cups water
• 2 cups maple syrup
Directions:
1. First, make the brine. Dissolve the sugar and salt in the water.
2. Arrange the pheasant in a large container and pour over the brine mixture. If the birds are not entirely covered, pour over more water.
3. Chill overnight (8–12 hours).
4. Take the birds out of the liquid and pat dry using kitchen paper. Set aside to dry for an hour.
5. Place the pheasants in the smoker.
6. In the meantime, add the maple syrup to a pan over moderately high heat and boil down until thick and syrupy.
7. After smoking the meat for an hour, baste the birds with maple syrup. Continue to base the meat every half an hour.
8. Enjoy warm or allow to cool.

Nutrition: Energy (calories): 620 | Protein: 55.36 g. | Fat: 8.6 g. | Carbohydrates: 79.38 g. | Calcium: 164 mg. | Magnesium: 73 mg. | Phosphorus: 542 mg. | Iron: 2.92 mg.

333.   Ultimate Duck Breasts

Preparation time: 5 minutes
Cooking time: 20 minutes
Servings: 6
Ingredients:
• 6 skin-on, boneless duck breasts (7.5-oz. 210-gms each)
• ¼ cup turbinado sugar
• ⅛ cup Kosher salt
• ¾ tbsp. garlic powder
• ⅓ cup light brown sugar
• 1½ tbsp. paprika
• ¾ tbsp. onion powder
• ½ tbsp. lemon pepper
• ½ tbsp. black pepper
• ½ tbsp. thyme, dried
• 1 tsp. chili powder
• ½ tbsp. cumin
Directions:
1. Rinse the duck breasts and gently pat dry with kitchen paper.
2. Score the fat layer in a crisscross pattern using a sharp knife.
3. Combine all rub ingredients in a small bowl.
4. Flip the duck breasts over, so they sit fat-side down, and coat the non-fat side liberally with the Prepared rub.
5. Arrange 1 or 2 duck breasts at a time on the grill, skin side down, and cook for approximately 5 minutes until a brown crust has developed. Once you have rendered as much fat as possible. Cook for a few more minutes, until medium-rare.
6. Allow the meat to rest for several minutes before slicing and serving.
7. Serve.
Nutrition: Energy (calories): 142 | Protein: 6.85 g. | Fat: 2.76 g. | Carbohydrates: 23.62 g. | Calcium: 42 mg. | Magnesium: 11 mg. | Phosphorus: 19 mg. | Iron: 1.77 mg.

117

334. Grilled Rabbit With Wine and Rosemary Marinade

Preparation time: 10 minutes
Cooking time: 40 minutes
Servings: 6
Ingredients:
• 1 rabbit cut into pieces
• For marinade:
• 3 garlic cloves, mashed
• 1 ½ tsp. rosemary
• 1 cup white wine, dry
• ½ cup olive oil
• 1 tbsp. white vinegar
• 1 tsp. mustard
• ½ tsp. cumin
• Salt and ground pepper to taste
Directions:
1. Whisk all marinade ingredients from the list.
2. Place the rabbit meat in the marinade and toss to combine well.
3. Cover with plastic wrap and refrigerate for several hours (preferably overnight).
4. Remove meat from marinade and pat dry on a paper towel.
5. Set the Smoke Temperature too High.
6. Place the rabbit pieces directly on the grill rack.
7. Grill for about 12–15 minutes per side.
8. The rabbit meat is ready when no longer pink inside, and the juices run clear.
9. Serve hot.
Nutrition: Energy (calories): 269 | Protein: 15.45 g. | Fat: 22.29 g. | Carbohydrates: 1.4 g. | Calcium: 17 mg. | Magnesium: 14 mg. | Phosphorus: 121 mg. | Iron: 1.55 mg. | Fiber: 0.2 g.

335. Goat Chops

Preparation time: 5 minutes
Cooking time: 8 minutes
Servings: 8
Ingredients:
• 8 (1-inch-thick) goat chops
• Marinade:
• 6 garlic cloves minced
• 1 tbsp. oregano, dried
• ¼ tsp. salt
• 1 tsp. ground black pepper
• ½ cup dry white wine
• 1 lemon, juiced
• 1 tbsp. grated lemon zest
• 1 onion, chopped
Directions:
1. Combine all the marinade ingredients in a mixing bowl. Add the goat chops and toss to combine. Leave the goat chops in the marinade for about 30 minutes.

2. Start the grill on smoke mode, leaving the lid open for 5 minutes for the fire to start.
3. Close the lid and preheat the grill to "high," with the lid closed for 15 minutes.
4. Place the goat chops on the grill grate and smoke for 8 minutes, 4 minutes per side.
5. Remove goat chops from heat and let them cool for a few minutes. Serve.
Nutrition: Energy (calories): 535 | Protein: 95.54 g. | Fat: 12.03 g. | Carbohydrates: 5.07 g. | Calcium: 113 mg. | Magnesium: 8 mg. | Phosphorus: 863 mg. | Iron: 13.07 mg. | Fiber: 0.5 g.

336. Smoked Goose Breast

Preparation time: 15 minutes
Cooking time: 45 minutes
Servings: 8
Ingredients:
• 8 goose breasts
Marinade:
• 4 tbsp. soy sauce
• 5 tbsp. brown sugar
• 4 tbsp. honey
• 1 tsp. garlic powder
• 1 tbsp. Dijon mustard
• ⅓ cup olive oil
• ½ cup pineapple juice
• 1 tsp. paprika
• ½ tsp. cayenne pepper
Directions:
1. Mix soy sauce, brown sugar, honey, garlic powder, and mustard.
2. Place goose breasts in a baking dish. Pour marinade over the goose, reserving 2 tbsp. of marinade for sauce.
3. Marinade for sauce. Reserve ⅓ of the marinade for sauce.
4. Marinate the goose breasts for 15 minutes.
5. Set aside pineapple juice. Mix with the rest of the marinade and paprika.
6. Heat the Traeger grill smoker.
7. Place breasts skin down in Smoker for 45 minutes.
8. Pour marinade over goose breasts. Cover the pan, and reduce heat to medium-low. Cook for 40 minutes. Rest for 5 minutes, then slice thinly. Drizzle with reserved sauce and pineapple juice.
Nutrition: Energy (calories): 991 | Protein: 155.26 g. | Fat: 36.01 g. | Carbohydrates: 13.46 g. | Calcium: 33 mg. | Magnesium: 193 mg. | Phosphorus: 1643 mg. | Iron: 37.9 mg. | Potassium: 2204 mg. | Fiber: 0.5 g.

337. Smoked Venison Tenderloin

Preparation time: 15 minutes
Cooking time: 2 hours
Servings: 4
Ingredients:
- 1 lb. venison tenderloin or backstrap
- 1 tbsp. ground black pepper
- ⅔ cup olive oil
- 5 garlic cloves, minced
- 1 tsp. thyme, dried
- 1 tsp. oregano, dried
- 1 tsp. paprika
- 1 tsp. freshly chopped peppermint
- 1 tbsp. Kosher salt
- 1 cup balsamic vinegar

Directions:
1. Cut the tenderloin or backstrap and place it in a bowl. Add the ground pepper, thyme, oregano, paprika, peppermint, salt, and garlic; add the olive oil, and toss, fully coating the meat. Refrigerate for 1–2 hours.
2. After 1–2 hours, take the tenderloin and place it on a hot smoker with the pepper and garlic. Cook it for 2 hours.
3. Next, add the balsamic, cover it with the lid, and reduce the heat.
4. Serve alongside wild rice and steamed vegetables.

Nutrition: Energy (calories): 558 | Protein: 34.8 g. | Fat: 38.97 g. | Carbohydrates: 13.71 g. | Calcium: 40 mg. | Magnesium: 51 mg. | Phosphorus: 365 mg. | Iron: 5.95 mg.

338. Smoked Rabbit

Preparation time: 15 minutes
Cooking time: 3 hours
Servings: 4
Ingredients:
- 1 (3 lb.) whole rabbit
- 1 tbsp. rosemary, dried
- ⅓ cup olive oil
- 1 tbsp. thyme, dried
- 1 tbsp. cracked black pepper
- 1 tsp. sea salt
- ½ cup dry white wine
- 1 cup apple juice
- 1 tbsp. oregano, dried
- 1 tbsp. freshly grated lemon zest

Directions:
1. Rinse and pat dry the rabbit. Cover it with the dried rosemary, olive oil, thyme, black pepper, and sea salt, ensuring the entire rabbit is coated.
2. Cover the rabbit with plastic wrap and place it in the refrigerator.
3. Consume within 2–3 days. Thaw overnight and refrigerate for 8 hours. Season the rabbit with white wine, apple juice, oregano, and lemon zest.

4. Cover with a layer of plastic wrap and refrigerate overnight; heat your barbecue/smoking machine to medium heat, and place the rabbit on the smoker. Smoke it for 3 hours, or until the liquid in the pan reduces by ¾.
5. Check every hour to baste the rabbit with the reduced liquid. When finished, remove from the smoker and let the rabbit cool down. Slice to serve.

Nutrition: Energy (calories): 301 | Protein: 6.85 g. | Fat: 24.64 g. | Carbohydrates: 14.3 g. | Calcium: 225 mg. | Magnesium: 22 mg. | Phosphorus: 161 mg. | Iron: 0.54 mg. | Fiber: 0.7 g.

339. Spatchcock Smoked Quail

Preparation time: 15 minutes
Cooking time: 1 hour
Servings: 4
Ingredients:
- 4 quails
- 2 tbsp. fresh parsley, finely chopped
- 1 tbsp. fresh rosemary, finely chopped
- 2 tbsp. fresh thyme, finely chopped
- ½ cup melted butter
- 1 tsp. garlic powder
- 1 tsp. onion powder
- 1 tsp. ground black pepper
- 2 tsp. salt or to taste
- 2 tbsp. scallions, finely chopped

Directions:
1. Remove the giblets from the quail; set them aside. Rinse the quails under cold running water, and pat dry with paper towels. Prepare the grill for cooking; place the quail on the grill rack and brush them with butter. Cook for about 1 hour, brushing with melted butter every 5 minutes, until evenly brown.
2. The internal temperature should reach 170°F. Meanwhile, prepare a marinade by combining the fresh herbs, scallions, garlic, onion powders, salt, ground black pepper, and salt; mix well.
3. Prepare the quail; pour the marinade over the quail, and place them in a glass baking dish, seam-side down. Cover with plastic wrap, and refrigerate overnight.
4. Serve with mashed potatoes and roasted vegetables.

Nutrition: Energy (calories): 339 | Protein: 20.87 g. | Fat: 27.28 g. | Carbohydrates: 2.84 g. | Calcium: 35 mg. | Magnesium: 32 mg. | Phosphorus: 303 mg. | Iron: 4.77 mg. | Fiber: 0.7 g.

340. Smoked Pheasant

Preparation time: 15 minutes
Cooking time: 5 hours
Servings: 5
Ingredients:
- 2 whole pheasants
- 4 tbsp. brown sugar
- 1 tbsp. kosher salt
- 1 tbsp. black peppercorns
- 4 cups water
- 2 cups maple syrup
- 1 cup pineapple juice
- 1 tbsp. Dijon mustard

Directions:
1. Rinse pheasant, pat dry. Rub all over with brown sugar, salt & pepper.
2. Place 4 cups of water in the bottom of a pot with high sides. Place pheasants in a pot, and bring to a boil for 20–30 minutes. Turn off the heat, and drain off the liquid through a strainer. Pat dry.
3. Place the breast side on a rack inside a roasting pan, with the rack sitting in low boiling water. Spoon on maple syrup, pineapple juice & mustard.
4. Cover with foil. Roast for 4 hours at 250°F, basting regularly with the juices in the pan. Remove foil and roast for 4 hours more, basting whenever possible. Enjoy it!

Nutrition: Energy (calories): 735 kcal | Protein: 66.77 g. | Fat: 10.48 g. | Carbohydrates: 92.69 g. | Calcium: 195 mg. | Magnesium: 95 mg. | Phosphorus: 657 mg. | Iron: 3.6 mg. | Fiber: 0.5 g. | Total Sugar: 83.52 g.

341. Rabbit Stew

Preparation time: 15 minutes
Cooking time: 2 hours and 30 minutes
Servings: 4
Ingredients:
- 1 (3 lb.) rabbit, cut into bite sizes
- ¼ cup olive oil
- 1 ½ onion, chopped
- 1 carrot, diced
- 1 stalk celery, diced
- 1 red bell pepper, sliced
- 2 garlic cloves, minced
- 1 cup red wine
- 4 cups chicken broth
- 2 bay leaves
- 2 tbsp. flour
- 1 tsp. thyme, dried
- 1 tsp. salt
- 1 tsp. ground black pepper

Directions:
1. Prepare your grilling machine.
2. In a large pot over medium heat, add olive oil and heat. Sauté onion, celery, carrot, red bell pepper, and garlic for 2 minutes, stirring constantly.

3. Add rabbit pieces, red wine, dried thyme, bay leaves, salt, & ground black pepper. Stir to coat rabbit. Add in enough broth so that rabbit is submerged, then cover.
4. Bring to a boil, then turn the heat to low. Simmer for at least 2 hours. Check occasionally to make sure the rabbit is submerged and that there is adequate liquid.
5. Mix 4 tbsp. flour and 1 cup of broth. Slowly stir into the rabbit.
6. Continue cooking on low heat uncovered for 30 minutes until the rabbit is tender.

Nutrition: Energy (calories): 1112 | Protein: 54.24 g. | Fat: 45.03 g. | Carbohydrates: 116.63 g. | Calcium: 58 mg. | Magnesium: 62 mg. | Phosphorus: 373 mg. | Iron: 3.72 mg. | Fiber: 2.1 g.

342. Grilled Antelope

Preparation time: 10 minutes and overnight
Cooking time: 15 minutes
Servings: 8
Ingredients:
7. 1 lb. antelope steak (sliced into 1-inch-thick slices)
Marinade:
- 4 tbsp. olive oil
- ½ tsp. rosemary, dried
- 2 garlic cloves, minced
- 1 lemon, juiced
- ¼ cup balsamic vinegar
- ½ tsp. salt or to taste
- 1 tsp. onion powder
- ¼ tsp. thyme
- 1 tsp. oregano
- 1 tsp. paprika

Directions:
1. Place all the ingredients in a zip lock bag and toss to coat the meat. Seal tightly and refrigerate for at least 1 hour or overnight.
2. Preheat a grill on medium-high heat, and brush the grill with some oil. Remove the meat from the marinade and place it on the grill.
3. Close the lid and cook until the meat is well grilled on both sides and is tender when pierced with a fork. Serve hot.

Nutrition: Energy (calories): 222 | Protein: 14.38 g. | Fat: 16.86 g. | Carbohydrates: 1.49 g. Calcium: 24 mg. | Magnesium: 17 mg. | Phosphorus: 124 mg. | Iron: 1.27 mg.

343. Elk Kebabs

Preparation time: 10 minutes
Cooking time: 12 minutes
Servings: 4
Ingredients:
• 2 elk steaks, cut into 2-inch cubes
• 1 large bell pepper, sliced
• 1 large yellow bell pepper, sliced
• 1 large green bell pepper, sliced
• 1 onion (sliced)
• 10 medium cremini mushrooms, destemmed and halved
• Wooden or bamboo skewers, soaked in water for 30 minutes, at least
Marinade:
• 1 tbsp. soy sauce
• 1 tsp. garlic powder
• ½ tsp. ground black pepper
• 1 tbsp. Worcestershire sauce
• 1 tbsp. lemon juice
• 1 tsp. onion powder
• 3 tbsp. olive oil
• 1 tsp. paprika
Directions:
1. In a large mixing bowl, combine all the marinade ingredients.
2. Add the elk and mushroom. Toss to combine.
3. Cover the bowl tightly with aluminum foil and refrigerate for 8 hours.
4. Remove the mushroom and elk from the marinade.
5. Thread the bell peppers, onion, mushroom, and elk onto skewers to make kabobs.
6. Preheat your grill with the lid closed for 15 minutes, using mesquite hardwood pellets.
7. Arrange the kebobs onto the grill grate and grill for 12 minutes, 6 minutes per side, or until the internal temperature of the elk reaches 145°F.
8. Remove kebabs from heat.
9. Serve warm and enjoy it!
Nutrition: Energy (calories): 838 | Protein: 15.05 g. | Fat: 28.3 g. | Carbohydrates: 132.74 g. | Calcium: 90 mg. | Magnesium: 22 mg. | Phosphorus: 79 mg. | Iron: 5.42 mg.

344. Turkey Pesto Panini

Preparation time: 5 minutes
Cooking time: 6 minutes
Servings: 2
Ingredients:
• 1 tbsp. olive oil
• 4 slices French bread
• ½ cup pesto sauce
• 4 slices Mozzarella cheese
• 2 cups chopped leftover turkey
• 1 Roma tomato, thinly sliced
• 1 avocado, halved, seeded, peeled, and sliced
Directions:

1. Start smoking your grill to medium-high heat.
2. Brush each slice of bread with olive oil on one side.
3. Place 2 slices of olive oil side down on aluminum foil.
4. Spread 2 tbsp. pesto over 1 side of French bread.
5. Top with all the ingredients and repeat with the remaining slices of bread.
6. Grill until the bread is golden and the cheese is melted, about 2–3 minutes per side.
7. Serve warm with your favorite salad or soup.
Nutrition: Energy (calories): 886 | Protein: 43.57 g. | Fat: 66.1 g. | Carbohydrates: 32.8 g. | Calcium: 232 mg. | Magnesium: 102 mg. | Phosphorus: 456 mg. | Iron: 5.69 mg. | Potassium: 951 mg.

345. Grilled Veggie Panini

Preparation time: 12 minutes
Cooking time: 20 minutes
Servings: 4
Ingredients:
• 8 slices sourdough bread
• 1 small zucchini, cut into strips
• 1 small yellow squash
• 1 red bell pepper
• 1 small red onion
• 3 basil leaves, chopped
• 2 tsp. olive oil
• Sea salt
• Pepper
• 8 slices Provolone cheese
• 2 tbsp. mayonnaise
Directions:
1. Preheat the entire grill to medium heat.
2. Toss vegetables, olive oil, basil, salt, and pepper in a large mixing bowl.
3. Add to the grill and cook for 5 minutes, often flipping, until vegetables are softened.
4. Top 4 bread slices with mayonnaise, grilled veggies, cheese, and the second slice of bread.
5. Place on the grill and cook for about 3 minutes per side.
6. Remove and serve warm.
Nutrition: Energy (calories): 374 | Protein: 16.29 g. | Fat: 20.62 g. | Carbohydrates: 31.77 g. | Calcium: 465 mg. | Magnesium: 52 mg. | Phosphorus: 674 mg. | Iron: 2.21 mg. | Potassium: 424 mg.

346. Greek Chicken Salad Pita Pockets

Preparation time: 10 minutes
Cooking time: 5 minutes
Servings: 6
Ingredients:
• 6 whole-wheat pita pockets, halved
• For the sandwich stuffing:
• 1 cup leftover grilled chicken thighs, chopped
• 4 cups shredded romaine lettuce
• ¼ cup grape tomatoes, chopped
• ½ cup cucumber, chopped
• ¼ cup black olives, sliced
• ⅓ cup crumbled feta
• ¼ cup extra-virgin olive oil
• 2 tbsp. red wine vinegar
• 1 lemon, juiced
• 2 garlic cloves, minced
• 1 tsp. oregano, dried
• Sea salt, to taste
• Pepper, to taste
Directions:
1. Whisk together dressing ingredients in a large mixing bowl.
2. Add the sandwich stuffing ingredients to a bowl and toss dressing until well-coated.
3. Fill each pita pocket with Chicken Salad and enjoy it!
Nutrition: Energy (calories): 226 | Protein: 8.84 g. | Fat: 11.73 g. | Carbohydrates: 23.01 g. | Calcium: 80 mg. | Magnesium: 37 mg. | Phosphorus: 140 mg. | Iron: 1.73 mg.

347. Prosciutto Pesto Hot Dog

Preparation time: 15 minutes
Cooking time: 15 minutes
Servings: 4
Ingredients:
• 4 smoked turkey hot dogs
• 4 large hot dog buns or split top hoagies
• 6 oz. fresh Mozzarella cheese
• ⅓ cup pesto, divided
• 3 oz. prosciutto, sliced thinly
• ¼ cup marinated artichoke hearts, chopped
• Olive oil, for drizzling
• Parmesan cheese, shaved for garnish
Directions:
1. Heat the entire grill smoker to medium heat.
2. Add hot dogs to one side, and reduce that side's heat to low. Grill until cooked through; about 5–7 minutes; turning occasionally.
3. Fry the sliced prosciutto until crispy on the other side of the grill; about 3 minutes. Drain on a paper towel-lined plate, and set aside.
4. Top the hot dogs with thin slices of mozzarella cheese, and remove once the cheese is melted.
5. Toast the buns on the grill for 2 minutes and remove.

6. Spread pesto onto the toasted buns.
7. Top with a mozzarella-covered hot dog.
8. Top with all the remaining ingredients.
9. Serve immediately!
Nutrition: Energy (calories): 267 | Protein: 19.76 g. | Fat: 17.13 g. | Carbohydrates: 10.22 g. | Calcium: 465 mg. | Magnesium: 41 mg. | Phosphorus: 376 mg. | Iron: 1.4 mg.

348. Summer Treat Corn

Preparation time: 10 minutes
Cooking time: 20 minutes
Servings: 6
Ingredients:
• 6 fresh whole corn on the cob
• ½ cup butter
• Salt, to taste
Directions:
1. Set the Traeger Grill to 400°F and preheat for 15 minutes with the lid closed.
2. Remove the silk and husk of the corn.
3. Brush each corn with melted butter and season generously with salt.
4. Place the corn on the grill for about 20 minutes, rotating every 5 minutes and brushing with butter halfway through.
5. Serve hot.
Nutrition: Calories: 334 | Carbohydrates: 43.5 g. | Protein: 7.7 g. | Fat: 18.1 g. | Sugar: 7.5 g. | Sodium: 171 mg. | Fiber: 6.3 g.

349. Crunchy Potato Wedges

Preparation time: 15 minutes
Cooking time: 16 minutes
Servings: 5
Ingredients:
• 4 Yukon gold potatoes
• 2 tbsp. olive oil
• 1 tbsp. garlic, minced
• 2 tsp. onion powder
• ½ tsp. red pepper flakes, crushed
• Salt and freshly ground black pepper to taste
Directions:
1. Set the temperature of Traeger Grill to 500°F and preheat with a closed lid for 15 minutes.
2. Cut each potato into 8 equal-sized wedges.
3. Add potato wedges and ingredients to a large bowl and toss to coat well.
4. Arrange the potato wedges onto the grill and cook for about 8 minutes per side.
5. Remove from grill and serve hot.
Nutrition: Calories: 157 | Carbohydrates: 25.7 g. | Protein: 3 g. | Fat: 5.8 g. | Sugar: 1.3 g. | Sodium: 46 mg. | Fiber: 2 g.

350. Twice Grilled Potatoes

Preparation time: 20 minutes
Cooking time: 4 hours
Servings: 6
Ingredients:
- 6 russet potatoes
- 2 tbsp. olive oil
- Salt, to taste
- 8 cooked bacon slices, crumbled
- ½ cup heavy whipping cream
- 4 oz. cream cheese, softened
- 4 tbsp. butter, softened
- 4 jalapeño peppers, seeded and chopped
- 1 tsp. seasoned salt
- 2 cups Monterrey Jack cheese, grated and divided

Directions:

1. Set the temperature of Traeger Grill to 225°F and preheat with a closed lid for 15 minutes.

2. With paper towels, pat dry the washed potatoes completely.

3. Coat the potatoes with olive oil and sprinkle with some salt.

4. Arrange potatoes onto the grill and cook for about 3–3½ hours.

5. Remove the potatoes from the grill and cut them in half lengthwise.

6. With a large spoon, scoop out the potato flesh from the skins, leaving a little potato layer.

7. In a large bowl, add potato flesh and mash it slightly.

8. Add bacon, cream cheese, butter, jalapeno, seasoned salt, and 1 cup of Monterrey Jack cheese and gently stir to combine.

9. Stuff the potato skins with bacon mixture and top with remaining Monterrey Jack cheese.

10. Arrange the stuffed potatoes onto a baking sheet.

11. Place the baking sheet on the grill and cook for about 30 minutes.

12. Serve hot.

Nutrition: Calories: 539 | Carbohydrates: 35.7 g. | Protein: 17.6 g. | Fat: 37 g. | Sugar: 2.8 g. | Sodium: 1355 mg. | Fiber: 5.5 g.

30 Days Meal Plan

DAY	BREAKFAST	LUNCH	DINNER	SNACK	DESSERT
1	Easy Eggs	Mustard Beef Short Ribs	Bacon-Wrapped Sausages in Brown Sugar	Grilled Corn	Grilled Pound Cake With Fruit Dressing
2	Smoked Pork Sausages	BBQ Meatloaf	Traeger Grilled Buffalo Chicken	Smoked Cashews	Grilled Pineapple With Chocolate Sauce
3	Grilled Ultimate Game Burger	Lemon Pepper Pork Tenderloin	Traeger Salmon With Togarashi	Smoked Popcorn With Parmesan Herb	Nectarine and Nutella Sundae
4	Breakfast Sausage	Beef Stuffed Bell Peppers	Traeger Grilled Aussie Leg of Lamb	Grilled Brussels Sprouts	Cinnamon Sugar Donut Holes
5	Tuna Burgers	Brandy Beef Tenderloin	Smoked Apple Pork Tenderloin	Roasted Tomatoes	Grill Chocolate Chip Cookies
6	Mini Portobello Burgers	Spicy Chuck Roast	BBQ Elk Short Ribs	Traeger Grill Funeral Potatoes	Blueberry Cobbler
7	Veggie Lover's Burgers	Chinese BBQ Pork	Traeger Smoked Shrimp	Grilled Watermelon Juice	Rum-Soaked Grilled Pineapple Sundaes
8	Smoked Mushrooms	Herbed Prime Rib Roast	Traeger Chili Lime Chicken	Smashed Potato Casserole	Charred Peaches With Bourbon Butter Sauce
9	Grilled Asparagus & Honey-Glazed Carrots	Smoked Beef Brisket in Sweet and Spicy Rub	Grilled Shrimp Kabobs	Smoked Coleslaw	Smoked Pumpkin Pie
10	Garlic Parmesan Grilled Cheese Sandwiches	Lemon Ginger Smoked Beef Ribs	Roasted Whole Ham in Apricot Sauce	Traeger Smoked Vegetables	Berry Cobbler

11	Sun-Dried Tomato and Chicken Flatbreads	Sweet & Spicy Beef Brisket	Smoked Sausages	Traeger Spicy Brisket	Grill Apple Crisp
12	Veggie Pesto Flatbread	BBQ Spiced Flank Steak	Traeger Smoked Lamb Chops	Grilled Broccoli	Ice Cream Bread
13	Cheesy Turkey Burger	Simple Smoked Beef Brisket With Mocha Sauce	Traeger Grilled Lingcod	Cranberry-Almond Broccoli Salad	Apple Cake
14	Smoked Healthy Cabbage	Chocolate Smoked Beef Ribs	Pulled Pork	Seasoned Potatoes on Smoker	Baked Caramel Pecan Brownie
15	Grilled Watermelon Juice	Smoked Beef With Smoked Garlic Mayo Dip	Traeger Smoked Lamb Shoulder	Easy Grilled Corn	Grilled Peaches and Cream
16	Grilled Chicken Quesadilla Sandwich	Simple Smoked Pulled Beef	BBQ Baby Back Ribs	Traeger Smoked Vegetables	Smoked Peach Parfait
17	Turkey Apple Burgers	Smoked Beef Churl Barbecue	Traeger Grilled Buffalo Chicken	Deviled Eggs	Grill Chicken Flatbread
18	Traeger Salmon With Togarashi	Honey Glazed Smoked Beef	Pork Collar and Rosemary Marinade	Grilled Brussels Sprouts	Apple Pie Grill
19	Grilled Sausage Ala Carte	Spiced Smoked Beef With Oregano	Roasted Pork With Balsamic Strawberry Sauce	Thyme-Rosemary Mash Potatoes	Grilled Fruit and Cream
20	Breakfast Sausage	BBQ Sweet Pepper Meatloaf	Lamb Skewers	Smoked Mushrooms	Grilled Pineapple With Chocolate Sauce
21	Buffalo Chicken Burgers	Blackened Steak	BBQ Pulled Pork Sandwiches	Atomic Buffalo Turds	Cinnamon Sugar Donut Holes
22	Smoked Popcorn With Parmesan Herb	Perfect Beef Tenderloin	Traeger Grilled Lingcod	Grilled Carrots	Blueberry Cobbler

23	Grilled Vegetable Pizza	Lemon Ginger Smoked Beef Ribs	Smoked Sausages	Cranberry-Almond Broccoli Salad	Grill Apple Crisp
24	Cheesy Lamb Burgers	Smoked Beef Brisket in Sweet and Spicy Rub	Traeger Grilled Buffalo Chicken	Smashed Potato Casserole	Ice Cream Bread
25	Tuna Burgers	Beef Stuffed Bell Peppers	BBQ Elk Short Ribs	Grilled Brussels Sprouts	Apple Cake
26	Veggie Lover's Burgers	Herbed Prime Rib Roast	Lemon Pepper Pork Tenderloin	Smoked Coleslaw	Baked Caramel Pecan Brownie
27	Mini Portobello Burgers	Sweet & Spicy Beef Brisket	Bacon-Wrapped Sausages in Brown Sugar	Grilled Corn	Grilled Pound Cake With Fruit Dressing
28	Smoked Pork Sausages	BBQ Meatloaf	Traeger Chili Lime Chicken	Smoked Cashews	Grilled Pineapple With Chocolate Sauce
29	Grilled Steak With American Cheese Sandwich	Versatile Beef Tenderloin	Smoked Pork Loin	Traeger Grill Funeral Potatoes	Rum-Soaked Grilled Pineapple Sundaes
30	Grilled Chicken Quesadilla Sandwich	Buttered Tenderloin	Smoked Baby Back Ribs	Seasoned Potatoes on Smoker	Nectarine and Nutella Sundae

Measurement Conversion Table

Volume Equivalents (Liquid)

US Standard	US Standard (ounces)	Metric (approximate)
2 tablespoons	1 fl. oz.	30 mL
¼ cup	2 fl. oz.	60 mL
half cup	4 fl. oz.	120 mL
1 cup	8 fl. oz.	240 mL
1 half cups	12 fl. oz.	355 mL
2 cups or 1 pint	16 fl. oz.	457 mL
4 cups or 1 quart	32 fl. oz.	1 L
1 gallon	128 fl. oz.	4 L

Volume Equivalents (Dry)

US Standard	Metric (approximate)
1/8 teaspoon	0.5 mL
¼ teaspoon	1 mL
half teaspoon	2 mL
¾ teaspoon	4 mL
1 teaspoon	5 mL
1 tablespoon	15 mL
¼ cup	59 mL
1/3 cup	79 mL
half cup	118 mL
2/3 cup	156 mL
¾ cup	177 mL
1 cup	235 mL
2 cups or 1 pint	475 mL
3 cups	700 mL
4 cups or 1 quart	1 L

Oven Temperatures

Fahrenheit (F)	Celsius (C) (approximate)
250°F	120°C
300°F	150°C
325°F	165°C
350°F	180°C
375°F	190°C
400°F	200°C
425°F	220°C
450°F	230°C

Weight Equivalents

US Standard	Metric (approximate)
1 tablespoon	15 g
half ounce	15 g
1 ounce	30 g
2 ounces	60 g
4 ounces	115 g
8 ounces	225 g
12 ounces	340 g
16 ounces or 1 pound or 1 lb	455 g

Conclusion

The overall best value is the Traeger Grill & Smoker cookbook. It's the cheapest way to get a cookbook with an extensive selection of recipes and offers excellent information about how to use your grill/smoker.

Traeger has won the hearts of anyone with love for cooking and grilling. Although Traeger is comparatively cheaper to start, it can be expensive to maintain. This cookbook has all the knowledge you'll need to prevent this problem and a wealth of other Traeger cooking techniques. You won't regret picking up a copy!

The Traeger Grill & Smoker cookbook is a great addition to any grilling enthusiast's collection. It has a lot of useful information about the management and care of your grill while giving you many delicious recipes. One important note would be the size of the book. The cookbook can easily be used on the one hand, but it is not very practical for transporting it from place to place. This cookbook is great for new and experienced grillers who want to add some new recipes to their repertoire!

The best time-saving snack recipes are included in this cookbook, providing individuals with treats that are not only tasty but healthy while also taking little time out of their day. If you are an individual that loves love while cooking, this cookbook is a must-read.

A cookbook from Traeger Grill & Smoker is a must-have for any serious griller, whether it be someone who has just started using the grill or has been using it for quite some time. With ingredients ranging from the most basic to the most exotic, this book will have something for everyone and will save you money on your next shopping trip.

Finding a cookbook with delicious and well-tested recipes for your Traeger Grill & Smoker has never been easier. The large variety of recipe choices is one of the best features of Traeger products. Regarding Traeger, you don't have to be a trial-and-error cook. You can be satisfied that you will get delicious results each time you try something new.

The cookbook was designed for anyone with an active passion for cooking who wants to expand their knowledge and enjoy great recipes with their Traeger Grill & Smoker. It is a comprehensive book that gives all the ins and outs of cooking the Traeger way.

The Traeger Grill & Smoker cookbook is perfect for any outdoor cooking enthusiast. It's designed to help people achieve a high-quality finish with every meal and does just that in an easy-to-follow, no-fuss way. The best part is that this book has a ton of recipes and tips packed into one place!

BONUS

These bonuses are **100% FREE**

To download your bonuses scan the **QR code** below

Thank you so much for reading this book.

Your support means a lot to me and
I would love to know your thoughts!

If you enjoyed reading it,
I invite you to scan the QR code below to leave a review.

Your opinion not only helps me grow but also guides other readers.

Remember that every review is more helpful than you know!

Thank you